T0323351

Economic Growth in Europe

Why has European growth slowed down since the 1990s while American productivity growth has speeded up? This book provides a thorough and detailed analysis of the sources of growth from a comparative industry perspective. It argues that Europe's slow growth is the combined result of a severe productivity slowdown in traditional manufacturing and other goods production, and a concomitant failure to invest in and reap the benefits from Information and Communications Technology (ICT), in particular in market services. The analysis is based on rich new databases including the EU KLEMS growth accounting database and provides detailed background of the data construction. As such, the book provides new methodological perspectives and serves as a primer on the use of data in economic growth analysis. More generally, it illustrates to the research and policy community the benefits of analysis based on detailed data on the sources of economic growth.

MARCEL P. TIMMER is Professor of Economic Growth and Development and Director of the Groningen Growth and Development Centre (GGDC) at the University of Groningen.

ROBERT INKLAAR is Assistant Professor in the Department of International Economics and Business at the University of Groningen.

MARY O'MAHONY is Professor of International Industrial Economics at Birmingham Business School at the University of Birmingham.

BART VAN ARK is Chief Economist of the Conference Board, New York, and Professor of Economic Development, Technological Change and Growth at the University of Groningen.

Economic Growth in Europe

A Comparative Industry Perspective

MARCEL P. TIMMER

ROBERT INKLAAR

MARY O'MAHONY

BART VAN ARK

CAMBRIDGE
UNIVERSITY PRESS

CAMBRIDGE UNIVERSITY PRESS
Cambridge, New York, Melbourne, Madrid, Cape Town, Singapore,
São Paulo, Delhi, Dubai, Tokyo, Mexico City

Cambridge University Press
The Edinburgh Building, Cambridge CB2 8RU, UK

Published in the United States of America by Cambridge University Press, New York

www.cambridge.org
Information on this title: www.cambridge.org/9780521198875

First published 2010

A catalogue record for this publication is available from the British Library

Library of Congress Cataloguing in Publication data
Economic growth in Europe : a comparative industry perspective /
Marcel P. Timmer ... [et al.].
    p. cm.
Includes bibliographical references and index.
1. Europe – Economic conditions – 20th century – Case studies.
2. Europe – Economic conditions – 21st century – Case studies.
3. Industrial policy – Europe – Case studies.   4. Technological
innovations – Economic aspects – Europe – Case studies.
I. Timmer, Marcel. II. Title.
HC240.E273 2010
338.94 – dc22   2010023577

ISBN 978-0-521-19887-5 Hardback

Contents

Figures

Tables

Preface and acknowledgements

Economic growth is a key factor in the improvement of our living standards and hence of great interest to academics and policy makers alike. This book aims to explain why growth across Europe has been disappointing since the mid 1990s, both compared to earlier periods and compared to the United States, which showed resurgent growth after 1995. In the process we present the EU KLEMS database, a rich data toolbox that can be used to explore these and other growth-related questions. The main message of this book is that an industry perspective on growth and the sources of growth is essential because of the great diversity in the drivers of growth in agriculture, manufacturing and services industries, including trade, transport, financial, business and personal services.

The empirical study of sources of economic growth has a long tradition in Europe, starting as far back as the seventeenth century when William Petty began to construct measures of economic performance including comparisons of output and productivity in industry, trade and transportation. Over the centuries, with the emergence of standardised national accounts and other internationally comparable statistical sources, the measurement of sources of growth has become more sophisticated. During the second half of the last century, growth accounting evolved as a standard methodology. In 1987, Jorgenson, Gollop and Fraumeni published a pioneering study laying out what has become known as the KLEMS approach. The KLEMS method measures the changes in the quantity and quality of capital (K), labour (L), energy (E), material inputs (M) and service inputs (S) as contributions to output growth. This approach has subsequently been particularly useful in tracing the effects of the development and deployment of information and communication technology (ICT) on the resurgence of the American economy since 1995 (Jorgenson *et al.* 2005).

While the KLEMS methodology has been replicated in studies for some individual countries, a standardised comparison of European countries has not been available until recently. This became increasingly pressing in the early 2000s as European productivity growth seemed to be on a declining trend, in the context of accelerating growth in the United States and increasing competition from emerging economies such as China and India. The slowing growth and faltering emergence of the knowledge economy in Europe led to an ambitious action programme of the European Commission, called the 'Lisbon Agenda', aimed at boosting competitiveness, primarily through innovation. Monitoring and evaluation of progress in achieving these goals required a comprehensive analysis of economic growth in Europe based on a detailed industry-level database. With evidence of the rising importance of ICT and market services for growth, there was also renewed attention given to measurement issues and the international comparability of national statistics. Clearly, there was an increasing need for new methods, comparable statistics and convergence of methods of measuring productivity. The aim of the EU KLEMS initiative set up in 2003 was to meet this demand.

This study is the result of the multi-year, multi-national endeavour involving a large consortium of researchers. It was supported by the European Commission, Research Directorate-General as part of the 6th Framework Programme, Priority 8, Policy Support and Anticipating Scientific and Technological Needs, and is part of the EU KLEMS Project on Growth and Productivity in the European Union. The grant made it possible to form a consortium of eighteen partners, including universities and research institutes across Europe, as well as Japan and the United States. The result of this collaboration is the EU KLEMS Growth and Productivity Accounts database, publicly available at www.euklems.net. This database includes measures of output and detailed capital and labour inputs, and derived variables such as labour and multi-factor productivity at the industry level. The measures are developed for twenty-five individual European Union member states, the United States and Japan and cover the period from 1970 onwards. This book combines a documentation of the EU KLEMS methodology and database with a number of analytical studies that have been carried out using the database. It can therefore be used as the primary reference work for the current and future versions of the EU KLEMS database. In particular Chapters 3 and 6 provide a detailed account of the growth accounting and level accounting methodologies used in the EU KLEMS project. The analysis in the book is primarily focused on the comparative output and productivity performance of the European Union, relative to the United States. In this respect, Chapters 2, 4 and 5 reflect our assessment of the comparative growth performance of the two regions during the period 1980–2005. The current book is a reflection of the significant work carried out by the EU KLEMS consortium that has led to the creation of the online database, and a series of academic and policy publications on growth and productivity. The data work for the EU KLEMS Growth and Productivity Accounts would not have been possible without the input of all consortium members and the persons belonging to these institutions. Our thanks go to Centre d'études prospectives et d'informations internationals (CEPII), Paris (Michel Fouquin, Laurence Nayman, Anita Wölfl); Centre for Economic and Business Research (CEBR), Copenhagen (Martin Junge, Svend Hougaard Jensen, Mickey Petersen); Netherlands Bureau for Economic Policy Analysis (CPB), The Hague (Henry van der Wiel, Ate Nieuwenhuis, Paul de Jongh); Deutsches Institut für Wirtschaftsforschung e.V. (DIW), Berlin (Bernd Görzig, Martin Gornig, Rainer Vosskamp); Federaal Planbureau (FPB), Brussels (Chantal Kegels, Bernadette Biatour, Jeroen Fiers, Bernard Klaus Michel, Luc Avonds); Istituto di Studi e Analisi Economica (ISAE), Rome (Carlo Milana); Instituto Valenciano De Investigaciones Economicas (IVIE), Valencia (Matilde Mas, Javier Quesada, Ezequiel Uriel, Lorenzo Serrano); Helsingin kauppakorkeakoulu (Helsinki School of Economics) (Matti Pohjola); Austrian Institute of Economic Research (WIFO), Vienna (Michael Peneder, Kurt Kratena, Martin Falk); Vienna Institute for International Economic Studies (WIIW), Vienna (Peter Havlik, Monica Schwarzhappel, Robert Stehrer, Sebastian Leitner); Amsterdam Business and Economic Research (AMBER), Free University Amsterdam (Eric Bartelsman, Hans Quene); University of Konstanz (Jörg Beutel); The Conference Board Europe, Brussels (the late Robert McGuckin III, Janet Hao); Harvard University (Dale Jorgenson, Mun Ho, Jon Samuels); Pellervo Economic Research Institute (PTT), Helsinki (Janne Huovari, Jukka Jalava) and individual contributors such as Kyoji Fukao (Hitotsubashi University), Tsutomu Miyagawa (Gakushuin University), Hak K. Pyo (Seoul National University) and Keun Hee Rhee (Korea Productivity Center). We are particularly grateful to our colleagues at the University of Groningen, the National Institute for Economic and Social Research (NIESR) and the University of Birmingham for all their support

during various phases of the project. At the University of Groningen our thanks go to Gerard Ypma, Ton van Moergastel and Edwin
Stuivenwold for their excellent work in getting the first EU KLEMS
database off the ground, and to Jop Woltjer for his seamless continuation of this work. Lourens Broersma, Carolina Castaldi, Erik Dietzen-
bacher, Abdul Azeez Erumbam, Reitze Gouma and Bart Los provided
additional help and advice. We are also grateful to Rob Willems for
administrative support to the project. At NIESR, our thanks go to Mari
Kangasniemi, Peter Loveridge, Ana Rincon and Catherine Robinson;
and at the University of Birmingham to Yasheng Maimaiti, Fei Peng
and Nicholas Zubanov.

An important element in the success of the EU KLEMS project has
been the co-operation with national statistical institutes across the
European Union. The growth accounting system will hopefully be
implemented by national statistical institutes and Eurostat as part
of their regular statistical systems. While we received very useful
advice from all statistical institutes across Europe, we have partic-
ularly received significant in-kind help from Statistics Netherlands
(Mark de Haan, Dirk van den Bergen, Bert Balk, Hans Kolfoort),
Statistics Finland (Pirkko Aulin Ahmavaara and Antti Pasanen), the
Office of National Statistics, UK (Anna Soo and Tuu Van Nguyen),
ISTAT, Italy (Cecilia Joan-Lasinio, Massimiliano Iommi, Antonella
Baldassarini), Statistics Luxembourg (John Haas) and Statistics Sweden (Hans-Olof Hagén and Tomas Skytesvall). Researchers from the
OECD played an important role, both as external observers and advi-
sors; we would like to thank in particular Colin Webb, Dirk Pilat,
Paul Schreyer and Nadim Ahmad. We are also grateful to Eurostat,
especially to Arturo de la Fuente, Frank Schönborn, Leonidas Akri-
tidis and Jukka Jalava for their support in arranging regular meetings
with the National Accounts Working Party as well as setting up the
statistical module of the EU KLEMS database at the Eurostat website.
We received strong support from the European Commission Services
throughout the project and are especially grateful to DG Research
(Ian Perry, Marianne Paasi) and DG ECFIN (Werner Roeger, Kieran
McMorrow, Douglas Koszerek) for their help and advice. Finally, the
project also owes much to a number of individuals for advice and support at various stages of the project, including Eric Bartelsman, Erwin
Diewert, Mun Ho, Mathilde Mas, Nicholas Oulton and Jack Triplett.

We owe special thanks to Dale Jorgenson from Harvard University, one of the pioneers of the growth accounting method. His unwavering support for the project from the embryonic initialisation phase to completion has been highly motivating and a continuous source of inspiration for the project participants. We are looking forward to continuing our collaboration and extending this type of work to other countries in the world.

Finally, we also would like to thank Rebecca Cooke and Chris Doubleday for excellent work on the final edit of this manuscript.

All viewpoints expressed in this book are those of the authors only, and any remaining errors are our responsibility.

1 | *Introduction and overview*

1.1 Introduction

The late 1990s saw a major change in the comparative growth performance of Europe and the United States. After the Second World War labour productivity growth in Europe outstripped that of the United States, leading to rapid catch-up. This provided a strong foundation for rapid improvements in the standards of living across the continent. However, since 1995 US labour productivity growth has nearly doubled compared to earlier periods, while European growth rates have declined. The slowing growth and faltering emergence of the knowledge economy in Europe led to an ambitious action programme of the European Commission, called the 'Lisbon Agenda', aimed at boosting competitiveness and productivity through innovation. It emphasised the need to increase spending on research and development and higher education, and was combined with the aims of completing the single market, opening up sheltered sectors, improving the climate for business and reforming the labour markets while ensuring growth was environmentally sustainable. The urgency was reinforced in reviews of the Lisbon Agenda, in the Sapir report on economic growth in Europe and in various post-Lisbon strategy debates and conferences (European Commission 2004; Sapir *et al.* 2004).

The purpose of this book is to provide a comprehensive analysis of economic growth in Europe over the past three decades that allows an evaluation of progress in achieving the Lisbon goals. We analyse why European growth has been slower since the 1990s, both relative to its own past and relative to that of the United States, and we review a number of aspects of Europe's productivity performance and prospects. The main methodology used is the growth accounting approach that decomposes output growth into the growth of inputs and productivity growth. In this method, growth can be traced to increased investment in capital goods and increased use of (skilled) labour, or to increases in the efficiency with which these inputs are used. Such productivity improvements can be the result of innovation and technical change, but also of reallocation of resources due to, for example, competitive pressure. We will argue that Europe's falling behind is the combined result of a severe productivity slowdown in traditional manufacturing and other goods production, and a concomitant failure to invest in and reap the benefits from information and communications technology (ICT), in particular in market services. These results stem from a detailed industry-level analysis employing new data on the sources of growth from the EU KLEMS Growth and Productivity Accounts. This database contains detailed measures of output, labour and capital inputs and derived variables such as labour productivity and multi-factor productivity. Such data have not been available on an internationally consistent basis until now. The book illustrates the scope for rich analysis and robust results that can be achieved from coherent measurement at the industry level.

Indeed, the main contribution of this book is to show the large differences in growth performance across industries and the implications for aggregate trends. The chapters provide a detailed analysis of Europe's productivity performance since the 1970s and highlight the importance of structural change and the shifting contributions of goods- and services-producing industries to aggregate growth. It unveils large variations across industries in the use of skilled labour and ICT capital and in the dynamics of productivity growth, not only between manufacturing and services, but also across detailed services industries such as trade, transport, financial, business and personal services. The EU KLEMS database has made these differences transparent for the first time and, as we will argue, should be the cornerstone for future analyses of European performance. Further study of the drivers of cross-country differences in productivity performance, such as the effect of restrictive entry regulations or innovation bottlenecks, will need to confront and explore this industry heterogeneity. The databases presented in this book should therefore be part of the standard toolbox of economists interested in growth and development across advanced countries, and the methodological perspectives we offer can provide a starting point for further work.

This chapter sets the scene for the remainder of the book and summarises its main findings. We start with an overview of the various perspectives on Europe's falling behind since the 1990s in section 1.2.

Much of this literature stresses the role of product and labour market regulations in driving productivity growth and the increasing importance of innovation in Europe's economy. To a large extent this work on the ultimate sources of growth relies heavily on coherent measures of input, output and productivity as derived within a growth accounting system. The analysis in this book follows a long history of theoretical and empirical research in this area, surveyed in section 1.3. Section 1.4 summarises the main findings of the book and outlines its main contributions to the literature. Section 1.5 concludes.

1.2 Perspectives on Europe's falling behind

Europe's growth performance relative to the United States since 1950 can be usefully divided into three periods: 1950–73, 1973–95 and 1995–2006. During the first period, rapid labour productivity growth in the European Union went together with a catching-up in terms of per capita income levels with the United States. The reasons for this dual catching-up process during the 1950s and 1960s have been extensively discussed in the literature (see, for example, Crafts and Toniolo 1996 and Eichengreen 2007). The arguments include elements of imitation of technology and incremental innovation combined with labour market institutions. Compared to other parts of the world, Europe after World War II already had a relatively well-educated population and a strong set of institutions for generating human capital and financial wealth, which allowed a rapid recovery of investment and absorption of new technologies developed elsewhere, notably in the United States, known as catching-up. The 'golden age' of post-World War II growth came to an end rather abruptly in the early 1970s, followed by a period of significantly slower growth lasting almost two decades on both continents (Maddison 1987). Table 1.1 shows that while US GDP per capita growth slowed from 2.4% in the period 1950–73 to 1.8% in 1973–95, EU-15 growth slowed substantially more from 4.7% to only 1.7%. The reasons for this slowdown in the growth rate in Europe include the gradual exhaustion of potential for catching-up and a slowdown of investment rates. Globally, pervasive changes in the international economic order through the breakdown of the Bretton Woods system of fixed exchange rates, coupled with a severe oil price shock in 1973, undermined the effectiveness of stabilisation policies. Further discussions on the global growth slowdown during this period

Table 1.1. *Growth of GDP, GDP per capita and GDP per hour worked,*
EU-15 and USA, 1950–2006

	GDP	GDP per capita	GDP per hour worked
1950–73			
EU-15	5.5	4.7	5.3
USA	3.9	2.4	2.5
1973–95			
EU-15	2.0	1.7	2.4
USA	2.8	1.8	1.2
1995–2006			
EU-15	2.3	2.1	1.5
USA	3.2	2.2	2.3

Notes: Average annual growth rates (in per cent). EU-15 refers to the fifteen countries
constituting the EU up to 2004.
Sources: Calculations based on the Conference Board and Groningen Growth
and Development Centre, Total Economy Database, January 2007, available at
www.ggdc.net.

are provided by Crafts and Toniolo (1996), Baily and Kirkegaard
(2004) and Eichengreen (2007).

While GDP per capita growth rates became quite similar during
1973–95, labour productivity growth in the EU-15 was still twice as
fast as in the USA as unemployment rose and working hours declined.
But after the mid 1990s, the patterns of productivity growth in Europe
and the United States differed dramatically. In the United States, average annual labour productivity growth accelerated from 1.2% during
the period 1973–95 to 2.3% during 1995–2006. Comparing the same
two time periods, annual labour productivity growth in the European
Union declined from 2.4 to 1.5%.

Two main perspectives on the causes of Europe's falling behind
arose around the turn of the millennium. One perspective focused
in particular on developments in labour and product markets. It has
been suggested that an employment–productivity trade-off manifested
itself in the era of increasing labour supply, arising from the reform of
labour markets and tax systems in Europe. During the 1990s, substantial labour reforms were carried out in various European countries.
These reforms appeared to be quite successful in terms of employment

creation as the declining trend in hours worked was reversed in many countries (see, for example, Garibaldi and Mauro 2002). It is frequently argued that the price paid for the employment miracle was a drop in labour productivity growth (Blanchard 2004; Dew-Becker and Gordon 2008). In addition, deep reforms took place in European product markets, in particular for manufacturing goods in the context of the single European market. Similar reforms in services markets though have been much slower and seen as an obstacle to growth. In particular, in the wake of the ICT revolution tighter regulation in product and labour markets has reduced flexibility and may delay the uptake of the new technologies available (Nicoletti and Scarpetta 2003; Griffith *et al.* 2007; Bassanini *et al.* 2009).

Another strand of the literature focuses more on institutional characteristics of educational and innovation systems in Europe and argues that the European slowdown is mainly related to difficulties in switching from growth based on imitation to growth based on innovation. As Europe gradually reached the technology frontier, future growth had increasingly to come from domestic innovation. Instead, Europe still relied on outdated inflexible industrial structures, with low and medium-tech manufacturing dominating and with declining productivity growth rates. This sector suffered from global competition from new EU member states and the emerging economies, especially India and China. In this view a strong innovation system based on increased R&D expenditures and reformed educational systems is the key to renewed European growth (Sapir *et al.* 2004; Aghion and Howitt 2006).

1.3 Growth accounting

Analyses of the European growth slowdown rely heavily on good measures of labour, capital and productivity, and the growth accounting approach appears to be especially useful in this regard. Using this methodology, measures of output growth can be decomposed into the contributions of inputs and productivity within a consistent accounting framework. It allows for an assessment of the relative importance of labour, capital and intermediate inputs to growth, and for measures of multi-factor productivity (MFP) growth to be derived. MFP measures play a major role in the analysis of growth and also feature prominently in this book. Under strict neo-classical assumptions,

MFP growth measures disembodied technological change, although in practice measured MFP can include a range of other effects. These include unmeasured inputs related to organisational change and other intangible investments, returns to scale, any externalities related to investment, as well as measurement errors. In addition MFP measured at the industry level includes the effects of reallocation of market shares across firms. All these effects can be broadly summarised as 'improvements in efficiency', as they improve the productivity with which inputs are used within the industry (see section 3.6 for a more detailed discussion). The reader is referred to the excellent summary of the historical roots and theoretical aspects of this method in Hulten (2001; updated 2010), including its production function origins, sources of biases, index number issues and links with growth models.

Application of the growth accounting methodology has come in several waves. The first coincided with the main theoretical breakthroughs from the end of the 1950s to the 1970s and includes the seminal contributions of Tinbergen (1942), Solow (1957), Denison (1962), Jorgenson and Griliches (1967) and Diewert (1976). Although this first wave dealt mainly with the USA, various growth accounting studies on the European countries followed, including Carré *et al.* (1975) for France and Matthews *et al.* (1982) for the United Kingdom. The second wave, partly overlapping with the first, included a series of international comparative studies, including Denison (1967), Christensen *et al.* (1981) and Maddison (1987). In 1987, Jorgenson, Gollop and Fraumeni (1987) published their standard work outlining the growth accounting approach based on the KLEMS methodology, which measured the growth contributions of capital (K), labour (L), energy (E), material inputs (M) and service inputs (S), as well as the composition of these inputs to identify quality changes. Jorgenson (1995a, b) provides a compendium of studies made in the first two waves.

The third wave of growth accounting, during the 1990s, was triggered by the intensifying debate on the sources of the rapid growth in East Asia and other emerging economies, and the future of what was perceived by some primarily as an unsustainable input-driven growth process (Krugman 1994; Young 1995; Collins and Bosworth 1996; Nelson and Pack 1999). Further impetus came from the rise of ICT as an increasingly important source of growth in advanced economies. The Solow productivity paradox – that 'you can see the computer age everywhere but in the productivity statistics' (Solow 1987) – led to a surge in studies trying to explain the US growth acceleration, as well as why Europe was lagging behind.

In the first round of studies, aggregate growth trends in the United States were analysed. Accelerating labour productivity growth was mainly attributed to increasing investment in ICT goods and improvements in MFP (Jorgenson and Stiroh 2000; Oliner and Sichel 2000). Industry-level MFP trends were still unavailable, but rough estimates by 'backing out' MFP growth in IT production suggested that most of the aggregate MFP acceleration could be traced back to rapid technological change in ICT-goods-production.[1] However, as more detailed industry-level data became available, the focus broadened to include not only ICT-goods-producing industries but also service industries that are heavy users of ICT. This research was initially based on an analysis of labour productivity (Nordhaus 2002; Stiroh 2002), but quickly the needed data on industry capital were developed and the focus shifted to MFP. Studies by Triplett and Bosworth (2004) and Jorgenson, *et al.* (2003; 2005) showed that the biggest contributors to aggregate ICT-capital deepening were a limited number of service industries, in particular trade, finance and business services. In addition to growth in ICT-goods manufacturing, rising MFP growth in these service industries appeared also to be important in explaining the US productivity acceleration.

After some delay, similar studies became available on European growth. The first set of growth accounting studies for Europe relied heavily on private data sources on ICT expenditure collected outside the System of National Accounts (Schreyer 2000; Daveri 2002). They found that although ICT-investment *growth* also accelerated in Europe, its lagging behind the USA was mainly due to lower *levels* of ICT investment. This conclusion was confirmed once investment series from National Accounts became available (Colecchia and Schreyer

---

[1] The latter point is stressed especially by Gordon (2000). Triplett and Bosworth (2004) and Jorgenson *et al.* (2005) show that this 'backing out' of ICT-production MFP from aggregate MFP can be highly misleading as it generates only a *net* measure of MFP growth outside ICT-production. Industry-level studies show that MFP growth rates outside ICT-goods manufacturing have also been high. However, high growth in some industries was cancelled out by low or negative MFP growth in many others, as discussed in more detail in the chapters below.

2002; van Ark *et al.* 2002; Vijselaar and Albers 2004; Timmer and van Ark 2005). Typically, they found that the contribution of ICT capital deepening to aggregate labour productivity growth in Europe was only half of what the contribution was in the USA. In contrast to the USA, aggregate MFP growth in Europe did not accelerate. This difference could only partly be attributed to the smaller ICT-producing sector in Europe compared to that in the USA and hence must be sought elsewhere in the economy (Pilat *et al.* 2002; van Ark *et al.* 2003; Timmer and van Ark 2005).[2]

A detailed study of labour productivity growth at the industry level by van Ark *et al.* (2003) suggested that much of the failure of Europe to achieve its own labour productivity growth revival in the late 1990s could be traced to the same industries that performed so well in the United States, particularly trade and finance; this was confirmed by O'Mahony and van Ark (2003). Labour productivity growth in these industries lagged behind severely in Europe, and given their high ICT intensity in the USA, Europe's problem seemed to be related to slow ICT adoption. In this type of study, industries were grouped into ICT-producing, ICT-using and non-ICT-using based on the ICT intensity of industries in the USA. The basis for allocation to particular groups was, however, weak and results were sensitive to the choices made (Daveri 2004). In addition, it presumed a common ranking of industries on the basis of ICT use across all countries. Without detailed information on ICT and non-ICT investment for individual industries and countries, it remained unclear which industries were responsible for the gap in ICT investment between Europe and the USA and sluggish European MFP growth. Inklaar *et al.* (2005) were the first to consider the experience in Europe using a comprehensive dataset that separated ICT and non-ICT investment at the industry level, but this was limited to four EU countries: France, Germany, the Netherlands and the UK.[3]

In conclusion, this section highlights that a significant research effort in the past was devoted to explanations of Europe's poor relative

---

[2] The ICT-producing sector might also have additional productivity-enhancing effects through technology spillovers to other sectors. However, there is little evidence so far: a case study of Finland did not find much support for this (Daveri and Silva 2004).

[3] At the same time various individual country studies appeared, such as Oulton (2002) on the UK and Daveri and Jona-Lasinio (2005) on Italy.

productivity performance, but much of this was carried out at a time when detailed industry-level data were not available, and much of the literature refers to a limited set of countries. With evidence of the increasing importance of ICT and market services for growth, there was also renewed attention to measurement issues (Griliches 1992; Sichel 1997; Triplett and Bosworth, 2004) and international comparability of national statistics. Work at the OECD highlighted problems in comparability of ICT investment and price deflators and output measurement of market services (Schreyer 2002; Ahmad 2003; Wölfl 2003). Clearly, there was an increasing need for new methods, comparable statistics and convergence in methods of measuring productivity. The aim of the EU KLEMS initiative set up in 2004 was to meet this demand. This resulted in the construction of the EU KLEMS Growth and Productivity Accounts that provide the main building block for the comparative analysis of economic growth in Europe in this book.

1.4 Book summary and contribution

This book provides the detailed analysis required to delve deeply into the reasons for Europe's poor productivity performance since the 1990s, both relative to its own past and relative to the USA. Our main focus is on the performance of the European Union as a whole, given the increasing integration of the European economies and the growing importance of pan-European policies. Throughout the book we analyse growth in the European Union on the basis of data for ten of the fifteen countries constituting the EU before 2004, namely Austria, Belgium, Denmark, Finland, France, Germany, Italy, the Netherlands, Spain and the United Kingdom. Together the ten countries provided 93 per cent of the EU GDP in 1995. Occasionally, though, we also provide analysis of individual countries to illustrate the diversity of growth paths within Europe.

The main dataset used in our analysis is the EU KLEMS database that provides comparable and harmonised statistics on inputs, outputs and productivity trends for a wide range of countries from 1970 onwards within a growth accounting framework. The EU KLEMS database was constructed by a consortium of seventeen research institutes across Europe in close co-operation with national statistical institutes, as described in the Preface. The acronym KLEMS stands for capital (K), labour (L), energy (E), material (M) and services (S) inputs at the industry level. The database is publicly available at www. euklems.net. In addition to growth statistics, we rely on new estimates of relative levels of productivity across countries that allow for analysis of catch-up and convergence. Throughout the book, we devote considerable attention to a discussion of the details of the data employed and of the main methodological perspectives, illustrated with numerical examples. This function is fulfilled in Chapter 3 for growth accounting and in Chapter 6 for level accounting. The international effort that went into constructing the databases and the choice of methods of analysis together mean that the discussion in this book presents more information on Europe's relative performance than has been available in the literature to date. This allows for a deeper investigation of the main differences between high- and low-performing countries and industries. More generally, it illustrates to the research and policy community the benefits of analysis based on detailed data.

We argue that an industry perspective provides important additional insights when compared to more aggregate analyses. For example, the industries that appear to be responsible for the European slowdown, mainly in manufacturing and other goods production, are not the same as those driving the increasing gap with the USA, which are mainly in trade and business services. Given the large variation in the technological characteristics and regulatory environments of these industries, this has profound implications for further policy analysis. In addition, we show throughout the book the consequences of using detailed input measures that take account of heterogeneity in inputs. For example, accounting for the changing skill distribution of the labour force and the increasing use of ICT-capital assets can lead to rather different measures of MFP growth. In addition, comparisons of MFP levels are highly sensitive to the use of cross-country price ratios across industries. The impact of the use of crude or more data-intensive measures of productivity in growth and convergence analysis is discussed throughout the book. We also stress the numerous measurement problems that still hinder this type of analysis and argue that the benefits from additional data detail have to be weighed against the reliability of these data and the desire to achieve international comparability. As such, the book provides new methodological perspectives and so is useful not only as a guide to the EU KLEMS database, but also as a primer on the use of data in economic growth analysis.

The main body of the book begins in Chapter 2 with a broad analysis of economic growth in Europe in the past three decades based on the EU KLEMS database, following van Ark *et al.* (2008). It first presents a growth accounting decomposition for the EU aggregate and compares it to one for the USA. When looking at these growth accounts from the perspective of the emerging knowledge economy, it appears to be useful to focus on the summed contributions of three factors: direct impacts from investments in information and communication technology; changes in labour composition mostly driven by greater demand for skilled workers; and multi-factor productivity growth, which might include the impact of intangible investments such as organisational changes related to the use of information technology. This chapter shows that the combined contribution of these three factors to labour productivity growth in Europe was only 1.1 percentage points during 1995–2005, whereas they accounted for 2.6 percentage points in the US. It highlights the important role of multi-factor productivity growth; whereas MFP growth in the United States accelerated from 0.7% in 1980–95 to 1.3% in 1995–2005, the same measure declined from 1.0 to 0.3% between these two periods in the European Union.

The remainder of the chapter delves more into what underlies these aggregate trends and argues that some of the reasons for the European slowdown are related to particular structural characteristics of the European economy. Employment and productivity growth strongly declined in goods-producing industries such as agriculture, mining and construction that had been major drivers of aggregate growth in the past. Also technologically less sophisticated manufacturing industries suffered in this period, especially in Spain and Italy, in the face of increasing global competition. The movement of labour towards low-productive services further dragged down aggregate growth. Whereas market services emerged as a new source of growth in the USA, this did not happen in the EU.

A consideration in greater depth of market services reveals that transatlantic growth differences were especially large in distributive trade and business services. This suggests new opportunities for European growth driven by innovations in market services, enabled by investment in ICT. Within Europe, this transformation is already taking place to some extent: market services in the Netherlands, Sweden and the United Kingdom have contributed almost as much to aggregate labour productivity growth as in the United States. In contrast, Germany, Italy and Spain have showed almost zero contributions from market services.

Chapter 3 begins with a description of the growth accounting methodology that forms the organising principle of the EU KLEMS database. It is based on production possibility frontiers where industry gross output is a function of capital, labour, intermediate inputs and the level of technology. The first section of this chapter outlines this methodology, bringing the reader through the necessary equations and the underlying assumptions. It then considers in more detail the data series required to implement the growth accounting method, dividing them into outputs and intermediate inputs, labour services and capital services. In each case both the data requirements and additional technical assumptions are discussed. The chapter illustrates the complexities involved in a measurement exercise of this type and in turn demonstrates the richness of the data, in particular in its detail on labour and capital composition. It emphasises the need to breakdown these inputs into their components in order to fully comprehend sources of growth in an international perspective. It is well known that all workers should not be treated as equally productive and the literature review above emphasises a similar need to divide capital inputs by type of asset. Not doing so can lead to biased research results and erroneous policy conclusions. While few would dispute this, its practical implementation raises difficult issues that these sections highlight.

The second part of Chapter 3 is devoted to a discussion of various measurement issues that the EU KLEMS database could not fully address. Examples include the measurement of output in non-market services (health, education and public administration), difficulties in comparing types of labour across countries and the issue of using ex-ante or ex-post rates of return in calculating capital services. The chapter also includes a detailed discussion of the interpretation of MFP and its limitations as a measure of technology. A separate section is devoted to an overview of measurement practices in Europe concerning market services output. This finds that differences are still large in Europe but greater harmonisation is being achieved.

In Chapters 4 and 5 the broad analysis of Chapter 2 is complemented by more detailed analysis using the information by industry available in the EU KLEMS database. Chapter 4 argues that despite important differences, the processes of economic growth in the EU and the USA share a set of common characteristics when viewed from a long-term perspective. To this end, common trends in the two regions since 1980 have been identified. Foremost is the shift in the shares of employment and output from goods-producing industries to market services, continuing the trend earlier identified by Kuznets (1971) and Maddison (1980). Their analyses relied strongly on the dichotomy between industry and services. We argue that the treatment of the services sector as a homogeneous and stagnant sector, in contrast to dynamic manufacturing, is no longer warranted. The use of ICT and skilled labour is increasing throughout the economy, and in particular in market services. We also find that in the past decades, distribution services had productivity growth rates at least as high as goods production. In contrast to personal services, these industries do not suffer from Baumol's cost disease (Baumol 1967), either in the EU or the USA. Finance and business services have the highest levels of skill and ICT use and increasing employment shares, but long-run productivity growth trends have been flat. Given the large differences in technical progress and input structures within the services industries, we conclude that reliance on an aggregate representation of the services sector is no longer warranted.

In Chapter 5 we return to the analysis of the European productivity growth slowdown and provide a detailed analysis of the sources of growth in Europe and the USA based on data for twenty-six individual industries. It outlines a decomposition method that allows the tracing of industry-level contributions to aggregate productivity growth. These contributions are derived by weighting growth in the volume of inputs and productivity in an industry by its share in aggregate value added. In this way, the aggregate growth accounts in Chapter 2 are enriched with industry-level detail. Aggregate analysis shows that during 1995–2005 ICT investments contributed twice as much to aggregate labour productivity growth in the USA as in Europe. In Chapter 5 it is found that in twenty-three of twenty-six industries, the contribution of ICT was higher in the USA than in the EU, which is driven by differences between the two regions in the shares of ICT in value added, rather than by differences in growth rates. This in turn reflects the earlier adoption of ICT technology in the USA, possibly related to the more intensive use of high-skilled (graduate) labour. Given their heavy use of ICT, financial and business services are responsible for more than half of the EU–USA difference in the contribution of ICT capital.

In chapters 2 and 5 it is also argued that trends in MFP growth are crucial in understanding performance in the EU relative to that in the USA. In the EU, MFP growth rates declined in eighteen of twenty-six industries between 1980–95 and 1995–2005. There was a declining trend in the contribution of MFP growth in most manufacturing industries, as well as strong decelerations in agriculture, mining and construction. In the period 1980–95, these industries were strong drivers of aggregate growth in the EU. Post and telecommunication was the only sector that showed an increased contribution across the two periods. In contrast to Europe, MFP growth in the USA accelerated in many industries, especially in market services. Whereas their combined contribution was about zero in the earlier period, market services contributed half of US MFP growth in the later period, in particular in wholesale, retail and automotive trade. During 1995–2005 MFP growth in the USA was higher than in the EU in eighteen of twenty-six industries. Based on so-called Harberger diagrams (Harberger 1998), US growth is shown to be widespread across industries and is characterised as having a yeast-like pattern, while in Europe growth is more localised in a few industries and so can be described as having a mushroom-like pattern.

In addition to slowing MFP growth, growth in Europe also suffered from decelerating non-ICT capital deepening. This decline was pervasive as contributions to aggregate labour productivity growth after 1995 decreased in nineteen of twenty-six industries. The contribution of the mining sector and business services, heavy users of non-ICT capital, diminished strongly, but there was also widespread decline across all manufacturing sectors. The reduction in the contribution of non-ICT capital deepening is probably linked to moderation of wage growth in Europe, which raised the price of capital relative to labour, and to increasing global competition in manufacturing.

While the analysis in the earlier chapters mainly concerns trends in growth, Chapter 6 provides additional information on productivity levels, particularly useful for those interested in issues of convergence and growth. Various growth theories argue that the potential for future growth is closely related to a country's distance from the technology frontier. If the gap is large, rapid growth can be achieved through the imitation and adaptation of technologies developed elsewhere. Countries near the technology frontier, however, need to base growth more on domestic innovation. This chapter contains extensive methodology and data sections reflecting the difficulties in measuring output, input and productivity levels across countries. It then presents the results on comparisons of productivity levels and ends with an application of the data in convergence regressions. It is shown that in 2005 the EU led the USA in eight industries: mining, post and telecommunication, finance and five manufacturing industries. In other major industries like construction, retail and automotive trade, European MFP levels are on a par. However, big gaps relative to the USA are found for industries like agriculture, business services and, in particular, electrical machinery. This wide range of relative productivity levels highlights the importance of a detailed industry analysis. Aggregate productivity statistics might suggest that the EU is trailing the USA in terms of innovation and technological prowess, but the technological distance between these two regions is highly industry-specific. This is also true for patterns of catch-up and convergence. Additional analysis of convergence trends in a set of twenty countries between 1980 and 2005 indicates that about half of the twenty-four industries show decreasing dispersion, while the other half show increasing dispersion of MFP levels. There is no dominant convergence trend in sectoral productivity growth across advanced countries.

The main finding from this chapter is that a sizeable labour productivity gap has opened up between the EU and the USA since the 1990s. In 2005, the (log) gap in labour productivity between the EU market economy and the USA was 37 percentage points. Of this gap, 8 percentage points were due to a higher-skilled labour force and 5 percentage points were due to higher capital intensity in the USA. The latter hides two opposing forces – although ICT intensity was much lower in the EU, non-ICT levels were higher. The remaining gap of 24 per cent is explained by the differences in the efficiency with which labour and capital are used, as measured by multi-factor productivity. Looking at the industry origins of this gap, it is clear that business services account for a significant part of this difference, as a large productivity gap has opened up in this sector.

Finally, Chapter 6 undertakes an econometric analysis of possible determinants of MFP growth using a technology-gap specification commonly used in the literature. The results of this analysis provide no evidence for spillover effects of ICT-capital or skills to productivity growth. Returns to investment in ICT and human capital seem to be captured fully by the investor and they cannot explain the differences found in MFP growth across countries.

Chapter 7 concludes this book with a brief discussion of prospects for productivity growth in Europe and an exploration of a number of issues that might help in understanding the drivers of productivity growth. It suggests that future growth in Europe will depend crucially on the path taken by market services. In disentangling productivity it points to important remaining deficiencies in measurement, including the output of the banking sector and of the non-market services sectors, and in developing measures of intangible capital inputs. Much work is already underway in these areas and these additions to the literature are briefly reviewed. The chapter also considers the role of demand and resource allocation in driving productivity growth. It stresses the need for more studies based on firm-level data to complement industry-level analysis for further disentangling the drivers of productivity. However, in line with the overarching message of this book, it is argued that the important differences in performance and characteristics of industries are equally significant for improving our understanding of firm-level analyses.

1.5 Concluding remarks

The analysis in this book ends in 2006, just before a major global financial crisis and economic downturn emerged. This begs the question of whether the growth and productivity analysis presented here still has relevance given the significant changes in economic conditions. There is no doubt that the crisis, which came to full effect by the end of 2008, had an immediate effect on investment and productivity over the short run. The question remains as to the implications of the crisis in the medium and long term. A pessimistic view would be to expect a move towards greater risk aversion among firms and their financiers, leading to a period of slow growth in investment and a reluctance to introduce new technologies and to innovate. This could have adverse impacts on firms' propensities to invest in the inputs that were most important in the previous decade, namely ICT, human capital and other intangibles. A more optimistic view would be that the economic downturn increases incentives for innovative entrepreneurs to redirect resources for exploring new techniques and applications. In this case the impact in the medium to long term might be increased investment in innovation and their related inputs. As yet, it is too early to tell how this will play out, as it will be related to the pace and pattern of global growth and competitiveness and to institutional rearrangements on financial and capital markets. Regardless, the analysis in this book indicates that future growth in Europe has to come to an important extent from improvements in market services productivity. As attested by the US experience of the past decade, strong productivity growth in service industries is a realistic possibility, and this may perhaps be extended beyond the most successful cases of the distribution and business services sectors to other services industries, including non-market services. Despite the contributions from the new analysis presented in this book, we still face major challenges in improving the measurement of output, inputs and productivity growth in these industries. It remains important that we continue to develop robust statistical data that allow investigators to examine these trends.

2 | Economic growth in Europe

2.1 Introduction

After World War II productivity growth in Europe boomed, providing a strong foundation for rapid improvements in the standards of living across the continent. But since the mid 1990s, Europe has experienced a significant slowdown in productivity growth. Average annual labour productivity growth (measured as GDP per hour worked) in the fifteen countries that constituted the European Union up to 2004 declined from 2.4% in the period 1973–95 to 1.5% in 1995–2006. Conversely, productivity growth in the United States significantly accelerated from an annual average of 1.2% in the period 1973–95 to 2.3% 1995–2006. While the USA was able to reap the benefits of the dawning knowledge economy, the European Union seems to have missed the opportunity to revive economic growth. In this chapter we will argue that there are distinct reasons for the European productivity slowdown and US acceleration since the mid 1990s. Our detailed industry-level analysis reveals that traditional manufacturing and other goods production no longer acted as major engines for the European economy. At the same time, Europe has been slow in taking up the benefits from the knowledge economy. In contrast to the USA, productivity growth in market services has not accelerated. We consider various explanations that are not mutually exclusive. The European growth slowdown might be related to long-term trends in the structure of the economy, such as the increasing demand for low-productive services and a gradual exhaustion of the potential for growth based on catching up in traditional technologies. In addition, the slower emergence of the new knowledge economy in Europe might be due to lower growth contributions from investment in information and communications technology (ICT), the small share of technology-producing industries in Europe, and slower multi-factor productivity growth which proxies for advances in technology and innovation. Underlying

18

these are issues related to the functioning of European labour markets and the high level of product market regulation in Europe. This chapter emphasises the key role of market service sectors in accounting for the productivity growth divergence between the two regions.

We focus on the European productivity experience, especially in the period since 1995, using a new and detailed database called the EU KLEMS Growth and Productivity Accounts. The level of detail in this database allows explicit consideration of a number of issues: changes in patterns of capital–labour substitution; the increasing importance of investment in information and communications technology; the use of more high-skilled labour; the different dynamics across industries, like ICT-producing industries, manufacturing and services; and the diversity of productivity experiences across the countries of Europe. The rest of the chapter is organised as follows. In the next section, we provide a brief overview of GDP per capita and productivity growth in Europe and the USA since 1950. In section 2.3, aggregate output growth is decomposed into growth of factor inputs and multi-factor productivity (MFP) based on the growth accounting methodology. We find that while MFP in Europe slowed down in the 1990s, it accelerated in the USA. In the remainder of the chapter we zoom in on industry-level sources of growth. We argue in section 2.4 that Europe's slowdown is mainly grounded in declining performance in goods-producing industries. At the same time, employment is shifted to less productive services industries, further dragging down aggregate growth. However, developments in the USA show that the potential for growth has increased, driven by ICT-enabled innovation in market services. Section 2.5 argues that a new EU–US productivity gap has opened up, in particular in trade and business services. A case study of retailing illustrates that realisation of this potential will crucially depend on changes in the regulatory environment. As some European countries have already followed the US growth path, diversity in growth patterns across Europe is increasing as discussed in section 2.6. Section 2.7 concludes.

2.2 European and US productivity growth since 1950

Slower labour productivity growth in Europe than in the United States reverses a long-term pattern of convergence. The comparative European experience in GDP per capita, GDP per hour and hours

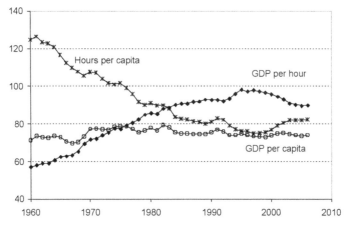

Figure 2.1. GDP per hour worked and GDP per capita, total economy, EU-15 as percentage of USA, 1960–2007. EU-15 refers to the fifteen countries constituting the European Union before 2004 (Austria, Belgium, Denmark, Finland, France, Germany, Greece, Ireland, Italy, Luxembourg, the Netherlands, Portugal, Spain, Sweden and the United Kingdom). Relative levels are based on purchasing power parities for GDP for 2002 from the OECD. (*Source*: Based on the Conference Board and Groningen Growth and Development Centre, Total Economy Database, January 2007, available at www.ggdc.net.)

worked per capita is illustrated in Figure 2.1. The GDP measures are compared to the US levels and are adjusted for differences in relative price levels using the GDP-based purchasing power parities for 2002 from the OECD.

In the 1950s and 1960s, rapid labour productivity growth in the EU went together with a catching-up in terms of GDP per capita with the USA. European productivity growth was characterised by a traditional catch-up pattern based on the imitation and adaptation of foreign technology coupled with strong investment and supporting institutions. However, the traditional post-war convergence process came to an end by the mid 1970s. In the light of this study, a striking observation is that while per capita income in Europe hovered around 75–80 per cent of the United States after 1973, the productivity gap between the EU and the USA continued to narrow. During this period labour productivity growth in the EU-15 was still twice as fast as in the USA. The labour productivity gap virtually closed, from 25 percentage points in 1973 to only 2 percentage points in 1995 (see Figure 2.1). In some

European countries (including Belgium, France and the Netherlands), GDP per hour worked in 1995 was even higher than in the USA. The combination of an unchanged gap in per capita income and a narrowing gap in labour productivity was – by accounting identity – related to a decline in Europe's labour force participation rates and a fall in working hours per person employed. Working hours per capita in the European Union countries declined from approximate equality to the US level in 1973 to only 76 per cent of the US level by 1995 (Crafts and Toniolo 1996; Baily and Kirkegaard 2004; Eichengreen 2007).

A substantial literature has explored why Europe's labour market institutions led to less work during this period. Blanchard (2004) stresses how the trade-off between preferences for leisure and work developed differently in Europe and the United States. Prescott (2004) estimates that the role of income taxes can account for virtually all of the differences in labour participation rates across European countries. Nickell (1997) shows that besides high payroll taxes, other labour market issues, such as generous unemployment benefits, poor educational standards at the bottom and high unionisation with little co-ordination, also play an important role in accounting for Europe's rise in unemployment since the mid 1970s. Europe's welfare state expanded rapidly in the 1970s, causing an increase in labour cost, a strong bias towards insiders in the labour market and an increase in structural unemployment in particular among young and elderly workers.

One result of Europe's slowing growth in labour input was a rapid increase in capital intensity, as the rise in wages supported the substitution of labour by capital. Figure 2.2 shows that in the market economy, Europe's capital services per hour worked was at 82 per cent of the US level in 1973, but increased rapidly to 95 per cent in the mid 1990s. Some European countries (including Austria, Belgium, Finland, France, Germany and the Netherlands) had levels of capital services per hour worked which were even above the US level in 1995.[1] As a result, the high labour productivity levels in the European Union by the mid 1990s should be interpreted with care. Economists draw a distinction between labour productivity, which can be measured by value added per hour worked, and multi-factor productivity, which is

---

[1] Figure 2.2 provides figures on the market economy, while Figure 2.1 refers to the total economy including non-market services; see section 2.3 for further discussion. Chapter 6 provides further evidence on level estimates.

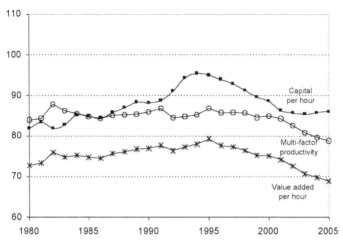

Figure 2.2. Productivity and capital intensity levels, market economy, EU-10 as percentage of USA, 1980–2005. Data for European Union refers to EU-10; see Table 2.1. (*Source*: Based on EU KLEMS database, March 2008, and GGDC Productivity Level database (Inklaar and Timmer 2009b) (see Chapters 3 and 6 for methods and sources).)

the level of output after accounting for both labour and capital inputs.[2] As we will argue in more detail below, even though Europe experienced relatively strong growth in labour productivity, the growth in multi-factor productivity was much lower. Figure 2.2 shows that relative MFP levels in the EU remained stagnant between 1980 and 1995. This indicates that Europe's higher labour productivity growth during this period may not have been so much the result of catch-up, access to superior technology or even faster innovation, as largely attributable to accumulated labour market rigidities.[3]

---

[2] This definition of multi-factor productivity is based on a value-added production function. A more general definition, including intermediate inputs, is discussed in Chapter 3.

[3] Using a model estimating diminishing returns to hours worked and employment and assuming hours worked and the employment rate being the same as in the United States, a study by Bourlès and Cette (2007) shows estimates of 'structural' hourly productivity for several continental European countries that are 10–15 percentage points lower than 'observed' productivity. While the results of such models may be sensitive to the specifications, these estimates are sufficiently large to suggest some role for labour market institutions in explaining Europe's productivity convergence between 1973 and 1995.

The second break in relative EU–US growth performance, which is the focus of this chapter, occurred in the mid 1990s when the catching up of labour productivity also came to a halt. In the United States, average annual labour productivity growth in the market economy accelerated from 1.9% during the period 1973–95 to 2.9% during 1995–2006, while growth in the European Union declined from 2.5 to 1.5%. By 2006, relative GDP per hour worked in the EU market economy had dropped about 10 percentage points compared to 1995. Similarly, Europe's capital input levels came down significantly from the mid 1990s.

The slowdown in labour productivity may be related to the rapid growth in labour input in many European countries, reversing the long-run declining trend. During the late 1980s and 1990s, several European countries introduced labour market reforms and instigated active labour market interventions to bring long-term unemployed people to work and raise the participation rate (Blanchard 2004). The slowdown in productivity growth and the decline in relative capital intensity in Europe since 1995 beg the question of whether, since limited employment growth accompanied higher labour productivity in Europe in the 1973–95 period, that pattern was reversing itself in the more recent time period (Dew-Becker and Gordon 2008). This trade-off might hold true for the short run, but there is little evidence that there is a long-run relationship between employment and productivity growth. While, in the short run, labour productivity growth might decline because of the dampening of real wage growth and consequent reduction in the rate of substitution of capital for labour, it is unlikely that the elasticity of labour input on productivity would be large in the medium and long term.[4] This will crucially depend on the endogenous developments in investment rates and technical change. As will be shown below, the rate of technical change in Europe, as measured by multi-factor productivity, also slumped. A related argument is that increases in employment have raised the share of less productive workers in the workforce, causing labour productivity to decline. However, there are

---

[4] Bélorgey *et al.* (2004) estimate a long-term productivity elasticity with regard to participation of −0.5 with regard to the employment rate and −0.35 with regard to hours worked per person. In contrast, McGuckin and van Ark (2005) find that the productivity response to a 1 per cent rise in participation is less than −0.3 and peters out in less than five years.

no signs of a significant slowdown in the skill level of the labour force pointing towards a strong rise in low-skilled labour in Europe. On the contrary, as will be shown in Chapter 4, the average skill level of the employed labour force continued to increase throughout the 1990s. Thus, the labour market is unlikely to be the main explanation for the long-term slowdown in labour productivity growth.

When put into a comparative perspective, the productivity slow-down in Europe is all the more disappointing as US productivity growth has accelerated since the mid 1990s. The causes of the strong US productivity resurgence have been extensively discussed elsewhere (as a starting point, see Jorgenson *et al.* 2005). In the mid 1990s, there was a burst of higher productivity in industries producing information and communications technology equipment and a capital-deepening effect from investment in ICT assets across the economy. This was driven by the rapid pace of innovation in information and communications technologies, fuelled by the precipitous fall in semiconductor prices.[5] With some delay, arguably due to the necessary changes in production processes and organisational practices, there was also a productivity surge in industries using these new information and communications technologies – in particular in market services industries (Triplett and Bosworth 2006). In Europe, the advent of the knowledge economy has been much slower. In the next sections, we exploit the EU KLEMS Growth Accounts database to develop a better view of how inputs and productivity trends at the industry level have contributed to the change in the growth performance of European countries, in particular in comparison with the United States.

2.3 Growth accounting for Europe and the United States

To assess the contribution of various inputs to GDP growth, we apply the neo-classical growth accounting framework pioneered by Solow (1957) and further developed by Jorgenson and associates (Jorgenson and Griliches 1967; Jorgenson, Gollop and Fraumeni, 1987). By using this framework, measures of output growth can be decomposed into the contributions of inputs and productivity within a consistent approach. It allows for an assessment of the relative importance of

---

[5] Aizcorbe and Kortum (2005) provide a vintage model that aims to explain the price decline.

labour, capital and intermediate inputs to growth, and for measures
of multi-factor productivity growth to be derived. The output contribution of an input is measured by the growth rate of the input,
weighted by that input's income share. Under neo-classical assumptions, the income shares reflect the output elasticity of each input and,
assuming constant returns to scale, they sum to one. The portion of
output growth not attributable to inputs is multi-factor productivity
growth. As a residual measure, multi-factor productivity has multiple
interpretations, but in some way it reflects the overall efficiency of the
production process.[6]

Our growth decompositions are based on the March 2008 release
of EU KLEMS database. In Chapter 3 of this book, growth accounting and the data sources and methodologies used in the construction
of this database will be discussed in detail, so we will be brief here.
The EU KLEMS database provides harmonised measures of economic
growth, productivity, employment creation and capital formation at
a detailed industry level for European Union member states and the
United States from 1980 to 2005. In particular, this database contains unique industry-level measures of the skill distribution of the
work-force and a detailed asset decomposition of investment in physical capital. Labour input reflects changes in hours worked, but also
changes in labour composition in terms of age, gender and educational
qualifications over time. Physical capital is decomposed into eight asset
categories, of which three are information and communications capital – information technology hardware, communication equipment
and software – and five are capital that does not involve information
and communications technology – including machinery and equipment, transport equipment and non-residential structures. Residential
capital, which does not contribute in any direct way to productivity
gains, is excluded from the analysis.

The EU KLEMS database has made it possible for the first time to
compare and analyse the role of high-skilled labour and information
and communications technology capital for productivity growth at an
industry level across countries. In this book, our focus is on the market
economy, which means that we exclude health and education services,
as well as public administration and defence. While we recognise that

---

[6] See section 3.6 for an elaborate discussion of the interpretations of multi-factor
productivity measures.

some output of these sectors is provided by (semi-) private institutions, and that the extent of the private industry share varies across countries, we refer to these sectors as 'non-market services'. Output measurement problems in these sectors are substantial, and in most countries output growth is measured using input growth, in particular for government services. In such cases, comparisons of productivity growth do not make much sense.[7] This exclusion implies a faster productivity growth in both the European Union and the United States since 1995 than for the total economy, but the difference in the pace of acceleration between the two regions does not change.[8] Also, in the remainder of the book, figures for the European Union are based on data for ten countries: Austria, Belgium, Denmark, Finland, France, Germany, Italy, the Netherlands, Spain and the United Kingdom. It excludes Greece, Ireland, Luxembourg, Portugal and Sweden from the set of fifteen countries which constituted the EU before 2004, because no industry-level accounts dating back to 1980 were available for these five countries. Together the ten countries (the EU-10) generated 93 per cent of the EU-15 GDP in 1995. In 2004, the EU expanded to include ten new member states, mainly in Central and Eastern Europe, and, in 2007, to include another two; the new members are not included in any EU aggregate in this book but they are included in various tables on an individual basis.

Table 2.1 provides a summary picture of the growth contributions of factor inputs and multi-factor productivity to labour productivity growth in the market economy in the ten European Union countries and in the United States for the periods 1980–95 and 1995–2005. Comparing the periods before and after 1995, output growth in the European Union has been more or less constant. As described at length in the previous section, hours worked in the European Union grew rapidly after 1995, to some extent making up for the shortfall in the earlier period. In contrast, the growth in hours worked slowed down very substantially in the United States – in particular after 2000 – even though the average growth rate in hours was comparable to that of the EU in the period 1995–2005. As a result labour productivity growth

---

[7] We also exclude real estate (ISIC 70), because output in this industry mostly reflects imputed housing rents rather than sales of firms. Consequently, residential buildings are taken out of the capital stock for the market economy.

[8] See Table 3.9 for more.

Table 2.1. *Decomposition of output growth, market economy, EU and USA, 1980–2005*

	European Union		United States	
	1980–95	1995–2005	1980–95	1995–2005
1 Market economy output ((2) + (3))	2.1	2.2	3.2	3.6
2 Hours worked	−0.5	0.7	1.3	0.7
3 Labour productivity ((4) + (5) + (8))	2.5	1.5	1.9	2.9
Contributions from:				
4 Labour composition	0.3	0.2	0.2	0.3
5 Capital services per hour ((6) + (7))	1.2	1.0	1.0	1.3
6 ICT capital per hour	0.4	0.5	0.7	1.0
7 Non-ICT capital per hour	0.8	0.4	0.3	0.3
8 Multi-factor productivity	1.0	0.3	0.7	1.3
Contribution of the knowledge economy to labour productivity ((4) + (6) + (8))	1.7	1.1	1.6	2.6

Notes: Contributions to growth of output volume in the market economy (annual average growth rates, in percentage points). Data for European Union refers to ten countries: Austria, Belgium, Denmark, Finland, France, Germany, Italy, the Netherlands, Spain and the United Kingdom. 'ICT' is information and communications technology.
Source: Calculations based on EU KLEMS database, March 2008; see Chapter 3.

in the US market economy doubled compared to a large slowdown in Europe after 1995.

Table 2.1 also shows that changes in labour composition contributed at most 0.3 percentage points to labour productivity growth both in the European Union and the United States during this entire time period. Even though this contribution is small, its positive sign implies that the process of transformation of the labour force to higher skills has proceeded at a steady pace both in Europe and the United States. This confirms the observation above that Europe did not raise its share of low-skilled workers during the employment expansion phase after 1995. Instead, the upward trend in the skill content of the employees shows that newcomers on the labour market have had, on average, more schooling than the existing labour force. Concerning the contribution of capital deepening to labour productivity growth, measured by capital services per hour, Table 2.1 shows somewhat larger differences between the European Union and the United States compared to labour composition. This contribution declined in Europe while rising in the United States between the two time periods. The specific contribution of information and communications technology per working hour in Europe has been lower than in the United States and, since 1995, it has accelerated more slowly (Timmer and van Ark 2005). This slower uptake in ICT-capital deepening is in part related to the overall decline in capital–labour ratios across Europe since the mid 1990s, as European employment grew rapidly, while investment rates remained essentially constant.[9]

The largest difference among sources of growth between the European Union and the United States shown in Table 2.1 is in the contribution of multi-factor productivity growth. Whereas multi-factor productivity growth in the United States accelerated from 0.7% in the period 1980–95 to 1.3% in 1995–2005, the same measure declined from 1.0 to 0.3% between these two periods in the European Union. Multi-factor productivity includes the effects of technological change, along with non-constant returns to scale. But as a residual measure it also includes measurement errors and the effects from unmeasured output and inputs, such as research and development and other intangible investments, including organisational improvements. Broadly, it indicates the efficiency with which inputs are used in the production process, and its reduced growth rate is therefore a major source of concern across Europe.[10]

When looking at these growth accounts from the perspective of the emerging knowledge economy, attention might be directed at the summed contributions of three factors: direct impacts from investments in information and communications technology, changes in labour composition, mostly driven by greater demand for skilled workers, and multi-factor productivity growth, which – as indicated above – might include the impact of intangible investments such as organisational changes related to the use of information technology. Table 2.1 shows that the combined contribution of these three factors to labour productivity growth almost fully explains the EU–US

---

[9] Chapter 5 provides a detailed analysis of capital–labour ratios in Europe at the industry level.
[10] See Chapter 3 for an elaborate discussion of the MFP concept.

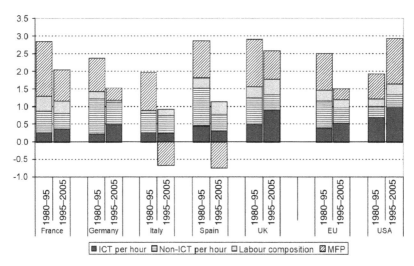

Figure 2.3. Sources of labour productivity growth, market economy, EU countries and USA, 1980–2005. (*Notes and sources*: See Table 2.1.)

labour productivity growth gap since 1995. In Europe they contributed only 1.1 percentage points during 1995–2005. In contrast, in the US economy the contribution of these three knowledge economy components was already 1.6 percentage points during 1980–95, and further increased to 2.6 percentage points during 1995–2005.

Table 2.1 also provides a first clue to the causes of the European slowdown. Rapid employment growth was not matched by increasing investment rates and the growth in capital per hour worked slowed down. While the use of ICT capital rapidly increased, this was counterbalanced by the slowing pace of non-ICT capital intensification. The biggest decline though was in the contribution from MFP, accounting for more than two-thirds of the labour productivity growth slowdown. This decline in the contribution of MFP was a widespread phenomenon in major European countries. Figure 2.3 provides a similar growth accounting decomposition of growth in the major European countries: France, Germany, Italy, Spain and the UK. All countries benefited from increased contributions from ICT, but this was counteracted by strong declines in the growth rate of non-ICT capital per hour worked. In addition, MFP growth rates decelerated, or even turned negative after 1995. As a result, all countries experienced declines in labour productivity growth, in particular, Italy and Spain. Only the growth pattern

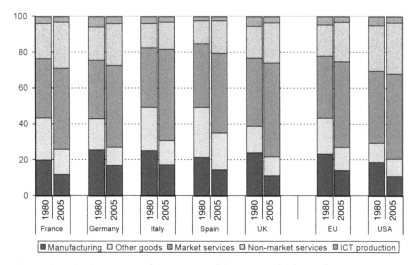

Figure 2.4. Major sector shares in total hours worked, total economy, EU countries and USA, 1980 and 2005. (*Notes and sources*: See Table 2.1.)

of the UK seemed to follow that of the United States with strong contributions from ICT capital and MFP growth. Previous industry-level analyses suggested that slowdown in continental Europe might be particularly due to a heavy reliance on traditional goods-producing industries. We therefore turn first to an analysis of structural change and the industry sources of aggregate growth.

2.4 Structural change and the European slowdown

Both Europe and the United States have experienced a major shift of production and employment from manufacturing and other goods-producing industries towards services. In Figure 2.4 we provide the shares in total hours worked in the five major sectors in 1980 and 2005. Data are provided for the major European countries, the EU-10 and the USA as before. Over the period 1980–2005, the share of labour input going to manufacturing typically declined by one-third or more. A similar decline can be seen for other goods-producing industries such as agriculture and mining. On the other hand, employment in non-market services slowly increased, while booming in market services. In 2005, the share of the latter in total hours worked was about half in both the EU-10 and the United States. While there are differences across European countries, even in Germany, a country in which manufacturing traditionally plays an important role, market services are now almost three times as big as manufacturing. Market services have grown fastest in the UK and employ almost five times the number of manufacturing workers. Market services include a wide variety of activities, ranging from trade and transportation services to financial and business services and also hotels, restaurants and personal services. In Chapter 4 we will provide more detailed evidence on these long-term trends in the structure of output and employment.

The shift from manufacturing to services has important implications for productivity growth. Traditionally, manufacturing activities have been regarded as the locus of innovation and technological change, and thus the central source of productivity growth. It was the key to post-World War II growth in Europe through a combination of economies of scale, capital intensification and incremental innovation. More recently, rapid technological change in computer and semiconductor manufacturing seemingly reinforces the predominance of innovation in the manufacturing sector. In contrast, the increasing weight of services in output was thought to slow aggregate productivity growth. Baumol (1967) called this the 'cost disease of the service sector'. The diagnosis of the disease argues that productivity improvements in services are less likely than in goods-producing industries because most services are inherently labour-intensive, making it difficult to substitute capital for labour. Although Baumol originally mainly referred to services activities like education, health and public services, this diagnosis was widely believed to hold for many other services sectors as well.[11]

To evaluate the effect of structural changes on productivity growth, we need to look at the contributions of individual sectors to the aggregate economy. Table 2.2 shows overall labour productivity for the market economy split into contributions from the ICT production sector (including production of electrical machinery and telecommunications services), manufacturing (other than electrical machinery),

---

[11] The latter has subsequently been qualified in the literature, e.g. Triplett and Bosworth (2006). As the discussion in this chapter and in Chapter 4 will show, the hypothesis is not supported by evidence from the EU KLEMS database. In particular in distribution services, productivity growth has been strong and pervasive for decades.

Table 2.2. *Major sector contributions to labour productivity growth in the market economy, EU and USA, 1980–2005*

	European Union		United States	
	1980–95	1995–2005	1980–95	1995–2005
Market economy	2.5	1.5	1.9	2.9
Contributions from				
ICT production	0.3	0.4	0.5	0.8
Manufacturing	0.9	0.5	0.5	0.6
Other goods	0.6	0.2	0.3	−0.1
Market services	0.7	0.5	0.8	1.8
Reallocation	0.0	−0.2	−0.1	−0.2

Notes: Major sector contributions to labour productivity growth in the market economy (annual average growth rates, in percentage points). Contributions based on growth in sectoral labour productivity weighted by the share in aggregate value added. The reallocation effect in the last row refers to labour productivity effects of reallocations of labour between sectors. The European Union aggregate refers to ten countries; see Table 2.1. Numbers may not sum exactly due to rounding.
Source: See Table 2.1.

other goods production (including agriculture, mining, utilities and construction) and market services (including trade, hotels and restaurants, transport services, financial and business services and social and personal services). The contributions are determined by labour productivity growth in each sector weighted by the sector's share in value added, along with an adjustment in the final row for the reallocation of hours between industries with different productivity. For a more detailed discussion of this methodology and detailed industry results the reader is referred to Chapter 5.

It can be seen from Table 2.2 that market services are the most important driver of differences in aggregate productivity growth rates between the EU and US. Even though the United States has a somewhat bigger share in the ICT-producing sector, the productivity growth rates of the EU and the USA in this sector are not substantially different, so that the impact on the aggregate growth differential was only 0.4 percentage points in the period 1995–2005. Also the contribution from goods production is comparable in the two regions. In contrast, market services contribute 1.3 percentage points to the transatlantic growth gap in this period. While in the USA, market services were rapidly transformed and productivity growth accelerated, developments in

Table 2.3. *Hours worked and productivity growth, major sectors, EU, 1980–2005*

	Total hours worked			Growth in hours worked		Labour productivity growth	
	1980	1995	2005	1980–1995	1995–2005	1980–1995	1995–2005
ICT production	10,600	8,696	7,878	−1.3	−1.0	4.9	6.5
Manufacturing	55,853	40,907	36,513	−2.1	−1.1	3.2	2.0
Other goods	48,646	34,059	32,585	−2.4	−0.4	3.5	1.6
Distribution services	47,406	48,152	51,186	0.1	0.6	2.5	1.7
Financial services	6,535	7,458	7,518	0.9	0.1	1.4	2.6
Business services	11,060	20,897	31,845	4.2	4.2	0.1	−0.2
Personal services	17,561	24,409	29,997	2.2	2.1	−0.5	−0.4
Market economy	197,661	184,579	197,522	−0.5	0.7	2.5	1.5

Notes: Hours worked in millions. Growth rates are annual averages. EU refers to EU-10; see Table 2.1.
Source: See Table 2.1.

Europe were only slow. Previous studies on the growth differential between Europe and the United States also stressed the differentiating role of market services (O'Mahony and van Ark 2003; Losch 2006; Inklaar *et al.* 2008). This will be discussed in greater depth in the next section.

Table 2.2 also shows clearly that the European slowdown is not so much related to developments in market services, as to those in goods production. In 1995–2005, the contribution of manufacturing and other goods production to aggregate growth was only 0.7 percentage points, which is only half the contribution in the period before. Partly this is related to the shift of employment from goods production to market services noted above, but there is also a decline in productivity growth in goods production itself. This is evident from Table 2.3, which provides growth rates of employment and productivity in the EU at the sector level. The revival of employment growth in Europe in the 1990s was clearly located in market services. Declining employment trends in goods production also continued in the 1990s as jobs were still being shed in agriculture, mining and manufacturing. Perhaps surprisingly, hours worked in distribution services and in finance increased only slowly and these sectors were not important in new employment creation. In contrast, hours worked in personal services, and in particular in business services, continued to grow strongly over the whole period. Unfortunately, productivity in these sectors barely improved in the past decades. While labour productivity in goods production still continued to improve after 1995, albeit at a slower pace, productivity growth in business and personal services was zero or even negative. Thus, aggregate growth in Europe in the 1990s was doubly hit: productivity growth declined in goods production, and employment shifted continuously towards business and personal services that historically had very low productivity growth.[12]

A simple way to gauge the importance of changing sectoral structures on aggregate productivity growth is to calculate counterfactual aggregate growth rates based on an alternative set of sector employment shares in the shift-share analysis described above.[13] When realised productivity growth rate is multiplied in each sector during 1995–2005 with sectoral employment shares in 1980, aggregate labour productivity growth during 1995–2005 becomes 0.5 percentage points higher than when using shares in 2005. This suggests an important role for structural change in explaining the European productivity slowdown. To the extent that the shift to market services is driven mainly by a higher income elasticity of these services, slowdown of growth in Europe was to be expected, as growth has to come increasingly from improvements in market services productivity. Developments in the USA since 1995 have shown that this is feasible.

2.5 Market services and the growing EU–US gap

In the previous section, we found that the EU–US productivity gap since the mid 1990s has mainly been located in market services. Contrary to Baumol's cost-disease hypothesis, labour productivity growth in some services industries has been strong, particularly in the USA. The fuelling of US productivity growth from market services is confirmed

---

[12] Chapter 5 provides a more in-depth analysis of the industry sources of aggregate growth.

[13] See Broadberry (1998) for a similar exercise, analysing slow growth in the UK, compared to Germany and the USA, since 1870.

Table 2.4. *Contributions of sectors to labour productivity growth in market services, EU and USA, 1980–2005*

	European Union		United States	
	1980–95	1995–2005	1980–95	1995–2005
Market services labour productivity	1.4	1.0	1.5	3.0
Distribution services contribution	1.1	0.7	1.2	1.5
from factor intensity growth	0.4	0.5	0.4	0.5
from multi-factor productivity growth	0.7	0.2	0.8	1.0
Financial services contribution	0.2	0.4	0.2	0.5
from factor intensity growth	0.3	0.2	0.7	0.5
from multi-factor productivity growth	0.0	0.1	−0.6	0.1
Business services contribution	0.0	−0.1	−0.1	0.7
from factor intensity growth	0.4	0.4	0.2	0.8
from multi-factor productivity growth	−0.4	−0.5	−0.3	0.0
Personal services contribution	−0.1	−0.1	0.2	0.2
from factor intensity growth	0.1	0.1	0.1	0.1
from multi-factor productivity growth	−0.2	−0.1	0.1	0.1
Contribution from labour reallocation	0.1	0.0	0.0	0.0

Notes: EU refers to EU-10; see Table 2.1. Factor intensity relates to the total contribution from changes in labour composition and capital deepening. The reallocation effect refers to the impact of changes in the distribution of labour input between industries. Growth rates are annual average volume growth rates and contributions in percentage points. Numbers may not sum exactly due to rounding.
Source: See Table 2.1.

in studies by Jorgenson *et al.* (2005) and Triplett and Bosworth (2006). Focusing on these industries reveals that transatlantic growth differences were especially large in distributive trade and in business services. This is shown in Table 2.4 where we focus on the contribution of four major groups of market services industries, namely distributive trade (including retail and wholesale trade and transport services), financial services, business services and personal services (including community and social services). In Europe, the distribution sector contributed 0.7 percentage points to labour productivity growth in aggregate market services in the period 1995–2005, compared to 1.5 percentage points in the United States. In business services a similar gap existed as this sector had a negative contribution in Europe while it contributed 0.7 percentage points in the United States. Interestingly in the light of the global financial crisis in 2007, the measured contribution from the finance sector to aggregate labour productivity growth was not disproportionate, adding about 0.5 percentage points in both the EU and the USA.[14] The contribution of personal services was negligible as productivity growth in this sector was close to zero in both regions, echoing Baumol's cost-disease hypothesis.

Drilling deeper into the data, it turns out that it is mainly multi-factor productivity and not factor intensity that is the key to the labour productivity growth differential between Europe and the USA. Differences in 'factor intensity' include the total contribution from changes in labour composition and deepening of all types of capital. In business services, this difference accounted for about half of the labour productivity growth gap, indicating higher investment and skill use in the USA. But in distribution services differences in inputs were not important. Rather, diverging MFP growth was driving the growing EU–US gap. In Chapter 5 this is discussed in more detail.

As multi-factor productivity growth represents a multitude of factors that are not explicitly measured in a growth accounts framework, it is useful to look at what lies behind MFP growth. While these factors may differ across sectors, the example of the retail sector may serve as an illustration of the complex interactions between productivity, investment and regulations. Over the past twenty-five years, the retail sector has undergone a substantial transformation on account of benefits from the increased use of ICT, commonly referred to as the 'lean retailing system' (Abernathy et al. 1999). This has turned the retail industry from a low-tech industry shifting boxes at infrequent intervals into one that trades information by matching goods and services to customer demand on a continuous basis. Various studies, including McKinsey Global Institute (2002), Baily and Kirkegaard (2004),

---

[14] The overestimation of finance output might even be higher in Europe than in the USA; see Chapter 3 for further discussion on this point.

McGuckin *et al.* (2005) and Gordon (2007) have discussed the reasons for superior performance in the US retail industry relative to that in Europe.

While there is significant evidence of a faster rise in ICT capital in the US retail sector than in Europe, the productivity impact of the greater use of barcode scanners, communication equipment, inventory tracking devices, transaction processing software, etc. may be understated when focusing solely on the contribution of investment as directly measured in growth accounts through the contribution of ICT capital to growth. ICT use also provides indirect benefits for growth through increasing the potential for innovation as measured by multi-factor productivity. These innovation effects were in part realised through 'softer' innovations, such as the invention of new retail formats, service protocols, labour scheduling systems and optimised marketing campaigns (McKinsey Global Institute 2002).

In Europe, lean retailing systems have not developed at a similar pace. Some stress that deregulation in upstream industries such as trucking in the 1980s was a necessary condition for the lean retailing model to work in the USA as it allowed more efficient ordering and shipping schedules. Others have emphasised the role of 'big box' formats, as exemplified most notably by the emergence of Wal-Mart, as the engine of productivity growth in US retailing (Basker 2007). From this perspective, Europe's lagging behind is due to more restrictive regulations concerning, for example, store opening hours, land zoning, labour markets and cultural differences, which inhibit a rapid increase in market share of new large-scale retail formats. The latter has been a main driver of growth in the USA, both because of increased competitive pressure on incumbent firms and higher productivity levels of new entrants (Foster *et al.* 2006).

With the acceleration in the USA, a new productivity gap in market services has opened up. In 2005, value added per hour worked in EU market services had dropped to only 70 per cent of the US level, and MFP to 80 per cent. The gap is particularly large in business services as European productivity levels are less than 60 per cent of those in the USA, suggesting abundant opportunities for renewed catching-up in Europe in the future. This is illustrated in Figure 2.5, which provides a decomposition of the EU–US labour productivity gap in the market economy in 2005. The contribution of each industry to the gap is calculated by multiplying the log gap in labour productivity

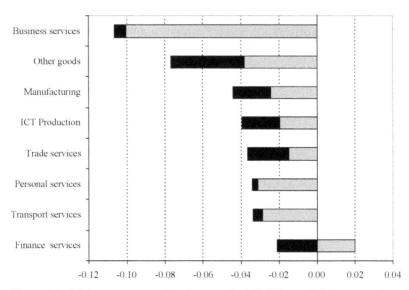

Figure 2.5. Major sector contributions to the EU–US gap in labour productivity, market economy, 2005. The contribution of each sector is calculated by multiplying the log gap in labour productivity (log level of EU over USA) by the share of each sector in market economy value added. The grey bar indicates the contribution of the log gap in multi-factor productivity and the black bar the contribution of the log gaps in capital and labour services per hour worked. (*Source*: See Figure 2.2.)

by its share in value added. The bars indicate the contribution of each sector to the overall labour productivity gap, decomposed into the contribution of differences in capital and labour services per hour worked (in black) and MFP (in grey). By far the biggest contributor to the EU–US labour productivity gap in the market economy is business services and especially the MFP gap in this sector looms large. Chapter 6 provides more details on the level accounting method and additional results.

2.6 Increasing European diversity

The productivity slowdown in Europe since the mid 1990s is largely driven by some of the large European continental countries, in particular Spain and Italy. In contrast, the Nordic economies (in particular Finland and Sweden), Ireland and – to a lesser extent – the United

Kingdom seem to have fared relatively well in productivity terms. This cross-country diversity makes it hard to tell 'a single European story' and understanding European performance requires an additional focus on individual EU member states (see also Gordon 2007). In Table 2.5 we provide a decomposition of growth in thirteen European countries based on the growth accounting methodology used above. There is a large variation in growth rates across European countries. Similar to the rows in Table 2.1, the first column of Table 2.5 shows the growth rate of output over the 1995–2005 period. The second and third columns divide that growth in output into changes in hours worked and changes in output per hour. As before, columns 4 to 7 divide up the growth in labour productivity into four sources and the final column shows the 'knowledge economy' contributions. Countries are ranked by growth rate of labour productivity.

One key observation to be drawn from this table is that the main difference in labour productivity growth between individual European economies is to be found in multi-factor productivity, not in differences in the use of capital per hour worked. Indeed the bottom row shows that the standard deviation for multi-factor productivity growth across the set of countries is larger than for factor inputs, confirming the earlier analysis by Timmer and van Ark (2005). For example, the difference in the contribution of capital deepening in information and communications technologies between a high investor like Finland and a low investor like Italy explains only 0.3 percentage points of a labour productivity growth difference of 2.9 percentage points. The remaining gap is fully accounted for by the difference in multi-factor productivity growth. Indeed differences in multi-factor productivity seem to have driven the divergence in labour productivity between European countries too. In Belgium, Denmark and Germany, MFP growth is less than 0.5 per cent per year and in Italy and Spain it is even negative. In contrast, MFP growth in Finland, Ireland and Sweden is greater than 1.5 per cent. Chapter 6 provides further analysis of catch-up and convergence in the European Union.

In addition to variance in aggregate productivity growth rates, European diversity manifests itself through differences in the sectoral origins of growth between countries. This is clearly illustrated by Figure 2.6, which provides for major European countries a breakdown of aggregate labour productivity growth by sector, by weighting

Table 2.5. *Gross value added growth and contributions, market economy, EU countries, 1995–2005*

| | Growth rate of value added | Value added contribution from | | Labour productivity contributions from | | | | Labour productivity contribution of the knowledge economy |
| | | Hours worked | Labour productivity | Labour composition | ICT capital per hour | Non-ICT capital per hour | Multi factor productivity | |
	$1 = 2 + 3$	2	$3 = 4 + 5 + 6 + 7$	4	5	6	7	$8 = 4 + 5 + 7$
Ireland	7.6	3.2	4.5	0.2	0.4	2.1	1.7	2.3
Sweden	3.9	0.3	3.6	0.3	0.6	1.1	1.7	2.5
Finland	4.3	1.1	3.2	0.1	0.6	-0.1	2.6	3.3
United Kingdom	3.2	0.6	2.6	0.5	0.9	0.4	0.8	2.2
Netherlands	2.8	0.7	2.1	0.4	0.6	0.1	1.0	2.0
France	2.4	0.4	2.1	0.4	0.4	0.4	0.9	1.6
Austria	2.5	0.5	2.0	0.2	0.6	0.1	1.2	1.9
Portugal	2.4	0.5	1.8	0.2	0.6	1.3	-0.3	0.6
Belgium	2.3	0.7	1.7	0.2	1.0	0.4	0.1	1.2
Denmark	2.2	0.7	1.6	0.2	1.0	0.2	0.1	1.3
Germany	1.0	-0.6	1.5	0.1	0.5	0.6	0.4	0.9
Spain	3.6	3.2	0.4	0.4	0.3	0.5	-0.7	0.0
Italy	1.2	0.9	0.3	0.2	0.3	0.5	-0.7	-0.2
Standard deviation	1.6	1.1	1.4	0.1	0.2	0.7	1.2	1.2

Notes: Growth rates are annual average volume growth rates and contributions in percentage points. 'ICT' is information and communications technology. Standard deviation based on all countries in the table. Numbers may not sum exactly due to rounding.
Source: See Table 2.1.

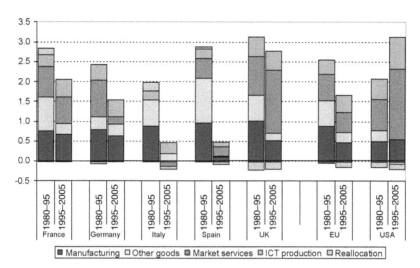

Figure 2.6. Major sector contributions to aggregate labour productivity growth, market economy, EU countries and USA, 1980–2005. (*Notes and sources*: See Table 2.2.)

sectoral productivity growth by the share in aggregate value added, following a similar approach as for Table 2.2.

In the past the bulk of aggregate productivity growth originated from goods production, but this no longer holds true. The contribution of manufacturing and other goods production in the EU has rapidly declined as discussed above, and this decline has been uneven across the European continent. In particular, traditional manufacturing industries in Italy and Spain, such as textiles and leather products, languished. While in the past, they benefited strongly from the opportunities offered within the EU, these labour-intensive sectors faced a particularly tough challenge in the 1990s as low-wage competition from Eastern Europe and China increased. Also in the UK, manufacturing productivity slowed down, in particular in chemicals and transport equipment. In contrast, manufacturing in France and Germany continued to flourish and industries like chemicals, machinery and car manufacturing are still important sources of productivity growth.

Less well known, but equally important, is the decline in the contribution from other goods-producing sectors: agriculture, mining and construction. Reasons for their decline vary widely across sector and country. In the past decades, the agricultural sectors in France, Italy

Table 2.6. *Major sector contributions to labour productivity growth in the market economy, EU countries and USA, 1995–2005*

			Contribution from			
	Market economy	ICT production	Manufacturing	Other goods	Market services	Reallocation
Ireland	4.5	1.0	2.2	0.2	1.4	−0.3
Sweden	3.6	1.1	1.0	0.2	1.4	0.0
Finland	3.2	1.7	0.7	0.4	0.4	0.0
United Kingdom	2.6	0.5	0.5	0.2	1.6	−0.2
Netherlands	2.1	0.4	0.6	0.0	1.3	−0.1
France	2.1	0.4	0.7	0.3	0.7	0.0
Austria	2.0	0.3	1.0	0.6	0.2	−0.1
Portugal	1.8	0.5	0.5	0.2	0.6	0.1
Belgium	1.7	0.3	0.7	0.2	0.6	−0.1
Denmark	1.6	0.3	0.3	0.3	0.7	0.0
Germany	1.5	0.4	0.6	0.3	0.2	0.0
Spain	0.4	0.1	0.1	0.0	0.2	−0.1
Italy	0.3	0.3	0.0	0.2	−0.1	−0.1
USA (pro memoria)	2.9	0.8	0.6	−0.1	1.8	−0.2

Notes: Growth rates are annual average volume growth rates and contributions in percentage points. The reallocation effect in the last column refers to effects of reallocations of labour between sectors. Numbers may not sum exactly due to rounding.
Source: See Table 2.1.

and Spain have been increasingly rationalised and rapid productivity gains were made as labour moved out. Naturally, this potential source of growth has been gradually exhausted and in the 1990s productivity growth rates in this sector dropped strongly. The importance of mining has been dwindling in all countries, and in the UK this was exacerbated by a strong declining productivity trend. Also in the construction sector, labour productivity growth rates dropped, in particular in France and Spain. In the latter country the decline was concomitant with strongly increasing employment in a building boom, suggesting a short-run employment–productivity trade-off. Only in the UK has the loss of the traditional drivers of growth been compensated by an increase in the contribution from market services, mainly due to strong performance in trade and business services industries.

In the smaller economies in Europe too the sectoral origins of growth varied widely in the period 1995–2005. Table 2.6 shows that in countries like Austria, Belgium and Ireland, manufacturing is still the most important engine of growth, just as in France and Germany. Other countries, such as Finland, Hungary and Sweden enjoyed additional high contributions from the production of ICT goods and services.[15] At the same time various countries had high contributions from growth in market services. As in the UK, market services contributed strongly to aggregate growth in Ireland, the Netherlands and Sweden. Incidentally, market services also appear to exhibit rapid productivity growth in other Anglo-Saxon economies, such as Australia and Canada (Inklaar et al. 2007). In contrast, Austria, Germany, Italy and Spain show almost no, or even negative, contributions from market services to aggregate labour productivity growth. In Germany, business services in particular performed extremely weakly. Clearly, disparate performance in market services is not only responsible for the EU–US productivity gap, but is also an important driver of divergence among

---

[15] If one were to account for the large share of ICT-goods production exported by these countries, the contribution of this sector would be lower than indicated here. If rapid productivity growth is mainly translated into lower prices for foreign consumers, terms of trade will decline and aggregate productivity gains are less than suggested here. In traditional growth accounting, countries are considered to be closed economies. See Diewert and Morrison (1986) and Kohli (1990) for approaches to growth accounting that take account of changes in terms of trade and Feenstra, Heston, Timmer *et al.* (2009) for a cross-country application.

members of the European Union. Additional detailed country analyses based on the EU KLEMS database are provided by Mas *et al.* (2008) on Italy and Spain; Görzig *et al.* (2010) on France, Germany and the UK; Kegels *et al.* (2008) on Austria, Belgium and the Netherlands; and Havlik *et al.* (2008) on Central and Eastern European countries.

2.7 Concluding remarks

In this chapter we analysed the severe productivity slowdown in the European Union in the 1990s. As a declining employment trend was reversed at the same time, because of deregulation of labour markets, a trade-off between jobs and productivity seemed to be at work. While this might be true for the short run, there is little evidence that this also holds in the longer run, in particular as technical progress, as measured by multi-factor productivity, declined as well. Instead we argue that the European productivity growth slowdown has certain structural characteristics, partly related to the end of the process of catch-up and convergence that has driven productivity growth in the past. This follows from a more detailed industry-level analysis of the sources of growth. There has been a strong decline in growth in agriculture, mining and construction. As employment continued the long down-ward trend, productivity growth rates in these sectors decelerated in the 1990s as opportunities for further rationalisation and technical change were gradually exhausted. Also manufacturing growth languished as Europe was faced with increasing global competition, especially in low- and medium-technology sectors. At the same time, employment moved out of the goods-producing sectors to market services, driven by shifts in domestic and global demand. This shift decreased aggregate productivity growth even more as market services historically had lower levels of productivity than goods-producing industries.

However, Europe is not necessarily down on a structurally low productivity growth path. In the 1990s, the US economy was resurgent, fuelled by rapid productivity growth in market services. This suggests new opportunities for growth driven by innovations enabled by investment in information and communications technology, especially in trade and business services. This growth path is not unique to the USA and has also been followed in some form by countries like the Netherlands, Sweden and the United Kingdom. With some delay, the benefits from the new knowledge economy are being spread throughout Europe, as use of ICT and the quality level of the labour force are increasing. At the same time it is clear that realisation of this new growth potential requires more than investment in ICT and skill formation. The case study of retail illustrated the complex interactions between productivity, investment and the regulation of labour, capital and product markets. It suggests that the more stringent regulatory environment in Europe became increasingly binding with the advent of new technology. At the same time it is obvious that a new phase of simple imitation of the US innovation system and regulatory practices may not be the most promising way to support higher dynamics of Europe's economies. Clearly, more research on drivers of productivity in services is needed and this is further discussed in Chapter 7.

3 | *EU KLEMS database*

3.1 Introduction

Until recently, internationally comparable studies of the relationships between skill formation, investment, technological change and growth have been hampered by the lack of a readily available standard database covering a large set of countries. As a result, researchers had often to compile their own databases, making replication and comparability of studies difficult. In our analysis of European growth and productivity in Chapter 2 we made use of a new database which can serve as a useful tool for empirical and theoretical research in the area of economic growth: the EU KLEMS Growth Accounts database. This database includes measures of output and input growth and derived variables such as multi-factor productivity at the industry level. The input measures include various categories of capital (K), labour (L), energy (E), material (M) and service inputs (S). The measures are developed for twenty-five individual European Union member states, the United States and Japan and cover the period from 1970 to 2005. The variables are organised around the growth accounting methodology, a major advantage of which is that it is rooted in neo-classical production theory. It provides a clear conceptual framework within which the interactions among variables can be analysed in an internally consistent way.

The data series, publicly available on www.euklems.net, can be used by researchers employing growth accounting to consider sources of output and productivity growth in cross-country comparisons or studies of particular industries and different time periods, such as discussed in the previous chapters. Although the primary aim of the EU KLEMS database is to generate comparative productivity trends, the data collected are also useful in a large number of other contexts, as the database provides many basic input data series. These input series are derived independently from the assumptions underlying the

46

growth accounting method. In evaluating research using any database, readers need to understand the theoretical and practical underpinnings of the database. The main purpose of this chapter is therefore to summarise the methodology employed in constructing the database and the practical limitations of the database and to indicate areas for further improvement. O'Mahony and Timmer (2009) provide a brief overview.

The remainder of this chapter is organised as follows. It begins, in section 3.2, with an outline of the growth accounting method, which is the organising principle underlying the construction of the database. Next, we describe the construction of the various variables, namely output and intermediate inputs (section 3.3), labour input (3.4) and capital input (3.5). We broadly indicate the sources and methodology followed, but for details by country the reader is referred to the EU KLEMS Sources and Methodology documents (Timmer van Moergastel, Stuivenwold *et al.* 2007) – see also the appendix to this chapter for summary information. Section 3.6 outlines general measurement issues variable by variable, while section 3.7 investigates the specific case of output measurement in market services. In section 3.8 a comparison is made between the EU KLEMS database and various international and national alternatives. Section 3.9 concludes.

3.2 Growth accounting methodology

The organising principle underlying the EU KLEMS database is the growth accounting methodology. Growth accounting allows a decomposition of output growth into the growth of various inputs and productivity. This approach has a long history dating back to a seminal article by Jorgenson and Griliches (1967) and put in a more general input-output framework by Jorgenson, Gollop and Fraumeni (1987). It was further grounded in economic theory by Diewert (1976) and Caves *et al.* (1982a). It is based on production possibility frontiers, where industry gross output is a function of capital, labour, intermediate inputs and the level of technology *T*. Each industry, indexed by *j*, can produce a set of products and purchases a number of distinct intermediate, capital and labour inputs to produce its output. The production function is given by:

$$Y_j = f_j\left(X_j, K_j, L_j, T\right) \tag{3.1}$$

where Y is output, K is an index of capital service flows, L is an index of labour service flows, X is an index of intermediate inputs, either purchased from domestic industries or imported, and T is the level of technology. All variables are also indexed by time, but the t subscript is suppressed wherever possible to facilitate exposition.

Under the assumptions of competitive factor markets, full input utilisation and constant returns to scale and using the translog functional form common in such analyses, we can define multi-factor productivity (A^Y) growth as follows:

$$\Delta \ln A_j^Y \equiv \Delta \ln Y_j - \bar{v}_{X,j}^Y \Delta \ln X_j - \bar{v}_{K,j}^Y \Delta \ln K_j - \bar{v}_{L,j}^Y \Delta \ln L_j \quad (3.2)$$

where $\Delta x = x_t - x_{t-1}$ denotes the change in the period from $t-1$ to t such that $\Delta \ln x$ indicates logarithmic growth rates, and $\bar{v}$ is the period average share of the input in nominal value of output. The value share of each input is defined as

$$v_{X,j}^Y = \frac{p_j^X X_j}{p_j^Y Y_j}$$

$$v_{L,j}^Y = \frac{p_j^L L_j}{p_j^Y Y_j} \qquad\qquad (3.3)$$

$$v_{K,j}^Y = \frac{p_j^K K_j}{p_j^Y Y_j}$$

and the period-average shares as

$$\bar{v}_{X,j}^Y = 0.5^*\left(v_{X,j,t}^Y + v_{X,j,t-1}^Y\right)$$
$$\bar{v}_{L,j}^Y = 0.5^*\left(v_{L,j,t}^Y + v_{L,j,t-1}^Y\right) \qquad (3.4)$$
$$\bar{v}_{K,j}^Y = 0.5^*\left(v_{K,j,t}^Y + v_{K,j,t-1}^Y\right)$$

In the remainder of this chapter we indicate the weight of a sub-component (subscript) in its relevant aggregate (superscript) by using subscripts and superscripts on weights v. A bar on a variable always indicates period averages. Because of our assumption of constant returns to scale to all input, shares add up to unity:

$$v_{X,j}^Y + v_{L,j}^Y + v_{K,j}^Y = 1 \qquad (3.5)$$

This allows us to use observed output shares in the estimation of multi-factor productivity growth. Although it is common in the productivity literature to impose constant returns to scale, one might also opt not to do this, and use cost shares rather than revenue shares to weight input growth rates (see section 3.6).

Rearranging (3.2) yields the standard growth accounting decomposition of output growth as the revenue-share weighted growth of inputs and the residual multi-factor productivity growth:

$$\Delta \ln Y_j = \bar{v}^Y_{X,j} \Delta \ln X_j + \bar{v}^Y_{K,j} \Delta \ln K_j + \bar{v}^Y_{L,j} \Delta \ln L_j + \Delta \ln A^Y_j \quad (3.6)$$

Each element on the right-hand side of (3.6) indicates the proportion of output growth accounted for by growth in intermediate inputs, capital services, labour services and MFP growth representing technical change.[1] The latter cannot be directly measured and is derived as a residual as in (3.2).

Aggregate labour input L_j is defined as a Törnqvist volume index of hours worked by individual labour types as follows:[2]

$$\Delta \ln L_j = \sum_l \bar{v}^L_{l,j} \Delta \ln H_{l,j} \quad (3.7)$$

with weights given by

$$v^L_{l,j} = \frac{p^L_{l,j} H_{l,j}}{p^L_j L_j} \quad (3.8)$$

where $\Delta \ln H_{l,j}$ indicates the growth of hours worked by labour type l and weights are given by the period-average shares of each type in the value of labour compensation, such that the sum of shares over all labour types is unity. As we assume that marginal revenues are equal to marginal costs, the weighting procedure ensures that inputs which

---

[1] This term reflects technical change and is sometimes also referred to as total factor productivity (TFP). In this book we use the term multi-factor productivity and indicate, if needed, to what set of inputs it refers. Because of our approach to capital measurement it only includes disembodied technical change (see also the discussion in section 3.6).

[2] Aggregate input is unobservable and it is common to express it as a translog function of its individual components. Then the corresponding index is a Törnqvist volume index (see Jorgenson, Gollop and Fraumeni 1987). For all aggregation of quantities we use the Törnqvist quantity index, which is a discrete time approximation to a Divisia index. This aggregation approach uses annual moving weights based on averages of adjacent points in time. The advantage of the Tornqvist index is that it belongs to the preferred class of superlative indices (Diewert 1976). Moreover, it exactly replicates a translog model which is highly flexible, that is, a model where the aggregate is a linear and quadratic function of the components and time.

have a higher price also have a larger influence in the input index. So, for example, a doubling of hours worked by a high-skilled worker gets a bigger weight than a doubling of hours worked by a low-skilled worker.

Similarly, aggregate capital input K_j is defined as a Törnqvist volume index of individual capital assets as follows:

$$\Delta \ln K_j = \sum_k \bar{v}_{k,j}^K \Delta \ln K_{k,j} \qquad (3.9)$$

with weights given by

$$v_{k,j}^K = \frac{p_{k,j}^K K_{k,j}}{p_j^K K_j} \qquad (3.10)$$

where $\Delta \ln K_{k,j}$ indicates the volume growth of capital asset k and weights are given by the period-average shares of each type in the value of capital compensation, such that the sum of shares over all capital types is unity.

Aggregate intermediate input X_j is defined analogously as a Törnqvist volume index of individual intermediate inputs as follows:

$$\Delta \ln X_j = \sum_x \bar{v}_{x,j}^X \Delta \ln X_{x,j} \qquad (3.11)$$

with weights given by

$$v_{x,j}^X = \frac{p_{x,j}^X X_{x,j}}{p_j^X X_j} \qquad (3.12)$$

where $\Delta \ln X_{x,j}$ indicates the volume growth of intermediate input x and weights are given by the period-average shares of each type in the value of intermediate input compensation, such that the sum of shares over all intermediate input types is unity.

For many applications it is useful to further break down the contribution of the various inputs. In the EU KLEMS database, the volume growth of labour input is split into the growth of hours worked and the changes in labour composition in terms of labour characteristics such as educational attainment, age or gender (see below). Let H_j indicate total hours worked by all types $H_j = \sum_l H_{l,j}$ then we can decompose the change in labour input as follows:

$$\Delta \ln L_j = \sum_l \bar{v}^L_{l,j} \Delta \ln \frac{H_{l,j}}{H_j} + \Delta \ln H_j = \Delta \ln LC_j + \Delta \ln H_j \quad (3.13)$$

The first term on the right-hand side indicates the change in labour composition and the second term indicates the change in total hours worked.[3] It can easily be seen that if proportions of each labour type in the labour force change, this will have an impact on the growth of labour input beyond any change in total hours worked.

To analyse the separate impact of ICT and non-ICT capital, asset types are allocated to two groups of assets: ICT assets (indicated by *ICT*) and non-ICT assets (indicated by N), such that

$$\Delta \ln K_j = \bar{v}^K_{ICT,j} \Delta \ln K^{ICT}_j + \bar{v}^K_{N,j} \Delta \ln K^N_j \quad (3.14)$$

with $\bar{v}^K_{ICT,j}$ the period-average share of ICT assets in total capital costs in industry j, and similarly for non-ICT assets. Volume growth of ICT and non-ICT capital is defined as

$$\Delta \ln K^{ICT}_j = \sum_{k \in ICT} \bar{v}^{ICT}_{k,j} \Delta \ln K_{k,j} \quad (3.15)$$

$$\Delta \ln K^N_j = \sum_{k \in N} \bar{v}^N_{k,j} \Delta \ln K_{k,j} \quad (3.16)$$

with $\bar{v}^{ICT}_{k,j}$ the period-average share of ICT asset k in total ICT capital costs in industry j, and $\bar{v}^N_{k,j}$ the period-average share of non-ICT asset k in total non-ICT capital costs. Each set of weights will sum to unity.

For many analyses it is also useful to group intermediate inputs into three groups, energy (E), materials (M) and services (S), such that

$$\Delta \ln X_j = \bar{v}^X_{E,j} \Delta \ln X^E_j + \bar{v}^X_{M,j} \Delta \ln X^M_j + \bar{v}^X_{S,j} \Delta \ln X^S_j \quad (3.17)$$

with $\bar{v}^X_{E,j}$ the period-average share of energy products in total intermediate input costs in industry j, and similarly for materials and services.

---

[3] The first term is also known as 'labour quality' in the growth accounting literature (see, for example, Jorgenson *et al.* 2005). However, this terminology has a normative connotation which easily leads to confusion. For example, lower female wages would suggest that hours worked by females have a lower 'quality' than hours worked by males. Instead we prefer to use the more positive concept of 'labour composition'.

Input volume growth of E, M and S is defined in terms of their components as

$$\Delta \ln X_j^E = \sum_{x \varepsilon E} \bar{v}_{x,j}^E \Delta \ln X_{x,j} \tag{3.18}$$

$$\Delta \ln X_j^M = \sum_{x \varepsilon M} \bar{v}_{x,j}^M \Delta \ln X_{x,j} \tag{3.19}$$

$$\Delta \ln X_j^S = \sum_{x \varepsilon S} \bar{v}_{x,j}^S \Delta \ln X_{x,j} \tag{3.20}$$

with weights $\bar{v}_{x,j}^E$ the period-average share of energy product x in total energy costs in industry j, summing to unity over all energy input products. Weights for materials and services input volumes are defined analogously.

Using the above formulas, the EU KLEMS database provides a full decomposition of growth in gross output into eight elements as follows:

$$\begin{aligned}
\Delta \ln Y_j = {}& \bar{v}_{E,j}^Y \Delta \ln X_j^E + \bar{v}_{M,j}^Y \Delta \ln X_j^M + \bar{v}_{S,j}^Y \Delta \ln X_j^S \\
& + \bar{v}_{ICT,j}^Y \Delta \ln K_j^{ICT} + \bar{v}_{N,j}^Y \Delta \ln K_j^N \\
& + \bar{v}_{L,j}^Y \Delta \ln LC_j + \bar{v}_{L,j}^Y \Delta \ln H_j + \Delta \ln A_j^Y
\end{aligned} \tag{3.21}$$

The product of its share in total output and its growth rate gives the contribution of each intermediate and capital input. The weights for intermediate inputs are given by their respective shares in total output: $\bar{v}_{E,j}^Y = \bar{v}_{X,j}^Y \bar{v}_{E,j}^X$; $\bar{v}_{M,j}^Y = \bar{v}_{X,j}^Y \bar{v}_{M,j}^X$; and $\bar{v}_{S,j}^Y = \bar{v}_{X,j}^Y \bar{v}_{S,j}^X$. Similarly the weights for capital inputs are given by $\bar{v}_{ICT,j}^Y = \bar{v}_{K,j}^Y \bar{v}_{ICT,j}^K$ and $\bar{v}_{N,j}^Y = \bar{v}_{K,j}^Y \bar{v}_{N,j}^K$. The contribution of labour input is split into hours worked and changes in the composition of hours worked.[4] Any remaining output growth is picked up by the multi-factor productivity term A.

It is useful at this stage to present an example of the growth accounting method. At various places in this chapter we use the case of the metal manufacturing industry in the UK as an example to illustrate the

---

[4] The growth accounting calculations in EU KLEMS include this division into volume and composition for labour input to summarise all aspects of labour composition. Alternatively, in keeping with the divisions for intermediate and capital input the contribution of labour could be subdivided into groups, e.g. high-skilled and low-skilled labour. The data necessary for such a division is also available in the database – see below for further details.

Table 3.1. *Example of decomposition of gross output growth, metal manufacturing in the UK, 1995–2005*

	Average share in gross output	Volume growth rate	Contribution to growth in gross output
Gross output	100.0	−0.7	−0.7
Intermediate inputs	64.3	−1.1	−0.7
Energy	5.6	1.2	0.1
Materials	47.8	−1.5	−0.7
Services	10.9	−0.6	−0.1
Labour input	31.5	−2.6	−0.8
Hours worked	31.5	−3.4	−1.1
Labour composition	31.5	0.8	0.2
Capital input	4.2	1.5	0.1
ICT	0.9	15.2	0.1
Non-ICT	3.3	−1.5	−0.1
MFP (gross output based)		0.8	0.8

Notes: Contribution of inputs calculated as the share of input times the volume growth rate. Shares are averaged over 1995 and 2005. Volume growth rates are annual compound growth rates over the period 1995–2005. Numbers may not sum exactly due to rounding.
Source: Calculations based on EU KLEMS database, March 2008.

various calculations involved. In Table 3.1 we provide a decomposition of gross output growth in this sector between 1995 and 2005 into the eight elements given in (3.21). The first column indicates the average share of each input in gross output. In metal manufacturing, intermediate inputs – in particular, materials – play a dominant role, taking up almost half of the total cost. Labour input is also important, while the cost share of capital input is relatively low.[5] These cost shares are used to weight the volume growth rate of each individual input given in the second column. Between 1995 and 2005 production in the metal industry contracted by 0.7 per cent on a yearly basis and most inputs

---

[5] This does not mean that little capital is involved in the production of metals. Rather it is an indication of the low rates of return of the capital involved. Returns to capital are determined residually by equating total output and total input costs and include any deviation from the zero profit condition (see section 3.7 for further discussion).

declined as well, especially hours worked. Only the use of ICT capital increased. The contracting labour force was, however, composed of more productive workers by the end of the period, as indicated by the positive growth in labour composition. Multi-factor productivity growth was also positive, indicating that all inputs (intermediate, capital and labour) were used in a more efficient way in the production process. It was calculated as the growth of output minus the weighted growth of inputs. The last column indicates the contribution of each input and MFP to growth in output. Overall, the decline in output was mainly due to the rapid decline in the use of material and labour inputs, accounting for 0.7 and 0.8 percentage points respectively. This was partly counteracted by the more efficient use of inputs, adding 0.8 percentage points to output. Later on in this chapter we provide more in-depth discussion of the way labour and capital services are calculated, and of various interpretations of multi-factor productivity growth.

In Figure 3.1 we provide a ranking of technical change in twenty-six industries in the European Union measured by growth in gross output MFP over the period 1980–2005. MFP growth rates are highest in post and telecommunication and agriculture at annual growth rates of about 2 per cent. Also in many manufacturing industries the efficiency with which inputs are used increased in the past decades. Only in hotels and restaurants, business services and other services is MFP growth negative, which might be due to the inherent limitation to innovation in these sectors as suggested by Baumol's cost-disease hypothesis (Baumol 1967), but might also be due to measurement problems. Baumol's conjecture is discussed in greater depth in Chapter 4, while interpretations of MFP and measurement issues are discussed in sections 3.6 and 3.7.

In order to decompose growth at higher levels of aggregation (see discussion below) we also define a more restrictive industry value-added function, which gives the quantity of value added as a function only of capital, labour and technology as

$$Z_j = g_j(K_j, L_j, T) \tag{3.22}$$

where Z_j is the quantity of industry value added. The crucial assumption made is that the gross output production function is separable in capital, labour and technology, breaking the symmetry between

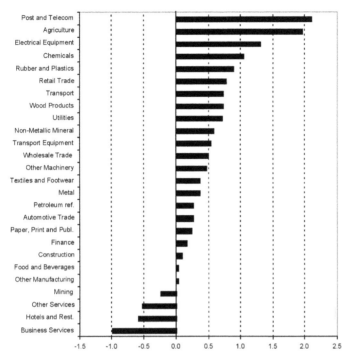

Figure 3.1. Growth rates of multi-factor productivity, twenty-six industries, EU, 1980–2005. Annual compound growth rates. Multi-factor productivity based on gross output. (*Source*: Calculations based on EU KLEMS database, March 2008.)

primary inputs, capital and labour, and intermediate inputs (see Jorgenson, Gollop and Fraumeni 1987) such that

$$Y_j = f_j\left(X_j, g_j\left(K_j, L_j, T\right)\right) \tag{3.23}$$

Under the same assumptions as for gross output, MFP growth can also be estimated from the value-added function (A^Z) and defined:

$$\Delta \ln A_j^Z \equiv \Delta \ln Z_j - \bar{v}_{ICT,j}^Z \Delta \ln K_j^{ICT} - \bar{v}_{N,j}^Z \Delta \ln K_j^N$$
$$- \bar{v}_{L,j}^Z \Delta \ln LC_j - \bar{v}_{L,j}^Z \Delta \ln H_j \tag{3.24}$$

where $\bar{v}^Z$ is the period-average share of the input in nominal value added. The value share of each input is defined as follows:

$$v_{ICT,j}^Z = \frac{p_j^{ICT} K_j^{ICT}}{p_j^Z Z_j}$$

$$v_{N,j}^Z = \frac{p_j^N K_j^N}{p_j^Z Z_j} \qquad\qquad (3.25)$$

$$v_{L,j}^Z = \frac{p_j^L L_j}{p_j^Z Z_j}$$

such that they sum to unity. In order to define the quantity of value added and remain consistent with the gross output function, the quantity of value added needs to be defined implicitly from a Törnqvist expression for gross output:

$$\Delta \ln Z_j = \frac{1}{\bar{v}_{Z,j}^Y} \left(\Delta \ln Y_j - \left(1 - \bar{v}_{Z,j}^Y\right) \Delta \ln X_j \right) \qquad (3.26)$$

where $\bar{v}_{Z,j}^Y$ is the period-average share of value added in gross output. The corresponding price index for value added is defined implicitly to make the following value identities hold:

$$p_j^Z Z_j = p_j^{ICT} K_j^{ICT} + p_j^N K_j^N + p_j^L L_j = p_j^Y Y_j - p_j^X X_j \qquad (3.27)$$

If the quantity of value added is defined as in (3.26), MFP measured for gross output (as in 3.2) and MFP as measured for value added (as in 3.24) are proportional to each other with the ratio of gross output over value added as the factor of proportion (Bruno 1984):[6]

$$\Delta \ln A_j^Z = \frac{1}{\bar{v}_{Z,j}^Y} \Delta \ln A_j^Y \qquad\qquad (3.28)$$

Essentially, MFP growth measured on a value-added function is based on the assumption that technical change only has an impact on the use of capital and labour. Put simply, any improvements in the use of intermediate inputs will thus end up in the measure of value-added MFP (see section 3.7 for further discussion).

Rearranging (3.24), the growth in industry value added can be decomposed into the contribution of capital, labour and technical

---

[6] However, note that this is only valid as long as value added volume growth rates are derived as in (3.26). This is not always the case; see section 3.6.

Table 3.2. *Example of decomposition of value added and labour productivity growth, metal manufacturing in the UK, 1995–2005*

	Average share in value added	Volume growth rates	Contribution to growth in value added	Volume growth rates per hour	Contribution to growth in value added per hour
Value added	100.0	0.0	0.0	3.4	3.4
Labour input		−2.6	−2.3	0.8	0.7
Hours worked	88.6	−3.4	−3.0	0.0	0.0
Labour composition	88.6	0.8	0.7	0.8	0.7
Capital input	11.4	1.5	0.2	4.9	0.6
ICT	2.5	15.2	0.4	18.6	0.5
Non-ICT	8.9	−1.5	−0.1	1.9	0.2
MFP (value-added-based)		2.1	2.1	2.1	2.1

Notes and source: See Table 3.1.

change in the use of labour and capital:

$$\Delta \ln Z_j = \bar{v}_{ICT,j}^{Z} \Delta \ln K_j^{ICT} + \bar{v}_{N,j}^{Z} \Delta \ln K_j^{N}$$
$$+ \bar{v}_{L,j}^{Z} \Delta \ln LC_j + \bar{v}_{L,j}^{Z} \Delta \ln H_j + \Delta \ln A_j^{Z} \tag{3.29}$$

Finally, various applications of the growth accounting methodology rely on a decomposition of labour productivity (value added per hour worked). This decomposition can be derived by subtracting $\Delta \ln H_j$ from the left- and right-hand sides of (3.29). Let z be labour productivity, defined as the ratio of value added to hours worked, $z = Z/H$, and k the ratio of capital services to hours worked, $k = K/H$; then

$$\Delta \ln z_j = \bar{v}_{ICT,j}^{Z} \Delta \ln k_j^{ICT} + \bar{v}_{N,j}^{Z} \Delta \ln k_j^{N} + \bar{v}_{L,j}^{Z} \Delta \ln LC_j + \Delta \ln A_j^{Z} \tag{3.30}$$

Equation (3.30) shows the four different sources of industry labour productivity growth, namely changes in labour composition, ICT capital deepening, non-ICT capital deepening and MFP growth.

In Table 3.2 a decomposition of growth in value added and value added per hour worked in UK metal manufacturing is provided, continuing the example in Table 3.1. Value added is dominated by labour inputs, accounting for almost 90 per cent of total value added. The volume growth rate of value added is derived on the basis of growth in intermediate inputs and output. The share of value added in gross output is 36 per cent, and consequently volume growth of value added turns out to be zero, following (3.26). As before, growth in hours worked is strongly negative, while growth in overall capital input is positive. The calculation of value-added-based MFP relies on the assumption that all technical change only takes place in the use of capital and labour, and not in the use of all inputs as was the case for gross output MFP. Due to the low share of value added in output, value-added-based MFP is much higher than gross output MFP (3.1 versus 0.8 per cent). The decomposition of value-added growth based on (3.29) is given in column 3. It shows that MFP growth fully counteracts the decline in the use of labour input. The last two columns of Table 3.2 provide a decomposition of growth in labour productivity (value added per hour worked) based on (3.30). Obviously, growth in labour input now only includes the changes in labour composition and contributes 0.7 percentage points to the 3.4 per cent growth in labour productivity. While growth in capital services is low, growth in capital services per hour worked is much higher because of the decline in hours worked. Capital input contributes 0.6 percentage points to growth in labour productivity.

In Figure 3.2 we provide a decomposition of labour productivity growth (value added per hour worked) in twenty-six industries in the EU over the period 1980–2005. Based on (3.30) the growth in value added per hour worked is divided into the contribution of growth in labour and capital services per hour worked (in black) and the change in productivity of these inputs as measured by the growth in MFP (in grey). Industries are ranked from highest to lowest growth rate. Labour productivity increased at a rate of more than 4 per cent annually in post and telecommunication, electrical equipment manufacturing, chemicals, agriculture, mining and utilities. On the other hand, labour productivity growth was low, or even negative, in business services, other services, hotels and restaurants and construction. All other industries had annual growth rates of at least 1.0 per cent per year. Differences in growth rates of labour productivity across industries were mainly driven by differences in the growth of MFP, as the correlation between labour productivity and MFP growth rates was 0.85, while the correlation with total factor inputs was only 0.48.

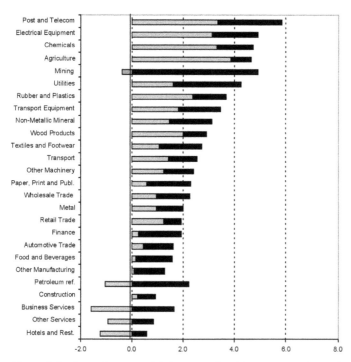

Figure 3.2. Growth rates of labour productivity, twenty-six industries, EU, 1980–2005. Annual compound growth rates of gross value added per hour worked by industry. In black, the contribution of growth in capital inputs per hour worked and changes in labour composition and, in grey, the contribution of growth in productivity of capital and labour (value-added based MFP). (*Source*: Calculations based on EU KLEMS database, March 2008.)

Growth in the use of inputs typically contributed about 1 to 2 percentage points to growth in labour productivity. Also industries that were stagnant in terms of labour productivity growth still increased the use of capital and labour services per hour worked.

The EU KLEMS database has been constructed largely on the basis of data from national statistical institutes (NSIs) and processed according to harmonised procedures. These procedures were developed to ensure international comparability of the basic data and to generate growth accounts in a consistent and uniform way. Cross-country harmonisation of the basic country data has focused on a number of areas including a common industrial classification and the use of similar price concepts for inputs and outputs, but also consistent definitions of various labour and capital types. Importantly, this database is rooted in statistics from the National Accounts and so broadly follows the concepts and conventions of the System of National Accounts (SNA) framework and its European implementation guide (ESA; European Commission 1996). As a result, the basic statistics within EU KLEMS can be related to the National Accounts statistics published by NSIs, although with adjustments that vary per group of variables: output and intermediate inputs, labour input and capital input. These adjustments are discussed in the relevant sections below.

3.3 Output and intermediate inputs

Volume series for output and intermediate inputs are based on deflation of nominal series by appropriate price indices. The volume series are given as indices with 1995 as the base year (1995 = 100). However, this does not mean that the series are valued at 1995 prices. This will depend on the base year of the underlying price indices. Nominal and price series at the industry level are taken directly from the National Accounts. As these series are often short (as revisions are not always taken back in time) different vintages of the National Accounts are bridged according to a common link methodology. In cases where industry detail for nominal series are missing, additional statistics from censuses and surveys are used to fill the gaps. Price indices for detailed industries that are not available from the National Accounts are based on more aggregated series for which data are available.

In this database we have chosen to report industry-level value-added volume indices for each country based on the National Accounts methodology of the particular country. This methodology might differ across countries and will not always be equal to the implicit definition as given in (3.26). This choice is driven by the fact that for many countries value-added volume series are often longer and have more industry detail than the gross output and intermediate inputs series. For series based on the European System of Accounts 1995 (ESA 95; European Commission 1996), differences are small as they are constructed by double deflation, separately deflating gross output and intermediate inputs, based on a chained Laspeyres volume index. But especially in the past, value-added volumes in the National Accounts were not always derived using the double deflation method. This is particularly true for some services industries and for data derived from earlier vintages of the National Accounts before the ESA 1995 revisions. Hence, redefining value added on the basis of gross output and intermediate input would have resulted in an unacceptable loss of data. Also, in some industries for some countries and years, nominal or real value added is negative. Where this is the case, volume indices cannot be derived and the series breaks down. In these cases, the volume series is missing, but the negatives are included at higher levels of aggregation.[7]

Output growth rates differ widely across industries. In Figure 3.3 we have ranked twenty-nine industries in the EU on the basis of growth of output volumes over the period 1980–2005. These growth rates varied from almost zero or even negative, as in the case of mining, textiles, petroleum refining and agriculture, to more than 4 per cent annual growth in the case of post and telecommunication and business services. Also in a number of other services, output growth was high such as in finance, trade and transport services. Fast-growing manufacturing industries include electrical machinery, transport equipment and rubber and plastics manufacturing. The growth of output is decomposed into the growth of intermediate inputs (black part) and of value added (grey part) based on (3.26). In general, the correlation between output and value-added growth was high, although in some industries the contribution of intermediate inputs is much higher than from value added. This is particularly true for transport equipment manufacturing, the output of which grew mainly on the basis of outsourcing of intermediate input production. On the other hand, output growth in health was predominantly based on increasing use of labour and capital inputs.

Series on intermediate inputs are broken down into energy, materials and services, based on supply-and-use tables using a standardised product classification. To ensure consistency with the National Accounts series, proportions of energy, materials and services inputs were applied to the total intermediate input series from the National Accounts. There has been some confusion in the literature on the price concept to be used for intermediate inputs. It is generally acknowledged that the intermediate input weights should be measured from

---

[7] To be more precise, in these cases we sum the chained Laspeyres series instead of applying Tornqvist aggregation.

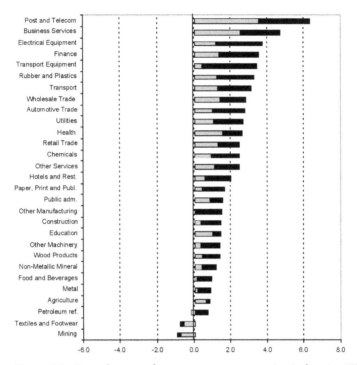

Figure 3.3. Growth rates of gross output, twenty-nine industries, EU, 1980–2005. Annual compound growth rates of gross output volumes by industry. In black, the contribution of growth in intermediate inputs and, in grey, the contribution of growth in value added. (*Source*: Calculations based on EU KLEMS database, March 2008.)

the user's point of view, i.e. reflect the marginal cost paid by the user. Most studies maintain that purchasers' prices should be used. These prices include net taxes on commodities paid by the user, and include margins on trade and transportation (see, for example, OECD 2001). However, when trade and transportation services are included as separate intermediate inputs, margins paid on other products should also be allocated to these services. Ideally, a distinction should be made between the intermediate product valued at purchasers' prices minus margins and the trade and transportation services valued at the margins. This is the approach taken in Jorgenson, Gollop and Fraumeni (1987) and in Jorgenson *et al.* (2005). However, in practice for the EU KLEMS database, we were not able to collect the necessary data for this breakdown, and used purchasers' prices to value intermediate inputs for all countries, except for the USA.

In growth accounting decompositions, the weights for the production factors labour and capital should reflect the marginal cost of labour and capital usage respectively. These weights are based on value-added components as given in the National Accounts. In the National Accounts the following definition holds: value added at basic price is equal to labour compensation of the employees plus gross operating surplus plus other net taxes on production. Operating surplus should be divided into compensation for self-employed labour, which is part of labour compensation, and the rest, which should be allocated to capital compensation. However, labour compensation of the self-employed is not separately registered in the National Accounts. We make an imputation by assuming that the compensation per hour of the self-employed is equal to the compensation per hour of employees. This assumption is made at the industry level and can be crude for some industries where the characteristics of the self-employed and employees differ widely.[8]

Similarly, other taxes on production should be allocated to both capital and labour inputs. However, this is not straightforward, as these consist of a variety of taxes levied on ownership and use of land, use of fixed assets, total wage bill, licences, pollution, etc. In the absence of detailed knowledge about the various tax types, taxes on production are allocated to capital compensation as they mainly fall on this factor input.

3.4 Labour services

The productivity of various types of labour, such as low- versus high-skilled labour, will differ across these types. Standard measures of labour input, such as number of persons employed or hours worked, will not account for such differences. Hence it is important that measures of labour input take account of the heterogeneity of the labour force in measuring productivity and the contribution of labour to

---

[8] Ideally, the imputation for self-employed should be constrained to the mixed income component of the gross operating surplus. However, data limitations did not allow us to do so. Only in the case of Belgium has this restriction been applied.

Table 3.3. *Classification of labour force for each industry*

Dimension	Number of categories	Categories
Employment class	2	Employees; self-employed
Gender	2	Male; female
Age	3	15–29; 30–49; 50 and over
Education	3	High-skilled; medium-skilled; low-skilled

output growth. In the growth accounting approach, these measures are called labour services, as they allow for differences in the amount of services delivered per unit of labour. It is assumed that the flow of labour services for each labour type is proportional to hours worked and that workers are paid their marginal productivities. Then the corresponding index of labour services input is given by a weighted growth of hours worked by each labour type and weights are given by the period-average shares of each type in the value of labour compensation as in (3.7). We cross-classify hours worked by employment class, educational attainment, gender and age into thirty-six labour categories, 2*3*2*3 types respectively (see Table 3.3). Age is included as a proxy for work experience. The definitions of high-, medium- and low-skilled are consistent over time for each country, but might differ across countries. The high–medium–low skill split is too restrictive, given the differences in educational systems throughout Europe. We therefore assume comparability only across the university graduates level (high-skilled), not at the other levels. Consequently, care should be taken in comparing shares of educational attainment across countries and further research is needed into the exact definitions used. In Table 3A.4 we provide a short overview of the definitions used for high-, medium- and low-skilled for each country in the EU KLEMS database.

In Table 3.4 we give an example of the calculations of the growth in labour services for UK metal manufacturing. For clarity, data are given for nine types of labour only, by summing over the gender and employment class dimensions. The table shows the total hours worked by each type and its share in total labour compensation. Although middle-aged medium-skilled workers dominate this particular labour force, a clear upskilling took place between 1995 and 2005.

Table 3.4. Example of labour services growth calculation, metal manufacturing in the UK, 1995–2005

	Hours worked (millions)			Share in labour compensation (per cent)			Contribution to labour services growth
	1995	2005	Annual growth	1995	2005	Average	
High-skilled, older than 49	13	20	4.5	2.2	4.4	3.3	0.1
High-skilled, 30 to 49	63	78	2.2	9.7	17.0	13.4	0.3
High-skilled, younger than 30	36	30	–1.7	3.2	3.8	3.5	–0.1
Medium-skilled, older than 49	128	131	0.2	13.1	15.9	14.5	0.0
Medium-skilled, 30 to 49	384	307	–2.2	36.7	37.8	37.3	–0.8
Medium-skilled, younger than 30	293	148	–6.8	19.4	11.9	15.6	–1.1
Low-skilled, older than 49	77	46	–5.1	4.7	3.8	4.3	–0.2
Low-skilled, 30 to 49	122	49	–9.2	8.7	4.4	6.5	–0.6
Low-skilled, younger than 30	44	16	–10.3	2.2	1.0	1.6	–0.2
Residual							–0.1
All workers	1,160	826	–3.4	100.0	100.0	100.0	–2.6

Notes: Contribution of labour types calculated as the average share of input times the volume growth rate. Numbers may not sum exactly due to rounding. Residual includes effects of shifts in male and female shares.
Source: Calculations based on EU KLEMS database, March 2008

High-skilled workers increased their hours worked, while hours by low-skilled workers declined strongly. By multiplying the average share in labour compensation and the growth in hours worked, the contribution of each labour type to growth in labour services is calculated. This is given in the last column. Total hours worked in metal manufacturing declined at a rate of 3.4 per cent per year while labour services declined at 2.6 per cent. The difference of 0.8 per cent is due to the change in the composition of the labour force, in this case upskilling.

Series on hours worked by labour types are not part of the core set of National Accounts statistics put out by NSIs, even at the aggregate level. Also, there is no comprehensive international database on skills which could be used for this purpose. Previous cross-country studies relied on rough proxies of skills, for example by distinguishing production versus non-production workers as in Griffith *et al.* (2004) or by combining a wide variety of disconnected sources such as in Nicoletti and Scarpetta (2003). Country studies in greater depth, such as Koeniger and Leonardi (2007), use consistent data for both wages and employment by skill from one particular source. This is also the strategy followed in EU KLEMS. For each country covered, a choice was made of the best statistical source for consistent wage and employment data at the industry level. In most cases this was the labour force survey (LFS), which in some cases was combined with an earnings survey when wages were not included in the LFS. In other instances, an establishment survey or social security database was used. Table 3A.5 provides additional detail on the sources used for each country. Care has been taken to arrive at series which are consistent over time. This involved significant additional effort, as most employment surveys are not designed to track developments over time, and breaks in methodology or coverage frequently occur.

In Figure 3.4, industries in the EU are ranked on the basis of the share of university graduates (high-skilled) in total hours worked in 1995. This share varies widely and is particular high in non-market services including health, education and public administration, but also in business and financial services. High-skilled shares are low in agriculture, construction, hotels and restaurants and retailing.

The data on self-employed hours tend to be less easily available and are not always reported in National Accounts or LFS. In some instances these have been estimated from other figures. For example, for France they have been estimated from hours worked by the employees corrected for overtime, and, for the UK, trends from employees have been

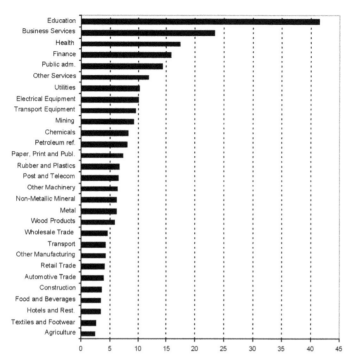

Figure 3.4. Share of high-skilled workers in total hours worked (percentage), twenty-nine industries, EU, 1995. (*Source*: Calculations based on EU KLEMS database, March 2008.)

used to estimate self-employed hours for the 1970s and 1980s. Further details on the methods used for individual countries are given in their respective sections in the EU KLEMS Sources document (Timmer, van Moergastel, Stuivenwold *et al.* 2007). Also labour compensation of the self-employed is not registered in the National Accounts, which, as emphasised by Krueger (1999), leads to an understatement of labour's share. We make an imputation by assuming that the compensation per hour of the self-employed is equal to the compensation per hour of employees. This is especially important for industries which have a large share of self-employed workers, such as agriculture, trade, business and personal services. Also, we assume the same labour characteristics for the self-employed as for employees when information on the former is missing. These assumptions are made at the industry level.

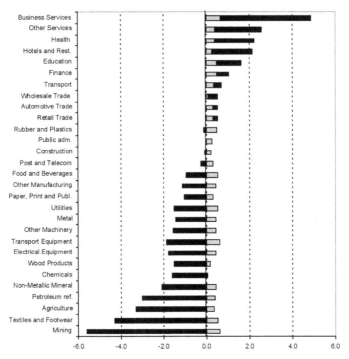

Figure 3.5. Growth rates of labour input, twenty-nine industries, EU, 1980–2005. Annual compound growth rates. In black, the growth in hours worked and, in grey, the contribution of changes in labour composition. (*Source*: Calculations based on EU KLEMS database, March 2008.)

Growth rates of labour services per hour worked across industries differ much less than levels of labour services. Figure 3.5 provides an overview of growth in labour services across industries in the EU over the period 1980–2005. In almost all industries changes in labour composition (grey part) contribute positively to growth in labour services. In most countries and industries there is a slow long-term up-skilling trend that seems to be driven by the gradually increasing supply of skilled labour. In contrast, growth in total hours worked (black part) varied widely. In business services, hours worked grew at an annual rate of almost 5 per cent. Also employment in many other services industries grew strongly, whereas in most manufacturing industries and traditional industries such as agriculture and mining employment declined. Growth in labour services is clearly dominated by changes in

Table 3.5. *List of asset types and depreciation rates*

Full name	Abbreviation	Range of depreciation rates across industries	
		Minimum	Maximum
Total assets	GFCF		
ICT assets	ICT		
Computing equipment	IT	0.315	0.315
Communications equipment	CT	0.115	0.115
Software	Soft	0.315	0.315
Non-ICT assets	Non-ICT		
Residential structures	Rstruc	0.011	0.011
Non-residential structures	OCon	0.023	0.069
Transport equipment	TraEq	0.061	0.246
Other machinery and equipment	OMach	0.073	0.164
Other assets[a]	Other	0.073	0.164

Note: [a] Other assets include products of agriculture and other tangible and intangible products not elsewhere classified, following the ESA 1995 (mainly mineral exploration and artistic originals).

hours worked and not by any contribution from changes in the labour force.

3.5 Capital services

As for labour, various types of capital will have differing productivities. While, say, a building delivers its services over a long period, ICT assets such as software are typically replaced within five years. To account for this difference the user-cost approach is employed and capital input is measured as capital services, rather than stocks. It is measured as the weighted growth of stocks of eight assets as in (3.14)–(3.16). These assets are residential structures, non-residential structures, transport equipment, information technology equipment, communication technology equipment, other machinery and equipment, software and other fixed capital assets. Table 3.5 provides more information on this classification. For each individual asset, stocks have been estimated on the basis of investment series using the perpetual inventory method (PIM) with geometric depreciation profiles.

Industry-level estimates of capital input require detailed asset-by-industry investment matrices. Aggregate investment by industry and aggregate investment by asset type are normally available from the National Accounts. However, the allocation of assets to using industries in the so-called capital-flow matrix is not always made public by the NSIs. The main reason for this is that the construction of this matrix is much less reliable than the aggregate series and depends on a wide variety of assumptions.[9] For each country, the basic investment series by industry and asset have been derived from capital-flow matrices and benchmarked to the aggregate investment series from the National Accounts. For some countries the classification of capital assets is not always detailed enough to distinguish investment in information and communications equipment. Additional information has been collected to obtain investment series for these assets, or assumptions concerning hardware–software ratios have been employed. Table 3A.6 provides additional detail on a country-by-country basis.

To transform the nominal investment series into volumes, price deflators for each asset type are needed. Price measurement for ICT assets has been an important research topic in recent years, as the quality of those capital goods has been rapidly increasing. Until recently, large differences existed among countries in the methodology for obtaining deflators for ICT equipment, and the use of a single harmonised deflator across countries was widely advocated and used (Colecchia and Schreyer 2002; Schreyer 2002; Timmer and van Ark 2005). This deflator was based on the US deflators for computer hardware, which were commonly seen as the most advanced in terms of accounting for quality changes using hedonic pricing techniques (Triplett 2006). However, in recent years, many European countries, such as France, Germany, the Netherlands and the UK, have made significant progress in either developing and implementing their own quality-adjusted deflators for IT equipment, using high-frequency matched models or hedonic-type deflators, or by using deflators based on adapted price indices from the US Bureau of Economic Analysis. These new deflators typically show price declines of about 10 per cent annually. For those countries (Austria, Belgium, Finland, Italy and

---

[9] For example, to distribute parts of equipment, computers and software the BEA use occupation-by-industry data, rather than investment survey data (see Meade *et al.* 2003).

Spain) which have not yet implemented a quality-adjusted investment deflator for computers, we continue to use the harmonisation procedure suggested by Schreyer (2002).

Additional research on prices of other ICT hardware and software suggests that official deflators in the National Accounts in the USA and elsewhere might still overstate price changes for these high-tech products. Abel *et al.* (2007) provide an analysis of pre-packaged software prices, Doms (2005) surveys research on telecommunication equipment prices and van Reenen (2006) provides a case study of network servers. As these studies are as yet infrequent and *ad hoc*, they are not included in the EU KLEMS database. This must await further research and the inclusion of improved price series in official National Accounts statistics.

According to the perpetual inventory method (PIM), the capital stock (S) is defined as a weighted sum of past investments with weights given by the relative efficiencies of capital goods at different ages:

$$S_{k,T} = \sum_{t=0}^{\infty} \partial_{k,t} I_{k,T-t} \qquad (3.31)$$

with $S_{k,T}$ the capital stock (for a particular asset type k) at time T, $\partial_{k,t}$ the efficiency of a capital good k of age t relative to the efficiency of a new capital good, and $I_{k,T-t}$ the investments in period $T - t$. An important implicit assumption made here is that the services provided by assets of different vintages are perfect substitutes for each other. As in most studies, a geometric depreciation pattern is applied in the EU KLEMS database. With a given rate of depreciation δ_k which is assumed constant over time, but different for each asset type, we get $\partial_{k,t} = (1 - \delta_k)^{t-1}$, so that

$$S_{k,T} = \sum_{t=0}^{\infty} (1 - \delta_k)^{t-1} I_{k,T-t} = S_{k,T-1}(1 - \delta_k) + I_{k,T} \qquad (3.32)$$

If it is assumed that the flow of capital services from each asset type k (K_k) is proportional to the average of the stock available at the end of the current and the prior period ($S_{k,T}$ and $S_{k,T-1}$), capital service flows can be aggregated from these asset types as a translog quantity index by weighting growth in the stock of each asset by the average shares of each asset in the value of capital compensation, as illustrated for two asset types in (3.14) above.

The estimation of the compensation share of each asset, v_i, is related to the user cost of each asset. The user cost approach is crucial in any analysis of the contribution of ICT capital to growth. An example might help to illustrate this approach. Suppose a firm leases a computer and a building for one year in the rental market. If the cost of leasing one euro of computers is higher than leasing one euro of buildings, then computers have a higher marginal productivity, and this should be accounted for. There are various reasons why the cost of computers is higher than the cost of buildings. While computers may typically be discarded after five or six years, buildings may provide services for several decades. Besides, prices of new computers decline rapidly, while prices of buildings normally do not. Hence the user cost of computers is typically 50 to 60 per cent of the investment price, while that of buildings is less than 10 per cent. Therefore one euro of computer capital stock should get a bigger weight in the growth decomposition than one euro of building stock. Using the rental price of capital services picks up this difference.

The rental price of capital services, $p_{k,t}^K$, reflects the price at which the investor is indifferent between buying and renting the capital good for a one-year lease in the rental market. In the absence of taxation the equilibrium condition can be rearranged, yielding the familiar cost-of-capital equation:

$$p_{k,t}^K = p_{k,t-1}^I i_t + \delta_k p_{k,t}^I - \left(p_{k,t}^I - p_{k,t-1}^I \right) \tag{3.33}$$

with i_t representing the nominal rate of return, δ_k the depreciation rate of asset type k, and $p_{k,t}^I$ the investment price of asset type k. This formula shows that the rental fee is determined by the nominal rate of return, the rate of economic depreciation and the asset-specific capital gains.[10] Ideally taxes should be included to account for differences in tax treatment of the different asset types and different legal

---

[10] The logic for using the rental price is as follows. In equilibrium, an investor is indifferent between two alternatives: earning a nominal rate of return r on an investment q, or buying a unit of capital collecting a rental p and then selling it at the depreciated asset price $(1 - \delta)q$ in the next period. Assuming no taxation the equilibrium condition is: $(1 + r_T)q_{i,T-1} = p_{i,T} + (1 - \delta_i)q_{i,T}$, with p as the rental fee and q_i the acquisition price of investment good i (Jorgenson and Stiroh 2000, p. 192). Rearranging this yields a variation of the familiar cost-of-capital equation: $p_{i,T} = q_{i,T-1}r_T + \delta_i q_{i,T-1} - (q_{i,T} - q_{i,T-1})$, which is identical to (3.33).

forms (household, corporate and non-corporate). The capital service price formulas above should then be adjusted to take these tax rates into account (see Jorgenson and Yun 1991). However, this refinement would require data on capital tax allowances and rates by country, industry and year, which is beyond the scope of this database. Available evidence for major European countries shows that the inclusion of tax rates has only a very minor effect on growth rates of capital services and MFP (Erumban 2008).

The nominal rate of return is determined ex-post as in the endogenous approach (Jorgenson *et al.* 2005). It is assumed that the total value of capital services for each industry equals its compensation for all assets. This procedure yields an internal rate of return that exhausts capital income and is consistent with constant returns to scale. This nominal rate of return is the same for all assets in an industry, but is allowed to vary across industries, and is derived as a residual as follows:

$$
i_{j,t} = \frac{p^K_{j,t} K_{j,t} + \sum_k \left(p^I_{k,j,t} - p^I_{k,j,t-1}\right) S_{k,j,t} - \sum_k p^I_{k,j,t} \delta_{k,j} S_{k,j,t}}{\sum_k p^I_{k,j,t-1} S_{k,j,t}}
$$

$$(3.34)$$

where the first term $p^K_{j,t} K_{j,t}$ is the capital compensation in industry j, which under constant returns to scale can be derived as value added minus the compensation of labour. In section 3.7, alternative methods for the calculation of rental prices are discussed.

In practice, the capital service prices implied by equation (3.33) can be negative. Negative rental prices are not necessarily theoretically inconsistent (see, for example, Berndt and Fuss 1986), but they can also be an indication of empirical problems in the estimation of labour and capital compensation shares (see below), or in the investment deflator. Most negative rental rates are caused by large swings in investment deflators, for example, in non-residential buildings. Others are due to very low, or even negative, capital compensation, related to negative value added or to over-adjustment of the labour compensation of self-employed people, for example in agriculture. Negative capital prices break down our aggregation framework and therefore need to be dealt with by an *ad hoc* procedure. In the EU KLEMS database, we use a simple heuristic rule and constrain the rental price to be non-negative, setting it to zero in cases where it is negative. See section 3.6 for further discussion.

In the EU KLEMS database a harmonised approach to capital measurement is used, based on one set of asset depreciation rates for all countries. These depreciation rates differ by asset type and industry, but not by country and not over time. Although depreciation rates most likely vary across countries and time on account of differences in the pace of structural change, there is no empirical evidence available that can be used to model this. Assuming identical rates across countries is clearly a second-best solution. The rates are based on the industry by asset type depreciation rates from the Bureau of Economic Analysis (BEA) as described in Fraumeni (1997). The advantage of using the BEA rates is that they are based on empirical research (albeit, for many assets, rather outdated), rather than *ad hoc* assumptions based on, for example tax laws, as in many European countries (see Statistical Commission and Economic Commission for Europe 2004). Detailed BEA asset lifetimes were aggregated based on capital stocks for each separate asset type, available from the BEA data (see Timmer, van Moergastel, Stuivenwold *et al.* 2007 for more details). Therefore, depreciation rates of the more aggregated assets in EU KLEMS might differ across industries. Table 3.5 provides the minimum and maximum rates over all industries in EU KLEMS for other machinery, transport equipment and non-residential buildings. The rates for the other asset types were the same for all industries. The rate for residential structures was set to 0.0114, the rate for 1-to-4-unit homes from the BEA. The three ICT assets, computers, software and communications equipment, were also assumed to have the same depreciation rate for all industries. These were set equal to the rates employed in Jorgenson *et al.* Stiroh (2005), that is, 0.315 for computers and software and 0.115 for communications equipment. These numbers are supported by a careful study by Doms *et al.* (2004) on depreciation of personal computers. The rate for other immaterial assets was set equal to software, infrastructure to non-residential buildings, and products of agriculture and other products to other machinery and equipment.

In Table 3.6 we give an example of the calculations of capital services growth for UK metal manufacturing. Volume growth rates of the stock of each asset between 1995 and 2005 are given in the first three

Table 3.6. *Example of capital services growth calculation, metal manufacturing in the UK, 1995–2005*

	Capital stock (in millions and 1995 prices)			Share in capital compensation (per cent)			Contribution to capital services growth
	1995	2005	Annual growth	1995	2005	Average	
Computing equipment	136	2,018	27.0	2.4	15.8	9.1	2.1
Communications equipment	60	195	11.8	0.2	0.4	0.3	0.1
Software	322	523	4.8	4.5	20.2	12.3	0.4
Non-residential structures	5,788	5,271	−0.9	19.8	0.0	9.9	0.0
Transport equipment	580	520	−1.1	4.3	6.0	5.1	−0.1
Other machinery	11,010	9,344	−1.6	68.9	57.6	63.3	−1.1
Total	17,897	17,870	0.0	100.0	100.0	100.0	1.5

Notes: Contribution of each asset type is calculated as the compensation share weighted sum of the volume growth rate of the stocks. The contributions in the table are based on annually changing weights rather than the period average; see main text. Numbers may not sum exactly due to rounding.
Source: Calculations based on EU KLEMS database, March 2008.

columns.[11] They indicate that the use of ICT assets has dramatically increased. In contrast, the stocks of more traditional non-ICT capital have declined, as depreciation was higher than additions through new investment. In 1995, the combined share of ICT assets in the overall capital stock was less than 3 per cent. Because of their high rental prices, the ICT share in capital compensation was more than 7 per cent. This share increased to over 36 per cent in 2005, indicating the increasing importance of ICT assets in UK metal production. In the last column the contribution of each asset to the growth in capital services is given. This is based on multiplying the volume growth rate of each asset by its average share.[12] Clearly, the growth in capital services is due to the increased use of ICT assets, in particular IT hardware. Growth in ICT more than compensated for the sharp decline in the use of other machinery. This example also illustrates the large differences that can arise when capital input measures are based on stocks rather than capital services. The overall capital stock in this industry did not grow at all, while capital services input increased at an annual rate of 1.5 per cent. This underlines the importance of taking into account the changing asset distribution of the capital stock, in particular the increased use of ICT assets when analysing growth patterns.

The importance of ICT assets in production can be seen in many other industries. In Figure 3.6 we provide a ranking of industries in the EU on the basis of the shares of ICT assets in value added in 1995. In some industries the role of ICT is rather limited, for example in agriculture, mining, construction, hotels and restaurants and various traditional manufacturing industries. On the other hand, ICT is used intensively in many services industries such as post and telecommunications, finance and business services, but also in a number of manufacturing industries such as machinery. However, there is no clear-cut division between ICT-using and non-ICT-using industries as often used in earlier analyses of growth (see section 1.3). Instead, the use of ICT assets has become firmly established in the daily production routines of many firms. At the same time it is also clear that although

---

[11] Stocks of other assets are zero in this industry.

[12] In the EU KLEMS database, weights are averaged on an annual basis rather than per period. This might lead to different decomposition results in cases where asset shares change quickly over time, such as in the case of ICT assets. The contributions in the table are based on annual changing weights rather than the period average.

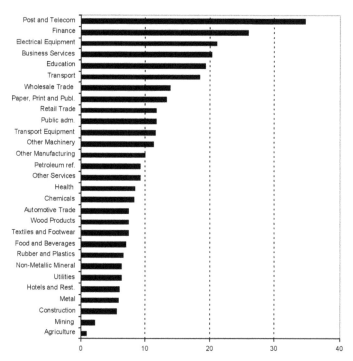

Figure 3.6. Share of ICT capital compensation in value added (percentage), twenty-nine industries, EU, 1995. (*Source*: Calculations based on EU KLEMS database, March 2008.)

ICT capital has been an important driver of growth in capital input, in many industries traditional non-ICT assets have played a major or even dominant role in the past decades. In Figure 3.7 we have ranked EU industries on the basis of growth in capital services inputs over the period 1980–2005. This growth is split into the contributions of ICT assets (in grey) and of non-ICT (in black). In only four industries the contribution of ICT is higher than that of non-ICT capital in the period 1980–1995. For the period 1995–2005 this increased to twelve industries (not shown).

Finally in this section we show full growth accounts for the EU and USA, showing contributions of inputs and MFP. In Tables 3.7 and 3.8 the results are shown for the EU and USA, respectively, by major sector. These illustrate the important contributions of both ICT capital and MFP growth in explaining productivity growth in many sectors.

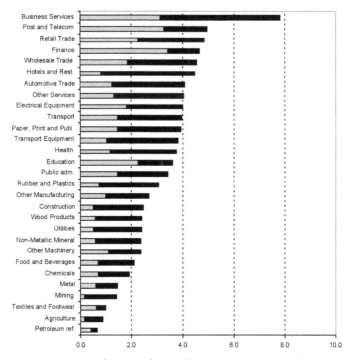

Figure 3.7. Growth rates of capital input, twenty-nine industries, EU, 1980–2005. Annual compound growth rates of capital input by industry. In black, the contribution of growth in non-ICT capital and, in grey, the contribution of growth in ICT capital. (*Source*: Calculations based on EU KLEMS database, March 2008.)

These findings were discussed in Chapter 2, and more detailed results by industry are discussed in Chapter 5 below.

3.6 Issues in measuring outputs, inputs and productivity

A crucial question in productivity analysis is whether the data used in the analysis are good enough to support the conclusions drawn from them. In general, productivity estimates will be biased if nominal outputs, prices, inputs or cost shares are not measured correctly (see Schreyer 2001 or Diewert 2007). As with all data series there are some unresolved measurement issues in EU KLEMS. Practical issues in using the data, together with health warnings, are discussed in the appendix to this chapter. Below we discuss some general measurement issues on a variable-by-variable basis. At the same time, it must be stressed that the

Table 3.7. *Growth accounting for major sectors, EU, 1980–2005*

	Growth rate of value added	Value added contribution from		Labour productivity contributions from			
		Hours worked	Labour productivity	Labour composition	ICT capital per hour	Non-ICT capital per hour	Multi-factor productivity
	1 = 2 + 3	2	3 = 4 + 5 + 6 + 7	4	5	6	7
1980–95							
Market economy	2.1	−0.5	2.5	0.3	0.4	0.8	1.0
ICT production	3.6	−1.3	4.9	0.3	1.0	1.0	2.7
Manufacturing	1.1	−2.1	3.2	0.3	0.2	1.0	1.6
Other goods	1.1	−2.4	3.5	0.2	0.2	1.3	1.8
Distribution	2.6	0.1	2.5	0.2	0.3	0.5	1.5
Finance & business	3.5	3.2	0.3	0.4	0.7	0.4	−1.2
Personal	1.7	2.2	−0.5	0.3	0.2	0.2	−1.2
1995–2005							
Market economy	2.2	0.7	1.5	0.2	0.5	0.4	0.3
ICT production	5.5	−1.0	6.5	0.2	1.3	0.8	4.2
Manufacturing	0.8	−1.1	2.0	0.3	0.3	0.6	0.8
Other goods	1.1	−0.4	1.6	0.2	0.2	0.7	0.5
Distribution	2.3	0.6	1.7	0.1	0.4	0.6	0.6
Finance & business	3.6	3.3	0.3	0.3	1.0	0.1	−1.1
Personal	1.7	2.1	−0.4	0.1	0.2	0.2	−0.9

Source: Calculations based on EU KLEMS database, March 2008.

Table 3.8. Growth accounting for major sectors, USA, 1980–2005

	Growth rate of value added	Value added contribution from		Labour productivity contributions from			
		Hours worked	Labour productivity	Labour composition	ICT capital per hour	Non-ICT capital per hour	Multi-factor productivity
	$1 = 2 + 3$	2	$3 = 4 + 5 + 6 + 7$	4	5	6	7
1980–95							
Market economy	3.2	1.3	1.9	0.2	0.7	0.3	0.7
ICT production	6.0	0.1	5.9	0.4	1.0	0.7	3.8
Manufacturing	1.7	−0.4	2.1	0.3	0.5	0.4	0.9
Other goods	2.2	0.4	1.8	0.3	0.2	0.2	1.1
Distribution	4.0	1.2	2.7	0.2	0.5	0.2	1.8
Finance & business	3.7	3.9	−0.3	0.2	1.6	0.4	−2.4
Personal	3.3	2.1	1.1	0.0	0.2	0.1	0.8
1995–2005							
Market economy	3.6	0.7	2.9	0.3	1.0	0.3	1.3
ICT production	8.4	−1.6	10.0	0.4	1.9	0.8	6.9
Manufacturing	1.1	−1.8	2.9	0.3	0.6	0.7	1.2
Other goods	1.4	1.8	−0.4	0.1	0.4	0.0	−0.8
Distribution	4.7	0.7	4.0	0.3	0.8	0.3	2.7
Finance & business	4.5	1.9	2.6	0.4	1.8	0.3	0.0
Personal	2.8	1.6	1.2	0.3	0.2	0.1	0.6

Source: Calculations based on EU KLEMS database, March 2008.

limitations of the EU KLEMS series vary widely by country, period and variable and prudent users of the data should familiarise themselves with the methods of construction as discussed on a country-by-country basis in Timmer, van Moergastel, Stuivenwold *et al.* (2007).

Output and intermediate inputs

As mentioned above, output series are taken primarily from National Accounts sources. However, this does not mean that these series are by any means perfect. In fact, there are significant unresolved measurement issues in the National Accounts, in particular for services. It is well known that the problem of measuring output is in general much more challenging in services than in goods-producing industries. Most measurement problems boil down to the fact that service activities are intangible, more heterogeneous than goods and often dependent on the actions of the consumer as well as the producer. A distinction should be made between services which are traded in a market (market services) and non-market services for which no prices exist. The measurement of nominal output in market services is generally less problematic, being mostly a matter of accurately registering total revenue. But the main bottleneck is the measurement of output volumes, which requires accurate price measurement adjusted for changes in the quality of services output. There is no doubt that problems in measuring market services output still exist, especially in finance and business services, but many statistical offices have made great strides in the measurement of the nominal value and prices. Output measures in the National Accounts should give a fairly accurate internationally comparable picture of developments in market services. This is discussed at greater depth in section 3.7, which contains an analysis of current practice and possible alternative measurement methods for two examples, the retail trade and financial services sectors.

If there are unresolved measurement issues in market sectors, these are magnified in the case of output in sectors where a large part of the services are provided by the public sector, namely public administration, education, health and social services.[13] The main problems in measuring output in non-market sectors relate to the absence of

---

[13] In EU KLEMS, as elsewhere, we refer to these sectors as 'non-market services', recognising that some output of these sectors is provided by the private sector and the extent of this varies across countries.

market prices that allow aggregation across diverse outputs, in addition to the need to incorporate quality improvements.[14] Typically, in the past, nominal output was measured by wages, sometimes including an imputation for capital costs. If output is measured by inputs, productivity growth should be zero by definition. More recently there has been a move to employ quantity indicators to measure volumes of output, with European Union countries facing a Eurostat target of removing the dependence on input measures. Until this process is complete, productivity measures for these sectors should therefore be interpreted with care, if at all.

Finally, on output measurement, it is important to note that for the most part the output of the real estate sector (NACE 70) is imputed rent on owner-occupied dwellings, so again productivity measures for this industry need to be interpreted with care.[15] Given the measurement problems in regard to non-market sectors and real estate, EU KLEMS presents aggregates for the market economy which exclude public administration, education, health and social services and real estate. The difference between growth rates of the total economy and the market economy can be important. In 1995, the market economy covered around 70 per cent of the economy in the EU and the USA. Typically, output growth in the non-market part of the economy is much lower than in the market economy, while growth in hours worked is higher. As a result, the growth of value added per hour worked in the market economy is normally higher than in the non-market economy. Table 3.9 shows that this is particularly true for the United States. Between 1995 and 2005 growth in labour productivity in the US market economy was 0.7 percentage points higher than growth in the total economy, while only 0.2 higher in the EU. This indicates that comparative analyses of productivity growth in the USA and the EU based on total economy numbers can be potentially misleading.

---

[14] For general discussions of the issues involved see Atkinson (2005) and O'Mahony and Stevens (2006); the reader is referred to Castelli *et al.* (2007) for discussion and possible resolution in the particular example of health sector output.

[15] Alternatively, one might define a separate household sector and impute capital services to owner-occupied dwellings and household durables as in Jorgenson, Gollop and Fraumeni (1987) and Jorgenson *et al.* (2005). See for a similar attempt for some European countries Jalava and Kavonius (2009).

Table 3.9. *Growth in market versus non-market economy, EU and USA, 1995–2005*

	Gross value added	Hours worked	Value added per hour worked
European Union			
Total economy	2.0	0.8	1.3
Market economy	2.2	0.7	1.5
Non-market economy	1.6	1.0	0.6
United States			
Total economy	3.2	1.0	2.2
Market economy	3.6	0.7	2.9
Non-market economy	2.2	1.6	0.6

Note: annual compound growth rates. Market economy excludes the following industries: public administration, education, health services and real estate.
Source: Calculations based on EU KLEMS database, March 2008.

For an analysis of the use of intermediate inputs in production it is important to note that series of energy, materials and services are derived by using their shares in intermediate inputs from supply and use tables (SUTs) applied to series of intermediate inputs from the National Accounts. SUTs are generally available on a frequent basis from 1995 onwards for many countries, but not for earlier years, and this necessitates interpolation and assuming constant shares to complete series in some cases. Also, because of the use of the purchasers' price concept the shares of services in intermediate inputs do not include trade and transportation margins (see section 3.3).

Labour input

Series on number of workers and hours worked by industry present relatively few problems, although there are still some unresolved issues regarding differences in sources and methods for annual average hours worked, which mainly affect level comparisons across countries (OECD 2008, Annex 1). Incorporating adjustments for composition of the labour force is more contentious. In EU KLEMS, skill levels are categorised high, medium or low – this categorisation is dictated by the need to keep the number of categories relatively low, given sample sizes in the underlying surveys. This fairly coarse categorisation can lead to biases in the aggregate composition adjustment if employment trends and wage shares differ within categories. The extent of these biases also relates to the comparability of educational attainment and qualifications across countries, since some sub-categories with relatively high wages may be classified to high skill in one country and medium skill in another. Therefore, comparisons of skill shares across countries should be interpreted with care.

The growth accounting section of EU KLEMS presents estimates of volume of labour input and labour services. Implicit in the construction of these series is the assumption that each type of labour is paid its marginal product. In some circumstances this assumption is not appropriate, for example if there is widespread monopsony power within an industry (Manning 2003) or an industry approximates a bilateral monopoly. These problems might be addressed by inclusion in regression equations of variables that proxy for collective bargaining. An alternative might be that users include different types of labour directly in an estimating equation. The additional variables section of EU KLEMS contains data on hours worked and wage shares by skill type, and for some countries the underlying data cross-classified by gender, age and skill are also available.

Capital input

The assets covered by the EU KLEMS capital account are fixed assets as defined in the ESA 95, with the exception of inventories, land and natural resources on account of a lack of data. Inventories can be especially important in trade and transportation industries, while the lack of land and natural resources data will mainly affect MFP estimates for agriculture and mining. It has little effect on input and productivity measures of most other industries, especially since land is often included with structures investment. Another particular problem concerns the issue of ownership versus use of capital assets. In general, assets are allocated to the industry of ownership, that is, in the case of leasing, the assets are accounted for in the capital stock of the leasing industry, and the using industry pays a rental fee which is recorded in its use of intermediate services. A particular example is infrastructure: public infrastructure is not allocated to the using industries but rather appears as part of the capital stock of public administration. This is an important asset in the transport industries and hence MFP growth in this industry includes the contribution of infrastructure to output growth.

Depreciation rates in EU KLEMS vary by asset and industry, but are held constant over time and across countries. Most likely these assumptions do not hold, as depreciation also depends on the degree of turbulence and innovation within an industry which induces premature scrapping because of obsolescence. However, there is little empirical evidence to buttress this argument and so it is difficult to measure (Görzig 2007). As a second-best solution, constant rates are assumed.

Another issue is the way in which capital service prices are calculated. The theoretical basis for the Jorgensonian implementation in (3.33) is fairly restrictive though, relying on perfect foresight. In the somewhat more realistic setting of Berndt and Fuss (1986), firms first choose their capital investments and when uncertainty about input prices, demand and technology is resolved in the next period, they choose their other inputs. This means that firms have to make an ex-ante judgement about the user cost of capital to inform their investment decision but the output elasticity of capital will depend on the realised, ex-post, user cost. In practice, this would mean that to explain investment behaviour, the opportunity cost of firms' own funds would be used, for example an estimate of the weighted average cost of capital. But to determine the productive effect of capital, an internal rate of return would be used. This prescription seems straightforward. However, it depends on further restrictive assumptions. In particular, Berndt and Fuss (1986) only consider investment in a single capital asset rather than the multitude of different assets (buildings, machinery, etc.) that are available in practice. As Oulton (2007) shows, the conclusions are much less clear-cut in a world with many assets with no single appropriate rate of return. Oulton (2007) ends up advocating a hybrid approach that uses an external rate of return to aggregate across different capital assets and an internal rate of return to determine the overall output elasticity of capital.

But aside from theoretical concerns, it is important to consider the difficulties in practical implementation as well.[16] A key assumption in

---

[16] See Diewert (2008) and Schreyer (2009) for a more extensive discussion of these topics.

the background to all these models is that we know the investment of a certain firm in each asset without error. In practice though, statistical agencies face the challenging task of allocating total investment in each asset across industries (rather than firms) and total investment by each industry across assets. This also assumes that we know exactly what the investments are and what the expenses are. In current practice, spending on research and development (R&D), typically an activity with a pay-off in the future, is classified as an expense rather than an investment.[17] Finally, to correctly implement (3.28), we need an accurate number for total capital income, but in industries where the number of self-employed workers is high, this is problematic since the self-employed earn 'mixed' income, i.e. compensation for both their labour and capital input. Taken together, it is clear that measurement error will play a sizeable role and by using (3.34), the measurement error will in part show up in variation of the internal rate of return, leading to, for example, drastically different user costs for the same asset across industries. Using an external rate of return, on the other hand, would avoid these problems.

Moreover, even in the (restrictive) worlds of the Berndt and Fuss and Oulton models, an external rate of return has a role to play. As mentioned above, firms make an ex-ante assessment of the future user cost of capital in making their investment decisions. And indeed, Gilchrist and Zakrajsek (2007) use corporate bond data to construct firm-specific user costs of capital and find a strong relationship between this user cost and firm investment. In any specific year, the actual ex-post rate of return will deviate from the ex-ante rate, but on average over time the two should be similar.[18]

Most studies show that, in practice, the choice between the ex-ante and ex-post measures does not make a big difference: on average, growth rates of capital services appear to be rather similar for both methods, although for some individual industries differences can be significant (Baldwin and Gu 2007; Oulton 2007; Erumban 2008; Schreyer 2009; Inklaar 2010). However, this is not necessarily the case when calculating the contribution of capital to output growth. Some studies show that in contrast to capital service input growth, estimates for MFP growth can be rather different, depending on whether ex-post

---

[17] See Chapter 7 for discussion of intangible capital.
[18] More precisely, a rational firm should not make systematic prediction errors.

or ex-ante shares are used to weight the contribution of capital to output growth. This can be the case in industries where the growth of capital input is much higher than the growth of labour and ex-ante and ex-post shares differ widely. Balk (2009) provides a defence of the ex-ante approach. Baldwin and Gu (2007), van den Bergen *et al.* (2008), Biatour and Kegels (2008) and Inklaar (2009) provide further sensitivity analyses for Canada, the Netherlands, Belgium and the USA respectively.

Multi-factor productivity

Multi-factor productivity (MFP) growth is measured as the difference between the volume growth of outputs and the volume growth of inputs. As such, it captures increases in the amount of output that can be produced by a given quantity of inputs. Put alternatively, it captures the reduction in input costs to produce a given amount of output. Under strict neo-classical assumptions, MFP growth measures disembodied technological change. Technical change embodied in new capital goods is captured by our measure of capital input through the use of quality-adjusted prices and user costs as weights in asset aggregation. A proxy for embodied technological change might also be of interest. One way to address this is by measuring capital input as the capital stock deflated at real acquisition prices and aggregated with nominal asset shares (Greenwood *et al.* 1997). The difference between the EU KLEMS capital input series and this new series would be a proxy for embodied technological change. The EU KLEMS database provides the basic investment and capital stocks series to construct these alternative measures of capital input.

MFP growth rates from growth accounts are occasionally negative, especially for some services industries. This might seem improbable as, under strict neo-classical assumptions, this indicates technological regress. However, being a residual measure, measured MFP growth, in practice, includes a range of other effects.[19] First, in addition to technical innovation it includes the effects of organisational change. For example, the successful reorganisation of a business to streamline the production process will generally lead to higher MFP growth in

---

[19] See Hulten (2001; 2010) for an elaborate history of the MFP concept. Balk (2003) provides another useful introduction to the concept.

the long run, but in the short run might decrease measured MFP as resources are diverted to the reorganisation process (for a discussion see Basu *et al*. 2004). More broadly, MFP includes the effects from any changes in unmeasured inputs, such as research and development and investments in other intangible investments (Corrado *et al*. 2006). This is further discussed in Chapter 7.

Second, MFP measures pick up any deviations from the neo-classical assumption that marginal costs reflect marginal revenues. If, for example, ICT investments have been driven more by herd behaviour than by economic fundamentals, as may have occurred in the run up to the dotcom bubble, marginal costs might be higher than marginal revenues. Our analysis in Chapter 6 suggests that this might indeed have been the case. Consequently, MFP is underestimated and the contributions of ICT investment to growth are overestimated. Conversely if there were above normal returns to ICT, for example due to network externalities, its contribution would be underestimated (O'Mahony and Vecchi 2005). Similarly, wages may not reflect marginal productivity in situations of regulated labour markets (Manning 2003). MFP also captures changes in returns to scale. For example, there is some evidence that scale is important for realising productivity growth in retail trade, possibly because of the large outlays required for modern inventory management systems. Foster *et al*. (2006) show that much of US productivity growth in retail trade is due to the spread of national chains. If a firm originally operates below its minimum efficient scale, increasing production will lead to an increase in measured MFP. One way to relax the underlying market-clearing assumptions and allow for mark-ups and varying returns to scale is by using cost shares rather than output value shares (Hall 1988; Crafts and Mills 2005). This requires independent estimates of the cost of capital through ex-ante rates of return as discussed above.

Third, in this database, MFP is measured at the industry level, not at the firm level. Industry-level MFP reflects not only the average change in MFP of each firm within the industry, but also includes the effects of reallocation of market shares across firms. Typically, it is found that within countries there is a large dispersion in productivity across firms (Bartelsman and Doms 2000; Bartelsman *et al*. 2004). MFP growth in a particular industry might increase through a shake-out of the least productive firms, for example because of increased competitive pressure after the liberalisation of domestic markets.

Fourth, and related to the above, is that MFP captures the combined effect of technological change and technical efficiency change as described by Malmquist distance functions.[20] In this approach technology is considered as a set of feasible combinations of input and output quantities based on a body of knowledge about production processes and organisational structures, rather than as a production function as in growth accounting. If firms do not behave optimally, they can be technically inefficient, that is, operating below the technology frontier. For example, privatisation of a public firm might lead to a reduction in input use while output remains the same. This is an improvement in the firm's technical efficiency, but does not indicate technical change in the sense described above.

Finally, MFP includes measurement errors in inputs and outputs, such as inadequate accounting for quality change in new services output, or high-tech inputs. We partly address this problem by using deflators for IT investment that correct for quality change. In the next section we discuss the – in our view – limited degree of mis-measurement of services output.

In conclusion, it can be stated that all effects on measured MFP discussed here can be broadly summarised as 'improvements in efficiency', as they improve the productivity with which inputs are used within the industry.

MFP measures can be derived at various levels of aggregation. Gross output decompositions are most meaningful at the lowest level of aggregation, viz. establishments. As soon as aggregates of gross output are decomposed, problems of comparability appear over time and across countries, depending on differences in the vertical integration of firms. Ideally, decomposing gross output should be done on a sectoral output measure which excludes intra-sectoral deliveries of intermediates (see Gollop 1979). Measures of sectoral output require detailed symmetric domestic input-output tables, which are not available on a sufficiently large scale for all European countries.[21] Also, a coherent framework for aggregation in an open economy has not yet been developed, as the standard methods ignore the role of imports. Therefore, value-added decompositions are most often made. For value-added

---

[20] See Coelli *et al.* (2005) for an accessible introduction to efficiency and productivity analysis.

[21] For the level comparisons in Chapter 6, these have been constructed for one particular year.

based MFP to represent technical change the value-added separability assumption needs to hold. Generally it is found that this assumption is too restrictive (see Jorgenson, Gollop and Fraumeni 1987 for an extensive discussion). Nevertheless, value-added based measures are widely used as they add up easily to aggregate GDP. Also, they do not require explicit series on gross output and intermediate inputs, although these data are needed where value added is derived by a proper double-deflation method.

Growth accounting and causality

It should be emphasised that growth accounting is useful as a descriptive tool but that it is merely accounting and says nothing about causality. For example, MFP growth in computer manufacturing may lead to a price decline in ICT assets, which induces investment in ICT and growth in capital services. Therefore improved technology partly has its effect through the capital contribution (Aghion and Howitt 2007). In addition, specific complementarities between various types of input are not taken into account, for example between skills and ICT capital. More fundamentally, proximate sources of growth such as productivity growth and investment are endogenous to deeper causes such as technical change, institutions, geography or macro-economic policies as discussed in Maddison (1995) and Aghion and Howitt (2009). This includes key contributions such as Acemoglu *et al.* (2002) and Krugman and Venables (1995), to name but two. But growth accounting provides a useful starting point for the identification of the contributions of the proximate sources of growth. Also it provides a consistent structure in which data on output and inputs can be collected, both across industries and between variables, and as such it is a powerful organising principle. Nevertheless, the method is constrained by its assumptions and so researchers may prefer to work with the underlying data. We believe that by also providing the basic input data of the growth accounts, EU KLEMS can support a much wider variety of approaches to the study of economic growth, alongside growth accounting.

3.7 Measurement issues in market services

Griliches (1994) paid particular attention to services sector output as a key source of uncertainty. Indeed, many recent studies look at measurement problems in services, for example Wölfl (2003), Triplett and Bosworth (2004; 2008), Abraham (2005) and Crespi *et al.* (2006). Triplett and Bosworth, in particular, conclude that in the USA, output measurement in services has improved considerably, even as numerous areas for further improvement still exist. This section provides an international comparative perspective on output measurement in services. We first discuss the current state of measurement practices in services across Europe and then we discuss our research on two of these service industries, namely retail trade and banking. Our overall assessment tends towards a 'glass half full': improvements in measurement practices have been substantial over the years and measurement methodologies have also become more similar. As a result, official statistics should give us a broadly reliable overview of growth trends in market services. Nevertheless, progress is still uneven across Europe and investment in service price measurement is less extensive than in the USA.

European measurement practices

There is no doubt that problems in measuring services output still exist, but today the data situation is much better than say two decades ago. In recent years, many statistical offices have made great strides in measuring the nominal value and prices of services output. However, progress has been uneven, both across industries and countries. For example, in most countries measurement problems are still most severe in finance and business services.[22] However, differences in progress across countries point to large potential gains from 'catching up' to best practice.

To provide an assessment of statistical practices in European countries, we have made use of a series of recent surveys of volume measurement practices by national statistical institutes (NSIs) in the European Union. These inventories were mandated by Eurostat. Using the Eurostat *Handbook on Price and Volume Measures in National Accounts* (Eurostat 2001), NSIs have graded their volume measurement techniques in each industry as an A-, B- or C-method. An A-method is considered to be most appropriate, a B-method is an acceptable alternative to an A-method, and a C-method is a method that is too biased

---

[22] See, for example, a study of measurement practices in the UK by Crespi *et al.* (2006).

to be acceptable, or one that is conceptually wrong. For example, for business and management consultancy services, an A-method would be the collection of actual or model contract prices, with such prices needing to account for changes in the characteristics of the contracts over time. A typical B-method could be the use of charge-out rates or hourly fees for business services or the price index of a closely related activity, such as accounting or legal services. A C-method would be any other deflation method, such as using the overall CPI or PPI (Eurostat 2001, pp. 107–8).

The inventories by the NSIs referred to above describe the state of measurement practices in each country around the year 2000. Most countries gave explicit grades for each industry and where possible, we cross-checked this grading with the description in the *Handbook*. Table 3.10 shows the share of output in each industry that is deflated using A-, B- and C-methods, averaged across those European countries for which these inventories were available.[23] The inventories reflected the situation around the year 2000 and it is not known to what extent subsequent revisions have changed the measurement practices both for current and historical series.

The top part of the table shows the average output share and the bottom part shows the range of shares across countries. The table shows that measurement practices in market services are far from perfect since A-methods, with the exception of hotels and restaurants, account for only a small share of output in most industries. It also shows that measurement is most problematic in finance and business services, where nearly half of the output is deflated with C-methods. As might be expected, there is also substantial variation in measurement across countries, but generally hotels and restaurants are the best measured (based on value data collected from surveys of businesses in the industry deflated by consumer price data on the hotel and restaurant expenditures) and finance and business services are the worst measured (see below). However, it is clear that the scope of measurement problems should not be overstated: only around 30 per cent of total market services output is deflated using inappropriate – and hence potentially misleading – methods while for the remainder at least acceptable measures are used.

---

[23] These are still fairly broad industries, hiding some of the heterogeneity within these industries. However, the main differences are across industries.

Table 3.10. *Share of value added in market services in European countries deflated using A-, B- or C-methods around the year 2000 (percentage)*

ISIC (rev. 3) code	Industry	A-method	B-method	C-method
Average				
50–2	Wholesale and retail trade	0	79	21
52	Retail trade	0	79	21
55	Hotels & restaurants	67	26	7
60–3	Transport & storage	9	67	24
64	Post & telecommunications	9	80	11
65–7	Financial intermediation	0	57	43
65	Banking	0	68	32
71–4	Business services	8	44	48
90–3	Social & personal services	15	44	42
	Market services	10	59	31
[Minimum–Maximum]				
50–2	Wholesale and retail trade	[0–1]	[0–100]	[0–100]
52	Retail trade	[0–1]	[0–100]	[0–100]
55	Hotels & restaurants	[18–87]	[0–82]	[0–70]
60–3	Transport & storage	[0–34]	[32–100]	[0–60]
64	Post & telecommunications	[0–73]	[27–100]	[0–70]
65–7	Financial intermediation	[0–0]	[0–94]	[6–100]
65	Banking	[0–0]	[0–100]	[0–100]
71–4	Business services	[0–37]	[5–96]	[0–95]
90–3	Social & personal services	[0–48]	[12–93]	[7–89]
	Market services	[3–15]	[12–83]	[5–86]

Notes: Classification into A-, B- and C-methods are by national statistical offices, based on Eurostat (2001). A-method is defined as most appropriate, B-method as acceptable and C-method as unacceptable. Average share is calculated based on information for Austria, Belgium, Denmark, Finland, France, Germany, Italy, the Netherlands, Sweden and the UK. For each country and each industry we use information on the share of value added deflated using A-, B- or C-methods, and for each industry (as well as the total average) these shares are averaged across countries.
Sources: Eurostat inventories on volume measurement practices of European national statistical institutes.

The bottom part of the table illustrates that differences across countries are very large. For example, there is one country that deflates almost three-quarters of output in post and telecommunications using an A-method while there is another country that deflates 70 per cent of output using a C-method. The country with the best measurement practices uses C-methods for only 5 per cent of market services output, while the country with the worst practices relies on C-methods for 86 per cent of all output. However, this latter country is only one of two outliers, which does suggest that convergence to best measurement practice within Europe would already allow for a more accurate assessment of productivity growth in market services. This would not so much require additional conceptual work, but more effective adoption of best practices among NSIs (see also Crespi *et al.* 2006). Moreover, researchers and other users would benefit substantially from more openness and transparency by NSIs about measurement practices. The unpublished, confidential and infrequent measurement inventories in Europe stand in sharp contrast to easily accessible publications as published in the *Survey of Current Business* of the US Bureau of Economic Analysis, which regularly reports on updates in the methodologies used in constructing the US National Income and Product Accounts.

After this general overview of A-, B- and C-methods, we look at two industries in some more detail, namely retail trade and banking. As Table 3.10 implies, measurement in retail trade is by and large acceptable, while in banking the problems are much more severe. This is also reflected in our own research, where we are able to make an international comparison of productivity growth in retail trade based on current and improved statistical methods, while in banking we are limited to comparing methods for the USA.

Retail trade

Productivity growth in the US retail trade industry since 1995 has been rapid, both compared to the earlier years (Triplett and Bosworth 2004) and compared to most European countries (van Ark *et al.* 2003). This has led to discussions about the underlying causes, but also raised the question whether or not this is merely a statistical artifact (European Commission 2004; Gordon 2007). The key problem is that in current National Accounts methodology, changes in prices of the most important input in retail trade, namely the purchases of goods for resale, are not accounted for. The failure to account for changes in prices of purchased goods has always been problematic, but is becoming more pressing for two reasons, namely changes in retailers' business models and rapid decline in sales prices of high-tech goods. First, changes in the business models of retailers are changing the demarcations among the activities of traders, manufacturers and customers. Triplett and Bosworth (2004) provide a simple example regarding the sale of bicycles, which in the past were delivered to the retailer fully assembled. Today they typically arrive in a box, and customers can choose between having the store arrange for assembly and doing it themselves. Failure to account for differences in prices of goods purchased by the retailer can lead to misstated growth rates if certain activities are shifted between stores and suppliers (Triplett and Bosworth 2004; Manser 2005).

The second reason is the rapid price declines of high-tech goods, such as computers. Paradoxically, improvements in the price measurement of sales can lead to deterioration in the measurement of trade productivity, when changes in purchase prices are not accounted for. This problem is akin to that of Triplett (1996) when he argued that more accurate price measures for the output of the computer manufacturing industry (computers) should be accompanied by better price measures for its inputs (e.g. semiconductors). Differences in measurement practices for the prices of high-tech goods across countries will also lead to artificial differences in measured productivity growth in retail trade. In particular, the more accurate adjustment for quality change for sales of high-tech goods in the USA, without similar adjustment for prices of purchases, is likely to lead to an overstatement of productivity growth in retail compared to Europe, where both sales and purchases prices are typically not adequately adjusted for quality change. Inklaar and Timmer (2008a) provide an attempt to measure this bias and their approach and results are summarised below.

In retail trade (and distributive trades more generally), different concepts of output are used. The broadest is sales of products. Gross margins, the output concept used in the National Accounts, are only a limited share of sales (around 25 per cent) and subtract the cost of goods sold. Value added is derived by subtracting the use of intermediate inputs such as packaging materials, energy and business services. Value added is only a limited share of gross margins (around 60 per cent). Measuring these output concepts in current prices is fairly straightforward, but the computation of output volumes poses greater problems. As long as prices for all output and all inputs are known, the choice of output measure is inconsequential. This can be illustrated using the example of double-deflated value added. Prices for value added are not observed directly, but statistical agencies use information on the gross output volumes and intermediate input volumes to implicitly estimate value added volumes. Similarly, given information on sales volumes and volumes of goods purchased for resale, double-deflated margins can be estimated:

$$\Delta \ln S = v_M \Delta \ln M + (1 - v_M) \Delta \ln C \qquad (3.29)$$

where S is the volume of sales, M the volume of margins, C the volume of goods purchased for resale and v_M the share of margins in sales. If all variables except M are known, M can be implicitly calculated. However, volumes of goods purchased for resale are not readily available so statistical agencies by and large use the volume of sales as a proxy for the volume of margins. In the Eurostat *Handbook* (Eurostat 2001), this is described as a B-method.

In Inklaar and Timmer (2008a), consumption expenditure data and matched consumer and producer prices are used to estimate the volume of goods purchased for resale, C, for France, Germany, the Netherlands, the UK and the USA. This would qualify as an A-method as it does not necessitate potentially implausible assumptions. While this is experimental, it does provide some indication of how much this could matter if implemented in official statistics. Table 3.11 shows average annual growth of real sales and double-deflated real margins. Real sales are currently used as a proxy for real margins, but this table illustrates that the differences between the two measures are substantial in most cases. It shows that moving from a B-method to an A-method can make quite a difference in the magnitude of output growth. The direction over time can also change: in Germany real sales growth slowed down after 1995 while real margins growth accelerated. However, the cross-country comparison is not strongly affected: countries with high output growth according to the sales proxy, like the UK and USA, also had comparatively high margins growth.

While the double deflation method is conceptually preferable, matching consumer and producer prices is difficult in practice and the degree of noise may be substantial. An alternative to this 'macro-level' matching of prices is to directly survey retailers on their purchase

Table 3.11. *Average annual growth of real retail sales and margins, 1987–2002*

	1987–95		1995–2002	
	Sales	Margins	Sales	Margins
France	2.4	0.1	2.6	−0.2
Germany	2.9	1.5	1.6	2.4
Netherlands	2.3	2.6	1.9	2.2
UK	3.0	6.3	5.2	6.5
USA	2.8	3.1	4.5	4.9

Note: Data for Germany refer to 1991–5 instead of 1987–95.
Source: Inklaar and Timmer (2008a), Table 5.

and sales prices. In the USA, this method is now applied in measuring a producer price for wholesale and retail trade (see, for example, Manser 2005).

Banking

The measurement of bank output is a particularly difficult area because much of this output is not explicitly priced.[24] Instead, borrowers pay a higher interest rate on their loans in return for screening and monitoring services while depositors receive a lower interest rate on their deposit accounts in return for transaction services and safekeeping. Eurostat (2001) acknowledges this problem and argues that there is no fully satisfactory method to distinguish price and volume movements of this implicitly priced output. As second-best alternatives, Eurostat (2001) outlines two methods currently in use. The most commonly used is the so-called 'deflated-balances' approach, where the trend in implicit bank output is given by the total amount of loans and deposits outstanding, deflated using a general price index such as the CPI. Given information on bank balance sheets, this method can be applied in a straightforward fashion. In the other method, which we call the 'activity-count' approach, the number of deposit transactions and loans are used as output indicators. Currently, the only country

---

[24] The discussion on banking is from Basu *et al.* (2009), Inklaar and Wang (2009) and Colangelo and Inklaar (2010).

to use the activity-count approach is the United States, with other countries relying on the deflated-balances approach.[25]

However, we would argue that the activity-count method has some preferable features compared to the deflated-balances method. Neither is perfect, but the assumption implicit in the deflated-balances approach is that every euro's (or dollar's) worth of loans corresponds to a constant amount of services over time. An example on residential mortgages can help demonstrate that this could well lead to a bias in output. If house prices in a country rise relative to the general price level, as occurred in numerous countries up to 2007, it seems likely that the average size of a mortgage will also increase. Indeed, in the USA, the average mortgage increased from $156,000 (at 2007 overall CPI prices) at the start of 2000 to $200,000 at the end of 2007, corresponding to a roughly constant loan-to-house-price ratio.[26] Under the deflated-balances approach, the services provided per mortgage would therefore have increased by almost 30 per cent over this period even though it seems unlikely that banks would have expended that much extra effort on screening and monitoring (prospective) borrowers.[27] The activity-count approach assumes constant services per loan over time, which seems to us a more plausible approximation.

To provide some indication of how much this may influence overall implicit bank output, we can make an actual comparison between the two methods for the USA only, based on Inklaar and Wang (2009). Their figures show that for the USA in particular after the late 1990s, when house prices started to increase rapidly, the two approaches displayed extensive divergence. According to the activity-count approach, implicit output in 2005 had increased by 14 per cent from 1997, while the deflated-balances approach showed an increase of 50 per cent.[28]

---

[25] One exception is the Netherlands, which uses the activity-count approach for deposits and the deflated-balances approach for loans. In addition, some countries may use even less suitable methods (C-methods in the Eurostat (2001) classification) such as deflating the net interest margin using a general price index. We do not discuss these methods here.

[26] These numbers refer to mortgages on all types of houses, financed using fixed-rate fifteen-year or thirty-year loans, from the Federal Housing Finance Agency.

[27] Arguably the subsequent financial crisis suggested that banks expended less, rather than more effort in this area.

[28] Note that this only refers to commercial banks and excludes fee-based output, which makes up about 40 per cent of total bank output in the latter part of the

Table 3.12. *Growth in implicit bank output volumes and in house prices relative to the overall price level, 2000–06*

	Implicit bank output	House prices
France	4.5	9.2
Germany	0.5	−1.7
Italy	3.9	3.5
Spain	10.7	6.7
UK	7.5	10.7
USA	5.4	7.1

Notes and sources: Annual average growth rates. Implicit bank output is calculated by deflating the change in total loans plus deposits by the CPI. For France, Germany, Italy and Spain, the loan and deposit data are from the ECB Statistical Data Warehouse; for the UK, from the Bank of England; US figures are from Inklaar and Wang (2009). House price data are from statistical agencies (France and Germany), Nationwide (UK), Case-Shiller (USA) and the BIS (Italy and Spain). The CPI is used as the overall price level for the house price numbers.

While we cannot show a similar figure for European countries we can provide some indication of how much it could matter. To this end, Table 3.12 shows output growth according to the deflated-balances method for a number of European countries and the USA for the period 2000–6. In addition, we show the average change in house prices relative to the overall price level. As this table makes clear, European countries, with the exception of Germany, had substantial growth according to the deflated-balances approach. Intriguingly, Germany was the only country where house prices declined relative to the overall price level over this period. In general the data are suggestive of a positive correlation between house prices and measured bank output. Of course, this is information for a few countries only, and mortgages are only a part of bank loans.[29] However, it does provide suggestive evidence that the deflated-balances approach overstates 'true' bank output growth when

period. However, this figure does serve to illustrate the contrast between the two approaches.

[29] In the USA, where real estate loans for both residential and commercial purposes are included, these loans make up about two-thirds of all loans. In

house prices increase rapidly. Conversely, as house prices decline, we would expect deflated-balances output growth to be too low.

This section illustrates that some work is still required to achieve theoretically and empirically robust measures of output in market service sectors. Nevertheless, we conclude that for many market service industries, output measures in the National Accounts should give a fairly accurate – albeit not perfect – internationally comparable picture of developments; see also Hartwig (2008). It is worth emphasising again that much progress could be achieved if all NSIs in the EU followed best practice.

3.8 Comparisons with alternative measures

Despite the publication of an OECD handbook on productivity measurement (Schreyer 2001), which is based on the growth accounting methodology, national statistical institutes (NSIs) have been slow in adopting this methodology and, to date, only few NSIs have published MFP-measures on a regular basis.[30] Because of the lack of the required statistics, various scholars have based their analyses on the OECD Structural Analysis Database (STAN) and its predecessor, the International Sectoral Database (ISDB). Interestingly, these databases were never designed for productivity analysis and as a result researchers have had to apply additional methods and make *ad hoc* adjustments, for example in the calculation of capital stocks or combining historical series.[31] Also, adjustments for changes in the composition of labour and capital could not be made on the basis of STAN and this was ignored, or additional data had to be found. This was done mostly for the purpose of one single study, which hindered validation and

---

the euro area, loans to households for house purchases make up about 40 per cent of all loans.

[30] These include Statistics Denmark, Statistics Netherlands, the Australian Bureau of Statistics, Statistics Canada and the US Bureau of Labor Statistics (BLS). Various other NSIs are currently experimenting with growth accounting statistics.

[31] Instead STAN was intended for tracking knowledge spillovers (in combination with other OECD databases such as ANBERD and the input-output database) and general structural analyses. It provides industry-level series on output, employment and aggregate investment for OECD member states. For a limited number of countries, capital stocks are given as well. It is mainly based on data published in the latest vintage of the National Accounts of each country.

replication of results by others. The EU KLEMS database was designed to fill this gap.

In Table 3.13 we indicate that using more data-intensive input measures, as in EU KLEMS, is not only conceptually appealing, but also leads to measures of MFP growth which can be radically different from cruder measures that have been used in other studies. The first column shows the EU KLEMS measure of MFP growth for the overall market economy for the 1995–2005 period for each country. In the next three columns we show the impact of the main refinements of the EU KLEMS database, namely accounting for changes in the average number of hours worked, changes in labour composition and changes in capital composition. The column labelled 'Crude MFP measure' shows what measured MFP growth would be without these refinements. The crude measure is calculated by subtracting the weighted growth in persons engaged and growth of the capital stock from growth in value added volumes. This is the measure most commonly used, for example, by Vandenbussche *et al.* (2006) and Färe *et al.* (2006). Changes in average hours and in labour composition are taken into account in a much smaller set of studies (such as Nicoletti and Scarpetta 2003; Griffith *et al.* 2004; Cameron *et al.* 2005), and changes in capital composition at the industry level are hardly ever accounted for.

The bottom row of the table shows that each of the three refinements made in the EU KLEMS database has a substantial effect on MFP growth. Crude MFP measures point to an average growth across countries of about 1.2 per cent per year, while the EU KLEMS results show growth of only 0.8 per cent. So what drives these adjustments? The mostly negative numbers in the 'average hours worked' column means that measured MFP growth is lower, and hence labour input growth is higher on a 'per person' than on a 'per hour' basis. In other words, most countries saw a decline in the average number of hours worked and MFP was on average underestimated by 0.2 per cent, as indicated in the last row. In contrast, the positive numbers for the labour and capital composition adjustments mean that crude MFP growth is overstated and labour and capital input growth are actually higher. In the case of labour composition, this means that there has been a shift of employment to workers with a higher wage, such as those with higher educational classifications, contributing about 0.2 percentage points. In the case of capital composition, it likewise means a shift towards capital with higher rental prices, such as ICT capital,

Table 3.13. *Alternative estimates of MFP growth in market economy, average 1995–2005*

| | EU KLEMS MFP measure | Contribution from changes in | | | Crude MFP measure | OECD STAN-based MFP measure | NSI MFP measure |
		Average hours worked	Labour composition	Capital composition			
Austria	1.14	0.00	0.20	0.19	1.52	n.a.	n.a.
Belgium	0.07	0.04	0.23	1.03	1.37	1.35	n.a.
Czech Republic	0.61	-0.13	0.19	0.60	1.27	2.09	n.a.
Denmark	0.01	0.19	0.23	0.36	0.80	1.58	0.22
Finland	2.49	-0.23	0.11	0.21	2.57	3.31	1.65
France	0.80	-0.51	0.37	0.29	0.95	1.31	n.a.
Germany	0.36	-0.51	0.05	0.41	0.31	0.98	0.37
Hungary	2.56	-0.20	0.43	0.22	3.01	n.a.	n.a.
Ireland	1.34	-0.32	0.24	0.81	2.07	n.a.	n.a.
Italy	-0.68	-0.21	0.19	0.35	-0.36	-0.26	-1.01
Netherlands	0.99	-0.26	0.43	0.21	1.37	1.64	1.27
Portugal	-0.41	-0.24	0.20	0.30	-0.16	n.a.	n.a.
Slovenia	1.44	-0.26	0.41	0.58	2.17	n.a.	n.a.
Spain	-0.82	-0.22	0.38	0.19	-0.47	-0.44	n.a.
Sweden	1.55	-0.19	0.30	0.48	2.14	n.a.	n.a.

UK	0.85	−0.29	0.45	0.33	1.35	n.a.	n.a.
USA	1.34	−0.11	0.31	0.33	1.87	n.a.	1.57
Average	0.80	−0.20	0.28	0.40	1.28		1.57

Notes and sources: The first five columns are based on data from the EU KLEMS database, March 2008. The contribution from changes in average hours worked is computed by multiplying the change in average hours worked by the share of labour compensation in value added. The contribution from changes in labour composition is computed analogously. The contribution from changes in capital composition is computed using the share of capital compensation in value added. The sum of EU KLEMS MFP growth (in the first column) and the three contributions gives the numbers shown in the column labelled 'Crude MFP measure'. The OECD STAN numbers in column 6 are computed using the 2008/9 edition of the database and refer to the non-agriculture business sector. MFP growth is calculated by subtracting the weighted growth in persons engaged and the weighted growth in the capital stock from the growth of value added in the non-agriculture, non-real-estate business sector. The share of labour compensation in value added in STAN is calculated by assuming that self-employed workers earn the same average wage as employees. The last column gives alternative estimates from national statistical institutes. Sources and coverage are as follows: Denmark from StatBank Denmark, non-farm business sector excluding real estate; Finland from Statistics Finland, total economy; Italy from Istat, total economy, excluding government; Netherlands from CBS Statline, commercial sector, 'neo-classical model' estimates; United States from BLS, private business sector. Germany is from Ifo Industry Productivity Database (Eicher and Strobel 2009).

contributing 0.4 percentage points. Although there are of course differences across countries, the sign and proximate size of the adjustments
is fairly comparable and crude measures always lead to overestimates,
except for Germany.

The final two columns of Table 3.13 provide a comparison of EU
KLEMS MFP growth estimates with estimates from other sources. The
most readily available alternative cross-country database on industry output and productivity is the OECD STAN database. The MFP
growth that can be calculated from this database is conceptually comparable to crude MFP as it is based on persons employed and capital
stock. Although for a number of countries, estimates of hours worked
are also given in the database, this is not the case for most. A more
serious problem in estimating MFP growth is that capital stocks are
often not available, so comparisons could only be made for nine countries. It should also be noted that STAN does not distinguish the market economy as a separate aggregate, but does provide data for the
non-agriculture, non-real-estate business sector, which is used here.[32]
Overall, the cross-country pattern is reasonably comparable in that
countries with high growth rates based on STAN data also show high
growth rates in EU KLEMS. But there are many differences as well. In
general, one can say that the differences in labour productivity growth
rates between STAN and EU KLEMS are relatively minor, underlying the complementary nature of the two databases for basic data.
Differences in output and employment growth are generally small,
although differences are possible because of differences in the vintage
of the National Accounts series used, and in the use of different index-
number formulas for industry aggregation. We use the theoretically
based Törnqvist indices, whereas in most National Accounts and in
STAN, chained Laspeyres-type indices are used. These differ only in
cases of very high or low growth rates. The greatest difference can
be found in capital stock estimates. STAN provides aggregate stock
estimates for those countries which publish these in their National
Accounts. The internationally harmonised approach to capital measurement in EU KLEMS often differs from the practice used in the
National Accounts of a particular country. The adjustments for capital

---

[32] The main difference of this aggregate from the market economy aggregate is
    that the market economy includes agriculture, forestry and fishing (division A
    and B) as well as other community, social and personal services (division O).

and labour composition in EU KLEMS provide additional information not available in STAN.

The last column shows MFP growth estimates by national statistical agencies. Of the seventeen countries covered here, five have national statistical agencies that produce official MFP growth estimates. As the notes to the table make clear in more detail, the industry aggregates to which these data refer vary, both from our market economy concept and from each other. So, for example, in the case of Italy, the number refers to the total economy, excluding government, while for the USA, the number is for the private business sector. In concept, the MFP measures from the NSIs are usually closer to the EU KLEMS concept as they correct for hours worked and often also include labour and capital composition, but not always. So, for example, the number for the Netherlands does not include the contribution from changes in labour composition, explaining most of the 0.3 percentage point difference between the EU KLEMS and the 'official' numbers. Also, NSIs often have alternative methods for calculating capital stocks, for example concerning depreciation patterns. Given these conceptual differences, the numbers are rather close and suggest little difference between growth accounts from NSIs and from the EU KLEMS database.

Publicly available growth accounting decompositions at the industry level developed by the academic community are also sparse. Recently, Eicher and Strobel (2009) released the Ifo Productivity Database that provides productivity estimates for German industries using a growth accounting methodology that is close in spirit to EU KLEMS. As shown in Table 3.13, their estimate of market economy MFP is almost identical to the EU KLEMS estimate. For the USA, the dataset provided by Jorgenson *et al.* (2005) is available for researchers and is also included in the EU KLEMS database after matching the US industry classification with the NACE classification used in EU KLEMS.[33] One difference is that the capital concept of Jorgenson *et al.* (2005) is broader than in most other studies because of the fact that it includes inventories, land and consumer durables. These assets are not included in the US data provided in EU KLEMS.

---

[33] This database is mainly based on SIC data and called usa-sic. EU KLEMS also provides a usa-naics database; see the appendix to this chapter for a discussion of the differences.

3.9 Concluding remarks

This chapter reviewed both the growth accounting methodology and the measurement methods employed in constructing the EU KLEMS database. It is designed as a reference guide for understanding the underpinnings of the analysis in the remainder of the book. It also serves as a useful guide to users of the EU KLEMS data – the latter should also consult the appendix to this chapter for specific guidance on use and coverage of the database. Our discussion illustrates the complexities involved in a measurement exercise of this type and in turn illustrates the richness of the data. In particular, this database is unique in its detail on labour and capital composition. It emphasises the need to break these inputs down into their components in order to fully comprehend sources of growth in international perspective. Although the primary aim of the EU KLEMS database is to generate comparative productivity trends, the data collected are also useful in a large number of other contexts, as the EU KLEMS database provides many basic input data series. These input series are derived independently from the assumptions underlying the growth accounting method. They can for example be used in studies of innovation, services outsourcing, skill formation and skill premia and investment in ICT assets.[34]

This chapter identified a number of outstanding measurement issues by reviewing both current practice and discussing potential alternatives. Some of these issues are unavoidable since the database relies heavily on National Accounts data and so need to await further developments in NSIs. In this respect, by collating various data sources within and across countries, the EU KLEMS database is useful in indicating priority areas for further improvement in basic series, including volume measures of services output, capital formation matrices and, more generally, consistency between output, labour and capital inputs at the industry level. Other caveats suggest prudence by the users, depending on the context in which the data are employed. As with all data analysis, a judicious use of econometric methods and sensible approaches to the use of the numbers should enable the database to be useful in a wide range of applications.

---

[34] See e.g. Kratena (2007), Jalava and Pohjola (2008) and Akkermans *et al.* (2009).

Appendix. The EU KLEMS database: contents of the March 2008 version

In this appendix we describe the main features of the EU KLEMS database and provide some health warnings for prudent use. Although the primary aim of the EU KLEMS database is to generate comparative productivity trends, it also provides many basic input data series. These input series are derived independently from the assumptions underlying the growth accounting method and might be useful also in other contexts. They can, for example, be used in studies of energy efficiency, services outsourcing, skill formation and skill premia and investment in ICT assets.

The EU KLEMS database is a public resource available through the Internet at www.euklems.net. Each year a new version is provided that contains updates, revisions and extensions of the previous versions. The first public release of the database was in March 2007. Most results in this book are based on the second public release in March 2008, and this section provides a brief overview of the contents of this version of the database. For up-to-date information on the latest version, the reader is referred to the EU KLEMS website. The March 2008 version covers twenty-five European Union countries, as well as Australia, Japan,[35] South Korea and the United States. In general, data for 1970–2005 are available for the 'old' EU-15 countries, while series from 1995 onwards are available for the states which joined the EU on 1 May 2004.

For the USA, two datasets are included in the database: the US SIC and the US NAICS series. This reflects the availability of various alternative data sources for output, labour and capital input, mainly from the Bureau of Economic Analysis (BEA) and Bureau of Labor Statistics (BLS). Until recently, these datasets showed important differences in some industries, even for relatively simple measures such as gross output and value added at current prices. Triplett and Bosworth (2004) and Jorgenson *et al.* (2005) provide a discussion of these differences and their possible origins, but they conclude that many questions still remain. In addition, the US statistical system switched from the SIC to the NAICS industrial classification at the end of the 1990s, which introduced breaks in the historical time-series. In EU KLEMS, the US

---

[35] See Fukao *et al.* (2007) for more information on the Japanese data.

NAICS series are benchmarked on the most recent NAICS-based industry accounts from the BEA National Income and Production Accounts
(NIPA) for output, labour input and investment flows. Missing historical detail was filled by linking with older SIC-based series. The US SIC
database is derived from the data described in Jorgenson *et al.* (2005)
that start from the SIC series, mainly from the BLS, and are extrapolated with NAICS-based series. In the near future, it is expected that
BEA and BLS series will be increasingly integrated because of closer
co-operation; and with the increasing availability of NAICS-based historical series, the difference will eventually become minimal.

Data are also provided for four country groupings: EU-25, EU-15,
EU-10 and Euro. EU-25 includes all member states of the European
Union (EU) as of 1 May 2004, EU-15 includes all member states of the
EU as of 1 January 1995, EU-10 includes all states which joined the EU
on 1 May 2004 and Euro includes all countries in the euro-zone as of
1 January 2001. The database also provides an aggregation for those
countries for which there is long-run capital and labour composition
data. The group of countries within the EU-IS and Euro groups for
which this is possible are called EU-15ex and Euroex respectively. To
aggregate across countries use is made of purchasing power parities
(PPPs) that reflect differences in output price levels across countries at
a detailed industry level. This price adjustment is often done by means
of GDP PPPs that reflect the average expenditure prices in one country
relative to another and are widely available through the work of the
OECD and Eurostat. However, it is well recognised that the use of
GDP PPPs, which reflect expenditure prices of *all* goods and services
in the economy, can be misleading when used to convert industry-level
output (see the discussion in Chapter 6). In the March 2008 version
of the EU KLEMS database, use is made of PPPs that reflect relative
output prices at a detailed industry level for 1997.

Table 3A.1 provides an overview of all the series included in the
EU KLEMS database. The variables covered can be split into three
main groups: (1) labour productivity variables; (2) growth accounting
variables; and (3) additional labour and capital variables. The labour
productivity series contain all the data needed to construct labour
productivity (output per hour worked) and unit labour costs. These
series include nominal, volume and price series of output and employment. Most series are part of the present European System of Accounts
(ESA 1995) and can be found in the National Accounts of individual

Table 3A.1. *Variables in EU KLEMS database*

(1)   Labour productivity variables

Values

GO	Gross output at current basic prices (in millions of local currency)
II	Intermediate inputs at current purchasers' prices (in millions of local currency)
VA	Gross value added at current basic prices (in millions of local currency)
COMP	Compensation of employees (in millions of local currency)
GOS	Gross operating surplus (in millions of local currency)
TXSP	Taxes minus subsidies on production (in millions of local currency)
EMP	Number of persons engaged (thousands)
EMPE	Number of employees (thousands)
H_EMP	Total hours worked by persons engaged (millions)
H_EMPE	Total hours worked by employees (millions)

Prices

GO_P	Gross output, price indices, 1995 = 100
II_P	Intermediate inputs, price indices, 1995 = 100
VA_P	Gross value added, price indices, 1995 = 100

Volumes

GO_QI	Gross output, volume indices, 1995 = 100
II_QI	Intermediate inputs, volume indices, 1995 = 100
VA_QI	Gross value added, volume indices, 1995 = 100
LP_I	Gross value added per hour worked, volume indices, 1995 = 100

(2)   Growth accounting variables

LAB	Labour compensation (in millions of local currency)
CAP	Capital compensation (in millions of local currency)
LAB_QI	Labour services, volume indices, 1995 = 100
CAP_QI	Capital services, volume indices, 1995 = 100
IIE	Intermediate energy inputs at current purchasers' prices (in millions of local currency)
IIM	Intermediate material inputs at current purchasers' prices (in millions of local currency)
IIS	Intermediate service inputs at current purchasers' prices (in millions of local currency)

(cont.)

Table 3A.1. *(cont.)*

IIE_QI	Intermediate energy inputs, volume indices, 1995 = 100
IIM_QI	Intermediate material inputs, volume indices, 1995 = 100
IIS_QI	Intermediate service inputs, volume indices, 1995 = 100
VA_Q	Growth rate of value added volume (per cent per year)
VAConH	Contribution of hours worked to value added growth (percentage points)
VAConLC	Contribution of labour composition change to value added growth (percentage points)
VAConKIT	Contribution of ICT capital services to output growth (percentage points)
VAConKNIT	Contribution of non-ICT capital services to output growth (percentage points)
VAConTFP	Contribution of TFP to value added growth (percentage points)
TFPva_I	TFP (value-added based) growth, 1995 = 100
GO_Q	Growth rate of gross output volume (per cent per year)
GOConII	Contribution of intermediate inputs to output growth (percentage points)
GOConIIE	Contribution of intermediate energy inputs to output growth (percentage points)
GOConIIM	Contribution of intermediate material inputs to output growth (percentage points)
GOConIIS	Contribution of intermediate services inputs to output growth (percentage points)
GOConH	Contribution of hours worked to output growth (percentage points)
GOConLC	Contribution of labour composition change to output growth (percentage points)
GOConKIT	Contribution of ICT capital services to output growth (percentage points)
GOConKNIT	Contribution of non-ICT capital services to output growth (percentage points)
GOConTFP	Contribution of TFP to output growth (percentage points)
TFPgo_I	TFP (gross-output based) growth, 1995 = 100

(3)   Additional labour and capital variables

CAPIT	ICT capital compensation (share in total capital compensation)
CAPNIT	Non-ICT capital compensation (share in total capital compensation)

Table 3A.1. *(cont.)*

CAPIT_QI	ICT capital services, volume indices, 1995 = 100
CAPNIT_QI	Non-ICT capital services, volume indices, 1995 = 100
CAPIT_QPH	ICT capital services per hour worked, 1995 reference
CAPNIT_QPH	Non-ICT capital services per hour worked, 1995 reference
LABHS	High-skilled labour compensation (share in total labour compensation)
LABMS	Medium-skilled labour compensation (share in total labour compensation)
LABLS	Low-skilled labour compensation (share in total labour compensation)
LAB_QPH	Labour services per hour worked, 1995 reference
H_HS	Hours worked by high-skilled persons engaged (share in total hours)
H_MS	Hours worked by medium-skilled persons engaged (share in total hours)
H_LS	Hours worked by low-skilled persons engaged (share in total hours)
H_M	Hours worked by male persons engaged (share in total hours)
H_F	Hours worked by female persons engaged (share in total hours)
H_29	Hours worked by persons engaged aged 15–29 (share in total hours)
H_49	Hours worked by persons engaged aged 30–49 (share in total hours)
H_50+	Hours worked by persons engaged aged 50 and over (share in total hours)

countries, at least for the most recent period. The main adjustments to these series were to fill gaps in industry detail and to link series over time, in particular in those cases where revisions were not taken back to 1970 by the NSIs. The variables in the growth accounting series are of an analytical nature and cannot be directly derived from published National Accounts data without additional assumptions. These include series of capital services, of labour services and of multi-factor productivity. The construction of these series was based on the theoretical model of production, requiring additional assumptions as spelled out in section 3.2. Finally, additional series are given which have been used in generating the growth accounts and are informative by themselves. These include, for example, various measures of the relative importance of ICT capital and non-ICT capital, and of the skilled labour within the EU KLEMS classification. The basic labour and capital input series with detailed data by labour and capital type are also publicly available at the EU KLEMS website, except for some countries for which confidentiality had to be maintained. Growth accounts and detailed labour and capital data are included for fourteen 'old' European Union countries (excluding Greece) and for the Czech Republic, Hungary and Slovenia of the new member states; Australia; Japan; South Korea and the United States. For all other countries only labour productivity and its underlying data series are included. Table 3A.2 provides more details on the period coverage for each variable and country.

At the lowest level of aggregation, data were collected for seventy-one industries. The industries are classified according to the European NACE revision 1 classification. But the level of detail varies across countries, industries and variables on account of data limitations. In order to ensure a minimal level of industry detail for which comparisons can be made across all countries, so-called minimum lists of industries have been used. All national datasets have been constructed in such a way that these minimum lists are met, but often more detailed data are available. For output and employment, the minimum number covered is sixty-two industries for the period from 1995, and forty-eight industries pre-1995. Growth accounts are available for thirty-one industries. These are listed in Table 3A.3. The EU KLEMS database provides data at a detailed industry level, but also provides higher-level aggregates, such as the total economy, the market economy, total market services and total goods production for all variables. Industry aggregations over nominal values and hours worked are made simply by summing. All aggregations of output and input volumes across industries use the Törnqvist quantity index. This is akin to the 'direct aggregation across industries' approach as developed by Jorgenson, Gollop and Fraumeni (1987, chap. 2). This approach is based on the assumption that value-added functions exist for each industry, but does not impose cross-industry restrictions on either value-added or inputs. This approach allows us to explicitly trace the source of aggregate growth to the underlying industry sources

Table 3A.2. *Country, period and variable coverage in EU KLEMS database, March 2008*

Country and regions	Abbreviation	Labour productivity variables	Growth accounting variables			
			MFP	Labour composition	Capital composition	Intermediate input composition
Australia	aus	1970	1982	1982	1970	-
Austria	aut	1970	1980	1980	1976	1970
Belgium	bel	1970	1980	1980	1970	1980
Cyprus	cyp	1995	-	-	-	-
Czech Republic	cze	1995	1995	1995	1995	1995
Denmark	dnk	1970	1980	1980	1970	1970
Estonia	est	1995	-	-	-	-
Finland	fin	1970	1970	1970	1970	1970
France	fra	1970	1980	1980	1970	1978
Germany	ger	1970	1970	1970	1970	1978
Greece	grc	1970	-	1992	-	1995
Hungary	hun	1992	1995	1995	1995	1995
Ireland	irl	1970	1995	1988	1970	1995
Italy	ita	1970	1970	1970	1970	1970
Japan	jpn	1973	1973	1973	1970	1973
Latvia	lva	1995	-	-	-	-
Lithuania	ltu	1995	-	-	-	-
Luxembourg	lux	1970	1992	1992	1970	1995
Malta	mlt	1995	-	-	-	-
Netherlands	nld	1970	1979	1979	1970	1987

(cont.)

Table 3A.2. (cont.)

Country and regions	Abbreviation	Labour productivity variables	Growth accounting variables			
			MFP	Labour composition	Capital composition	Intermediate input composition
Poland	pol	1995	–	1995	–	1995
Portugal	prt	1970	1995	1992	1970	1977
Slovak Republic	svk	1995	–	1995	–	1995
Slovenia	svn	1995	1995	1995	1995	1995
South Korea	kor	1970	1977	1970	1977	1970
Spain	esp	1970	1980	1980	1970	1980
Sweden	swe	1970	1993	1981	1993	1993
United Kingdom	uk	1970	1970	1970	1970	1970
United States (NAICS-based)	usa-naics	1977	1977	–	1970	–
United States (SIC-based)	usa-sic	1970	1970	1970	1970	1970
West Germany	dew	1970	1970	1970	1970	1978
EU-25	EU-25	1995	–	–	–	–
EU-15	EU-15	1970	–	–	–	–
EU-10	EU-10	1995	–	–	–	–
EU-15ex	EU-15ex	1970	1980	1980	1980	1980
Euro-zone	Euro	1970	–	–	–	–
Euro-zone ex	Euro-ex	1970	1980	1980	1980	1980

Notes: This table indicates for each country and variable the first year for which data is available in the EU KLEMS database, March 2008. '–' indicates not available. See Table 3A.1 for sets of labour productivity and growth accounting variables.

Table 3A.3. *Industry list for growth accounting variables*

Description	EU KLEMS code
TOTAL INDUSTRIES	TOT
Market economy	Markt
Electrical machinery, post and communication services	Elecom
Electrical and optical equipment	30–33
Post and telecommunications	64
Goods producing, excluding electrical machinery	Goods
Total manufacturing, excluding electrical	MexElec
Consumer manufacturing	Mcons
Food products, beverages and tobacco	*15–16*
Textiles, textile products, leather and footwear	*17–19*
Manufacturing n.e.c.; recycling	*36–37*
Intermediate manufacturing	Minter
Wood and products of wood and cork	*20*
Pulp, paper, paper products, printing and publishing	*21–22*
Coke, refined petroleum products and nuclear fuel	*23*
Chemicals and chemical products	*24*
Rubber and plastics products	*25*
Other non-metallic mineral products	*26*
Basic metals and fabricated metal products	*27–28*
Investment goods, excluding high-tech	Minves
Machinery, n.e.c.	*29*
Transport equipment	*34–35*
Other goods production	OtherG
Mining and quarrying	C
Electricity, gas and water supply	E
Construction	F
Agriculture, hunting, forestry and fishing	A–B
Market services, excluding post and telecommunications	Mserv
Distribution	Distr
Trade	50–52
Sale and repair of motor vehicles and motorcycles; retail sale of fuel	*50*
Wholesale trade and commission trade, except of vehicles	*51*
Retail trade, except of vehicles; repair of household goods	*52*

(*cont.*)

Table 3A.3. *(cont.)*

Description	EU KLEMS code
Transport and storage	60–63
Finance and business, except real estate	**Finbu**
Financial intermediation	J
Renting of m&eq and other business activities	71–74
Personal services	**Pers**
Hotels and restaurants	H
Other community, social and personal services	O
Private households with employed persons	P
Non-market services	**Nonmar**
Public admin., education and health	L–N
Public admin. and defence; compulsory social security	L
Education	M
Health and social work	N
Real estate activities	70

Notes: EU KLEMS code based on NACE rev. 1 industrial classification.

and is used in Chapter 4 to trace the industry origins of aggregate growth.[36]

Some general remarks on usage of EU KLEMS data are warranted. The data are suitable for both growth accounting and econometric exercises but the issues touched on in chapters 3 and 6 caution that the user should be aware of their limitations. As with all data series there are some unresolved measurement issues. As a general rule the reliability of the data is likely to be lower the finer the industry detail, i.e. the more we move from the industry level identified in the published National Accounts, and is often lower for services industries than for manufacturing. This is because to break down the National Accounts series, we often had to rely on additional data sources, which are more abundant and complete for manufacturing than for services. To this could be added that the further back in time the series, the greater the likelihood of error. Thus whereas growth accounting exercises

---

[36] See Jorgenson *et al.* (2005, chap. 8) for an elaborate discussion.

that quantify the contribution of ICT to output growth in transport equipment manufacturing over the period 1995 to 2005 might be reasonable, a precise number for the change of energy input use in business services between 1970 and 1971 might not be. These issues may be less important in econometric analysis with judicious use of methods.

Below we discuss some other practical measurement issues on a variable-by-variable basis. At the same time, it must be stressed that the limitations of the EU KLEMS series vary widely by country, period and variable and prudent users of the data should familiarise themselves with the methods of construction as discussed on a country-by-country basis in Timmer, van Moergastel, Stuivenwold *et al.* (2007). As discussed in Chapter 3, there remain issues in measuring market services output, in particular in finance and business services, and these problems are very severe for non-market services. Therefore the user should be wary of drawing strong conclusions. The data cannot be used as evidence that, say, health services in one country are more efficient or better than in another country in some overall sense. In addition, since the output of the real estate sector (NACE 70) includes imputed rent on owner-occupied dwellings, productivity measures for this industry need to be interpreted with care. Given the measurement problems in regard to non-market sector and real estate, users might want to restrict attention to the market economy numbers in EU KLEMS, which exclude public administration, education, health and social services and real estate. However, the choice of which data to use will depend on the research questions being asked. For example, EU KLEMS data may well be useful in considering the use of ICT or skilled labour in the health sector across countries.

For an analysis of the use of intermediate inputs in production it is important to note that estimates prior to 1995 in EU KLEMS are sometimes based on historical input-output tables which were not integrated with the National Accounts and which were only available for benchmark years, necessitating interpolation and on occasion the assumption that EMS shares are constant over time or across a sub-set of industries.

With respect to the labour input data, it is important to note that the level of independent industry detail is much lower for labour composition than for other variables, as dictated by the survey samples. In many cases the detail is restricted to fifteen industries, largely one-digit sectors but with manufacturing divided into three groups. The fifteen groups are the following (NACE 1 codes): A–B; C & E; 15–19 and 36–37; 20–28; 29–35; F; 50–55; 60–63; 64; J; 70–74; L; M; N; and finally O & P. As growth accounts are provided at a more detailed industry level, there is an implicit assumption that hours and wage shares in sub-industries are equal to those for aggregate industries. Researchers estimating labour demand equations should be aware that an attempt to do so at too fine an industry level would just reproduce this assumption. In addition, it should be noted that much of the information on self-employed workers is not based on survey data but imputed from employees, as the self-employed are often not (sufficiently) covered in labour force surveys. Similarly, for most countries, labour-type characteristics are only available for the number of employees, rather than hours worked, with the implicit assumption that hours do not vary by characteristic. While employment and earnings are consistently measured so that growth accounting and wage share equations are not affected, this would affect, say, an analysis of female participation rates, as women typically work (much) less hours than men. In addition, labour composition measures tend to be somewhat volatile over time since the underlying surveys are not designed to generate time-series. For some uses, period averages might be preferred to a focus on year-on-year changes. Table 3A.4 provides for each country, the definition of high-, medium- and low-skilled workers. Table 3A.5 outlines for each country the sources used for the data on wages and employment by type.

Industry-level estimates of capital input require detailed asset-by-industry investment matrices. Within EU KLEMS, various assumptions have been used to generate the capital-flow matrix, in particular for the breakdown of computing equipment (IT) and communications equipment (CT) by industry. In most cases, European Union countries provide estimates of software by industry for recent years, although the extent of backdating and industry coverage varies. In some cases it was necessary to use assumptions about the hardware–software ratios from other countries, so that IT and CT could be distributed across industries. Hence there is greater likelihood of error and non-comparability in these series than for other assets, especially in earlier periods. Table 3A.6 provides additional detail on a country-by-country basis.

Table 3A.4. *Definitions of high-, medium- and low-skilled*

	Definition of high-skilled	Definition of medium-skilled	Definition of low-skilled
Austria	College/university degree, technical/poly-technical degree, postgraduate courses.	Vocational middle schools, completed upper level of Gymnasium, vocational higher schools.	Primary education.
Belgium	University and non-university double-cycle tertiary education.	Higher/upper secondary education and non-university single-cycle tertiary education.	All people up to lower secondary education.
Czech Republic	University.	Higher post-secondary; secondary with GCE; apprenticeship and persons with unknown education.	Lower secondary and primary education.
Denmark	Long-cycle higher education.	Medium- and short-cycle higher education plus vocational education and training.	Basic school.
Finland	Tertiary schooling (or parts thereof).	Upper secondary level with or without matriculation.	Lower secondary or unknown.
France	University graduates.	Higher education below degree; low intermediate, vocational education.	No formal qualifications.
Germany	University graduates.	Intermediate.	No formal qualifications.
Hungary	Tertiary education (ISCED groups 5–6).	At most, upper secondary education (ISCED groups 3–4, excl. 3c programmes shorter than three years).	At most, lower secondary education (ISCED groups 0–2 & 3c programmes shorter than three years).

(cont.)

Table 3A.4. (*cont.*)

	Definition of high-skilled	Definition of medium-skilled	Definition of low-skilled
Italy	University graduates.	Higher education below degree; intermediate vocational plus advanced education; low intermediate.	No formal qualifications.
Japan	University graduates.	Junior college and upper secondary.	Lower secondary.
Netherlands	University degree and higher vocational.	Intermediate vocational plus advanced education and low intermediate.	No formal qualifications (Basis onderwijs).
Poland	Doctor and master's degree, bachelor's degree or any other degree of equal status.	Post-secondary, vocational secondary and basic secondary levels.	At most, lower secondary education (ISCED groups 0–2 & 3c programmes shorter than three years).
Slovak Republic	PhD, master's and bachelor's degree.	Higher professional education, secondary general, vocational and specialised education with and without matura, persons without information on educational attainment level.	Basic education.
Slovenia	University & non-university colleges.	Vocational secondary school degrees 2–5, vocational school for highly skilled workers and other secondary schools.	Vocational secondary school degree 1, primary school and no schooling.
Spain	University graduates.	Upper secondary schooling.	Lower secondary schooling and below.

Sweden	Postgraduates and undergraduates.	Higher and intermediate vocational.	Intermediate education and no formal qualifications.
United Kingdom	University degree.	HND, HNC, BTEC, teaching or nursing qualification, A level or equivalent, trade apprenticeship, O level or equivalent, BTEC, BEC, TEC General, City & Guilds.	No qualifications.
United States	College graduate and above.	High school and some years of college (but not completed).	Less then high school and some years of high school (but not completed).
West Germany	16–17 years of education.	Vocational degree.	Without degree.

Table 3A.5. *Sources used for employment and wages by type*

	Source used for division of employment by type	Source used for division of labour compensation by type
Austria	Microcensus data for the period 1980–2003 and individual Census of Population data for the years 1991 and 2001.	Microcensus data for 1997. Time-series are drawn from the wage and salary statistics.
Belgium	Unpublished social security data for the period 1997–2004; published Ministry of Labour data and LFS data used before 1997.	Unpublished social security data for split by gender and age class. Micro-data from Structure of Earnings Survey and LFS for distribution by skill level.
Czech Republic	Eurostat Labour Force Survey data, 2nd quarter of each year.	Structural Earnings Survey.
Denmark	Administrative data for the period 1980–2003.	Administrative data for the period 1980–2003.
Finland	Data from Statistics Finland's longitudinal census.	Data from Statistics Finland's longitudinal census.
France	Labour force surveys: 1982–9, 1990–2002, 2003, 2004.	Labour force surveys: 1982–9, 1990–2002, 2003, 2004.
Germany	Income survey, social security data and the Socio-Economic Panel Study, supplemented with micro-data.	Income survey, social security data and the Socio-Economic Panel Study, supplemented with micro-data.
Hungary	Eurostat Labour Force Survey data, 2nd quarter of each year.	Structural Earnings Survey.
Italy	Census of Population of 1971, 1981, 1991 and 2001.	Micro-data of the Bank of Italy surveys on household income, 1977–2004.
Japan	Monthly Labour Survey, supplemented with General Survey on Working Conditions, Basic Survey on Wage Structure and Employment Status Survey.	Monthly Labour Survey, supplemented with General Survey on Working Conditions, Basic Survey on Wage Structure and Employment Status Survey.

Table 3A.5. *(cont.)*

	Source used for division of employment by type	Source used for division of labour compensation by type
Netherlands	System of Labour Accounts, Labour Force Sample Survey (LFSS) and Labour Force Survey (LFS).	Micro-data for the years 1979, 1985, 1989, 1996, 1997 and 2002 from Wage Structure Inquiry; for 1992–2002 from the Inquiry of Work Conditions of the Ministry of Social Affairs and Employment.
Poland	Eurostat Labour Force Survey data, 2nd quarter of each year.	Structural Earnings Survey.
Slovak Republic	Eurostat Labour Force Survey data, 2nd quarter of each year.	Structural Earnings Survey.
Slovenia	Eurostat Labour Force Survey data, 2nd quarter of each year.	Structural Earnings Survey.
Spain	Labour Force Survey.	Wage Structure Survey.
Sweden	Statistics Sweden, employment at A60 level with breakdowns for age, gender and skill levels for the period 1993–2004.	Statistics Sweden, income levels for employment breakdowns.
United Kingdom	Labour Force Survey 1979–2004 and General Household Survey 1974–80.	Labour Force Survey 1993–2004 and General Household Survey 1972–1993/4.
United States	Census of Population; the Current Population Survey.	Census of Population; the Current Population Survey.
West Germany	Social security data and the German socio-economic panel, supplemented with information on employment by gender and occupation from the *Statistiches Jahrbuch*. Combined data with ILO occupation data.	Social security data and the German socio-economic panel, supplemented with information on employment by gender and occupation from the *Statistiches Jahrbuch*. Combined data with ILO occupation data.

Table 3A.6. *Sources used for capital stock estimation*

	Benchmark stock year	IT and CT investment	ICT deflator	Remarks
Austria	1976 net stock.	Before 1994 using US BEA asset proportions.	Harmonised BEA for IT/CT.	
Belgium	GFCF back to 1853.	Before 1995, asset shares constant.	Harmonised BEA for IT/CT.	Software before 1994 based on 1995 industry shares.
Czech Republic	1995 net stock.	Estimated on rough GFCF.	Harmonised BEA for IT.	
Denmark	1970 net stock.	Available from National Accounts.	Harmonised BEA for IT.	
Finland	1970 stock broken down using GFCF.	Using US BEA asset proportions.	Harmonised BEA for IT/CT.	
France	GFCF back to 1846.	Available from National Accounts.	National.	
Germany	1991 net stock.	IT/CT based on survey.	National.	
Hungary	2000 net stock.	Based on National Accounts stock estimates.	Harmonised BEA for IT.	CT ratio based on other countries.
Italy	1952 stock.	Available from National Accounts.	Harmonised BEA for IT.	Industries 50–2/K/60–4 estimated by higher aggregates.
Japan	1955 wealth stock.	Available from IO-tables, intrapolated in between.	National.	
Netherlands	1952 net stock.	CT estimated.	National.	

Slovenia	1999 gross stock.	Available from National Accounts.	National.	Before 1999, industry investment shares used.
Spain	1964 stock.	CT and software estimated by commodity flow.	Harmonised BEA for IT/CT.	Industries 50–2/K/60–4 estimated by higher aggregates.
Sweden	1993 net stock.	Available from National Accounts.	National.	
United Kingdom	1948 stock.	IT/CT based on survey.	National.	Industries 50–2/K/60–4 estimated by higher aggregates in earlier years.
United States NAICS	GFCF start in 1901.	Available from National Accounts.	National.	
United States SIC	GFCF start in 1901.	Available from National Accounts.	National.	After 2000, growth rates based on NAICS.
West Germany	1970 net stock.	Estimated based on survey.	National.	

Source: Based on situation in March 2007 release. See document 'Sources of the March 2007 Release' on www.euklems.net for detailed descriptions of methodologies used (Timmer, van Moergastel, Stuivenwold *et al.* (2007).

Table 3A.7. *Total economy shares and industry characteristics, twenty-six industries, EU, 1980 and 2005*

Industry	EU KLEMS code	Shares in total economy (per cent)				Shares in industry value added (per cent)		
		Value added		Hours worked		Labour compensation 2005	High-skilled compensation 2005	ICT-capital compensation 2005
		1980	2005	1980	2005			
Agriculture	AtB	3.6	1.3	9.9	4.1	82.8	5.7	0.1
Mining	C	1.8	0.6	0.9	0.2	25.7	4.8	1.4
Food and beverages	15t16	2.2	1.8	2.9	2.2	68.2	6.7	2.6
Textiles and footwear	17t19	2.4	0.8	3.4	1.1	79.8	5.6	2.1
Wood products	20	0.5	0.3	0.8	0.5	77.7	10.9	1.8
Paper, print and publ.	21t22	1.6	1.4	1.9	1.3	67.7	11.5	4.6
Petroleum ref.	23	0.5	0.3	0.2	0.1	39.5	7.5	5.5
Chemicals	24	2.1	1.8	1.5	0.9	56.6	10.0	3.6
Rubber and plastics	25	1.0	0.9	0.9	0.8	71.1	10.6	2.6
Non-metallic mineral	26	1.3	0.7	1.3	0.7	68.1	9.9	2.2
Metal	27t28	3.8	2.7	3.8	2.5	72.9	9.7	1.8
Other machinery	29	2.7	2.2	2.9	1.8	75.2	10.3	3.1
Electrical equipment	30t33	2.6	1.9	2.8	1.7	74.6	15.9	5.7
Transport equipment	34t35	2.1	1.9	2.4	1.5	76.6	15.8	3.1
Other manufacturing	36t37	0.9	0.9	1.3	0.9	77.9	8.6	2.6
Utilities	E	2.2	2.1	0.9	0.6	31.0	6.1	3.8

Construction	F	7.3	6.2	8.6	8.0	76.0	6.1	1.2
Automotive trade	50	2.3	1.7	2.4	2.4	76.8	8.8	2.6
Wholesale trade	51	3.7	3.9	4.5	4.7	67.7	7.2	4.8
Retail trade	52	4.2	4.4	8.1	8.1	83.6	8.5	2.0
Hotels and rest.	H	1.7	2.4	3.4	5.1	78.6	7.5	1.1
Transport	60t63	5.3	5.2	4.8	5.0	70.9	6.7	5.2
Post and telecomms	64	2.4	2.7	1.6	1.4	51.5	8.8	16.6
Finance	J	4.7	6.1	2.7	3.0	56.6	17.5	11.4
Real estate activities	70	8.0	10.7	0.5	1.1	6.8	2.4	0.7
Business services	71t74	5.6	11.6	4.6	12.6	72.3	28.4	6.6
Public administration	L	9.1	6.8	7.0	6.6	82.3	22.0	2.4
Education	M	6.3	6.3	4.3	5.4	93.8	56.4	1.2
Health and social work	N	5.1	6.5	5.9	8.9	83.2	23.9	1.7
Other services	O	2.7	3.7	2.9	4.8	74.0	17.8	2.9
Private households	P	0.3	0.4	1.0	2.0	100.0	15.9	0.0
Total economy		100.0	100.0	100.0	100.0	66.2	16.0	3.8

Data refer to a set of ten EU countries (EU 15ex). *Source:* EU KLEMS database, March 2008.

This appendix describes the March 2008 release of the EU KLEMS database. The database will be revised and updated each year and gradually expanded in terms of country coverage. In the near future, extensions are planned to include other major countries in the world economy such as Brazil, China, India, Indonesia, Mexico, Russia and Turkey (see www.worldklems.net).

While the EU KLEMS data can provide descriptive analysis of growth and its contributors as in this book, potentially its greatest benefit will be in future research where it is linked to additional databases. To explain differences in productivity growth, additional information on innovation inputs and outputs will be needed. Castaldi and Los (2009) provide data on patents and R&D stocks that match the EU KLEMS definitions and are available from the EU KLEMS website. Investment in intangibles, such as innovative property through research and development and firm-specific economic competences such as organisational capital and brand equity, has become increasingly important for growth, and preliminary evidence will be discussed in Chapter 7. Another promising avenue for further research is in the linking of firm-level based variables that might affect industry productivity trends – some preliminary data on concentration and average age of firms derived from aggregating company-based information is now available on the EU KLEMS website. For studies of outsourcing and international trade, further integration of trade statistics is needed, and a particularly challenging extension would be the inclusion of environmental pollution indicators. These types of data are part of the World Input-Output Database (WIOD) that will be available in the near future (at www.wiod.net) and will be closely linked to the EU KLEMS database. This database can be instrumental in studying the relationships between economic growth, socio-economic development and environmental quality within an international framework.

4 | Structural change

4.1 Introduction

In Chapter 2 we analysed the differences in growth performance between the European Union and the USA. While many idiosyncrasies in the growth patterns can be observed, there are also common long-term trends in the structure of the economy. The purpose of this chapter is to look for similarities, rather than for differences, in the process of structural change in the two regions.[1] This will be done by building upon the seminal work of Simon Kuznets and Angus Maddison. More than twenty-five years ago, these two economists established a number of empirical regularities in the structural transformation of advanced economies since the Second World War (Kuznets 1971; Maddison 1980). The best-known facts are the shifts of output and labour from agriculture to industry and later from industry to services. In addition, the services sector is characterised by limited scope for innovation and technical change with productivity growth rates that are much lower than in industry and agriculture.[2] The Kuznets–Maddison stylised patterns of growth have been a crucial ingredient in much work on economic growth, development economics, international trade, business cycles and labour markets. For example, sectoral differences in productivity are an important cornerstone in models of real exchange rates (Obstfeld and Rogoff 1996). They also underpin the hypothesis of the cost disease of the services sector described by Baumol (1967) and motivate the recent surge in multi-sector endogenous growth models, e.g. Ngai and Pissarides (2007) and Restuccia *et al.* (2008).

---

[1] This chapter relies heavily on a study by Jorgenson and Timmer (2009). This study also considers developments in Japan.

[2] See Krüger (2008) for a recent survey. Kuznets and Maddison focused mainly on advanced countries. Chenery *et al.* (1986) provide the seminal study of sectoral change in developing countries.

129

In this chapter we examine whether the stylised facts put forward by Kuznets and Maddison more than twenty-five years ago are still accurate descriptions of structural change in the EU and USA since 1980. Given the fact that the agricultural sector has become relatively small, our main focus will be on the developments in industry and services. In particular, we will look at the increasing share of services in output and employment at the expense of industry and at comparative productivity growth in industry and services. In addition, we will study changes in the structure of production technologies. Recent evidence suggests that technical change has favoured particular inputs of production and affected the production structures in a rather asymmetric way. In particular, the last two decades have been characterised by a growing importance of skilled labour and information and communications technology (ICT) assets.[3] Much of this work has been based on aggregate trends or manufacturing industries only. For the USA, Jorgenson *et al.* (2005) found that non-manufacturing industries are also heavy users of these so-called 'knowledge-based' inputs. We will search for common sectoral patterns in the use of skills and ICT capital across the EU and USA.

In our analysis we rely on the EU KLEMS database that was described in Chapter 3. This database provides comparable output and input statistics since the 1970s at a detailed industry level. Importantly, it contains new, more sophisticated measures of labour, capital and intermediate inputs that facilitate tracking of sectoral trends in both labour and multi-factor productivity.[4] The EU KLEMS database also allows us to greatly broaden the analysis of structural development by incorporating changes in the use of factor inputs in the production process. When considering sectoral developments in Europe, it is important to aggregate across European countries. Specialisation may generate differences in country patterns as relatively small countries freely trade with each other. Therefore, we study developments in the European Union as a whole, rather than in individual European countries as in Kuznets (1971) and Maddison (1980). The data

---

[3] For example, Autor *et al.* (1998), Machin and van Reenen (1998) and Jorgenson and Vu (2005).

[4] For historical analysis back to 1950 and an extension to non-OECD countries, see the GGDC Ten-sector database at www.ggdc.nl. This database provides output and employment for major sectors for Europe, Asia and Latin America (Timmer and de Vries 2009).

for the European Union used in this chapter refer to the following ten European countries for which long-term sectoral capital data are available: Austria, Belgium, Denmark, Finland, France, Germany, Italy, the Netherlands, Spain and the United Kingdom.[5]

Traditionally, the main distinction in sectoral studies is among agriculture, industry and services. However, in the past decades the importance of agriculture has rapidly declined while services have become by far the largest sector in advanced economies. Therefore a more detailed view of the services sector is essential and we will look at four of these services industries separately. In addition, we study the development of the ICT-goods producing sector which has played an important role in recent economic growth. In all, the economy is subdivided into seven sectors: ICT production; manufacturing excluding ICT production; other goods production (including agriculture, construction and utilities); distribution services; finance and business services; personal services; and non-market services (including public administration, education, health and real estate).[6] Table 4.1 provides the precise composition of each group in terms of the NACE rev. 1 industry classification scheme.

At the most general level we largely confirm the trends identified by Kuznets and Maddison, finding a continuing shift of employment and output from industry to services. Also, productivity growth in goods production is still higher than in services. But we argue that the distinction between goods and services has become obsolete and that this is not only because services now typically employ about three-quarters of the labour force. A more detailed industry analysis reveals very substantial heterogeneity within the services sector. Finance and business services have become highly skill- and ICT-intensive, but with little multi-factor productivity growth and steadily increasing prices. On the other hand, distribution services have become a major engine

---

[5] This group of countries is called EU15ex in the EU KLEMS database.

[6] In EU KLEMS, as elsewhere, we refer to these sectors as 'non-market services', recognising that some output of these sectors is provided by the private sector and the extent of this varies across countries. Non-market services should not be confounded with household production or home services. We rely on data collected within the System of National Accounts that exclude household activities by design. Real estate is grouped with non-market services as, for the most part, the output of the real estate sector is imputed rent on owner-occupied dwellings. Input in this sector consists mainly of residential buildings, and meaningful productivity estimates cannot be made.

Table **4.1.** *Description of sectors*

Description	Abbreviation	NACE rev. 1 code
ICT production (incl. electrical machinery manufacturing and post and communication services)	ELECOM	30–33 and 64
Manufacturing (excl. electrical machinery)	MexElec	15–29 and 34–37
Other production (incl. agriculture, mining, utilities and construction)	OtherG	A–C and E–F
Distribution (incl. trade and transportation)	DISTR	50–52 and 60–63
Finance and business services (excl. real estate)	FINBU	J and 71–74
Personal services (incl. hotels, restaurants and community, social and personal services)	PERS	H, O and P
Non-market services (incl. public administration, education, health and real estate)	NONMAR	70 and L–N

Source: Table 3A.3.

of productivity growth alongside manufacturing. The characterisation of services as stagnant in terms of productivity and input structures is no longer true. The remainder of the chapter is organised as follows. Section 4.2 is devoted to changes in sectoral output and employment shares. In section 4.3 we discuss trends in labour and multi-factor productivity. Section 4.4 studies patterns in the use of various types of labour and capital inputs, in particular, skilled labour and ICT capital. Section 4.5 concludes the chapter.

4.2 Trends in output and employment

The shift from agriculture to industry featured prominently in the earlier literature on modern growth and is still an important characteristic of growth in developing countries (Temple 2005). Currently, however, agriculture typically employs 6 per cent or less of the labour force in the EU and the USA. Instead the shift from industry to services has dominated the process of structural change since the 1970s. In

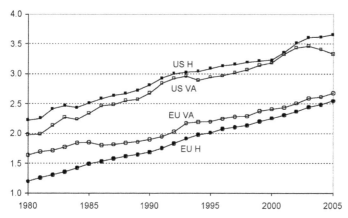

Figure 4.1. Ratio of services and goods production, EU and USA, 1980–2005. Ratio of variable in services (market and non-market) over goods production. VA denotes value added and H denotes hours worked. (*Source*: See Table 4.2.)

Figure 4.1 we show the ratio of value added in services (including market and non-market services) to goods production over the period from 1980 to 2005. In both the EU and the USA, the importance of services has steadily increased. A similar trend is found for hours worked (Figure 4.1). This confirms the first Kuznets–Maddison fact. At the same time, the figure makes clear that services have become a very sizeable sector. In 2005, they had at least double the output and employment of goods production in the EU and more than triple in the USA.

The growing importance of market services is the result of a number of interacting demand forces (Schettkat and Yokarini 2006). Higher per capita income leads to higher demand for services. There is also an increasing marketisation of traditional household production activities, including services like dining outside the home, cleaning and care assistance. Finally, many manufacturing firms are outsourcing aspects of business services, trade and transport activities. Ngai and Pissarides (2007) provide a model that stresses the importance of differences in technology across sectors, rather than non-homothetic tastes, as the driving force of structural change. Whatever the underlying causes of structural change, it has important implications for productivity growth and sectoral shares in GDP. Given lower productivity in services than in manufacturing Baumol predicted that service activities

Table 4.2. *Gross value added by sector as a percentage of GDP*

	EU		USA	
	1980	2005	1980	2005
Total	100.0	100.0	100.0	100.0
ICT production	4.9	4.6	6.1	4.7
Goods	36.1	25.9	31.5	22.0
Manufacturing	21.1	15.7	19.2	12.0
Other goods	14.9	10.2	12.4	10.1
Services	59.0	69.5	62.4	73.3
Market services	30.6	39.3	32.9	40.2
Distribution	15.6	15.1	16.9	14.5
Finance & business	10.3	17.7	11.2	19.5
Personal	4.7	6.5	4.8	6.3
Non-market services	28.4	30.2	29.5	33.1

Note: For sector definitions, see Table 4.1.
Source: Calculations based on EU KLEMS Database, March 2008; see Chapter 3.

would capture an ever-larger share of inputs and that prices of services would continue to grow faster than prices of goods. He called this the 'cost disease of the service sector'.

Table 4.2 presents value added as a percentage of GDP for our seven sectors in 1980 and 2005 for each region; similarly shares of hours worked are shown in Table 4.3. This more detailed view reveals striking differences among the four service industries. In 1980 non-market services already had the highest shares in output and employment in both regions and these increased slowly through 2005, taking up around 30 per cent of value added, with lower shares in employment. Personal services also increased their shares in the overall economy, accounting for 6–8 per cent of GDP. Their share in employment is about double at 11–15 per cent of hours worked, indicating low levels of productivity in personal services compared to other industries. The biggest increase in shares is in finance and business services, doubling their employment shares to over 12 per cent in the EU and 17 per cent in the USA, and even higher shares in GDP. By contrast to these three services industries, shares of the distribution sector remained constant or slightly declined. In 2005, this sector accounted for around 15 per cent of value added and 20 per cent of employment.

Table 4.3. *Hours worked by sector as a percentage of total hours worked*

	EU		USA	
	1980	2005	1980	2005
Total	100.0	100.0	100.0	100.0
ICT production	4.4	3.1	5.1	3.3
Goods	43.5	27.3	29.4	20.8
Manufacturing	23.2	14.4	18.8	10.9
Other goods	20.2	12.9	10.6	9.9
Services	52.1	69.6	65.4	75.9
Market services	34.4	47.7	40.3	47.3
Distribution	19.7	20.2	20.4	19.3
Finance & business	7.3	15.6	10.5	16.8
Personal	7.3	11.9	9.4	11.2
Non-market services	17.7	21.9	25.2	28.7

Note and source: See Table 4.2.

The increase in the shares of most services came at the expense of traditional goods production. Shares of manufacturing and other goods production declined rapidly in all regions. In 2005, other goods accounted only for about 10 per cent of GDP, while manufacturing accounted for 12 per cent in the USA and 15 per cent in the EU. Decreases in employment were equally strong. We have also singled out the ICT-producing sector. As we will show later, ICT has become an important driver of productivity growth in recent decades. The production of ICT goods and services makes up only a minor part of GDP and this share has been declining slightly in the EU and the USA. The decline is particular strong in hours worked, accounting for 4 per cent or less in 2005 in both regions.

The shares of the various sectors across the regions display a remarkable similarity in 2005. The major surprising difference is to be found in the employment share of non-market services, which is much higher in the USA than in the EU, reflecting the well-known higher expenditure on healthcare in the USA and its population's higher participation rate in tertiary education. In fact, the gap in the employment share of services between the EU and the USA has often been highlighted as an 'anomaly' (Pissarides 2007; Rogerson 2008). Explanations for this anomaly should focus on the non-market services sector, rather than the market services sector. By 2005, transatlantic differences in services employment were mainly to be found in industries like health and education.

4.3 Trends in productivity

One of the empirical regularities documented by Kuznets and Maddison is the slow growth of labour productivity in services compared to industry. Traditionally, manufacturing activities have been regarded as the locus of innovation and technological change and thus the central source of economic growth. This was the key to post-World War II growth in Europe through realisation of economies of scale, capital intensification and incremental innovation (Crafts and Toniolo 1996). More recently, rapid technological change in computer and semi-conductor manufacturing seemingly reinforced the predominance of innovation in the manufacturing sector. By contrast, productivity growth in services was assumed to be low or even zero. Baumol's cost disease suggests that productivity improvements in services are less likely than in goods-producing industries because most services are inherently labour-intensive, making it difficult to substitute capital for labour in service industries. Although Baumol (1967) originally mainly referred to services activities like education, health and public services and made a careful distinction between progressive and stagnant industries, it was widely believed to hold for all services industries. Related to this, but in an international context, sectoral productivity differences in growth are assumed to drive cross-country differences in price levels. The famous Harrod–Balassa–Samuelson hypothesis states that because of productivity differentials between traded and non-traded sectors, there is a tendency for countries with higher productivity in tradables compared to non-tradables to have higher price levels.[7]

In a seminal study, Triplett and Bosworth (2006) show that after 1995 fifteen out of twenty-two two-digit services industries in the USA experienced acceleration in labour productivity that at least equalled the economy-wide average. Hence the authors titled their study 'Baumol's Disease has been Cured'. In this chapter we will look for similar patterns in Europe and study sectoral trends in productivity since 1980.

---

[7] See, for example, Obstfeld and Rogoff (1996), pp. 210–11.

The EU KLEMS database provides the opportunity to examine trends in both labour and multi-factor productivity (MFP). Multi-factor productivity provides a measure of the efficiency of labour and other inputs and is often used as an indicator of technological change. The hypotheses of Baumol and Harrod–Balassa–Samuelson hinge crucially on sectoral differences in multi-factor productivity, but because of a lack of data they have often been tested by looking at labour productivity. In our analysis of productivity we exclude the non-market services industries, as productivity growth in these industries is not well measured in the National Accounts. Typically, growth of real output is proxied by the growth of inputs, such as number of employees, often with an arbitrary productivity adjustment. Recently, there has been a move within the statistical community to employ output quantity indicators to measure volumes of output. Until this process is more advanced, productivity measures for non-market services should therefore be interpreted with care, if at all (see also the discussion in Chapter 3 and Chapter 7).[8]

Industries are highly diverse in terms of their productivity performance, as shown in Table 4.4 and Figure 4.2. Table 4.4 provides average annual growth rates for the period 1980–2005 and Figure 4.2 presents trends with 1980 indexed to 100. By far the fastest growth in labour productivity is found in ICT production, with annual average growth rates of 3 per cent in the EU and more than 5 per cent in the USA. The trend for this sector is not shown in Figure 4.2 as it would dwarf all other curves. The second fastest growing sector in the USA has been distribution services, which has more than doubled its labour productivity level since 1980. In fact, growth in this sector has been higher than in manufacturing. On the other hand, labour productivity growth in other services industries has been very low. Finance and business services and personal services rank at the bottom in both regions during the entire period.

The wide range in sectoral labour productivity growth is surprising. With common Cobb–Douglas technologies and assuming that labour is homogeneous, can move freely across sectors and is paid its marginal product, labour productivity should grow at a similar rate

---

[8] See, for example, commentary by Lengellé (1980) on Maddison for an early statement of this problem, and Atkinson (2005) for a recent extensive discussion.

Table 4.4. *Labour and multi-factor productivity growth, 1980–2005*

	Labour productivity		Multi-factor productivity	
	EU	USA	EU	USA
Total	1.9	1.7	0.6	0.4
ICT production	5.5	7.5	3.2	5.0
Goods	2.7	1.8	1.2	0.7
Manufacturing	2.7	2.4	1.3	1.0
Other goods	2.7	0.9	1.1	0.4
Services	1.2	1.4	0.1	−0.1
Market services	1.3	2.1	0.0	0.5
Distribution	2.2	3.2	1.1	2.2
Finance & business	0.3	0.9	−0.9	−1.4
Personal	−0.4	1.2	−1.0	0.7
Non-market services	1.0	0.1	0.3	−0.8

Notes: Average annual compound growth rates. For sector definitions, see Table 4.1.
Source: See Table 4.2.

in all sectors (Temple 2005). This suggests that sectors differ substantially in their production technologies: elasticities of substitution between labour and capital may not be unity (as in the Cobb–Douglas case) and/or rates of technical change might differ across sectors. We measure technical change as the growth in multi-factor productivity as outlined above. Figure 4.3 and Table 4.4 show that indeed there is a large cross-sectional variation in the rates of MFP growth.[9] As before, the graphs are indexed to 100 in 1980. Given the fact that all sectors have increased their use of skilled labour and of capital services (see next section), productivity growth of hours worked is higher than multi-factor productivity growth. As outlined in Chapter 3, MFP growth takes into account changes in the composition of the labour force and in the use of capital services as well as hours worked. In some cases, the difference can be huge. For example, in US manufacturing, average labour productivity growth was 2.4 per cent. Taking into account the large increase in the use of skilled labour and capital,

[9] Our analysis of factor input shares in section 4.4 highlights other structural differences in sector technologies.

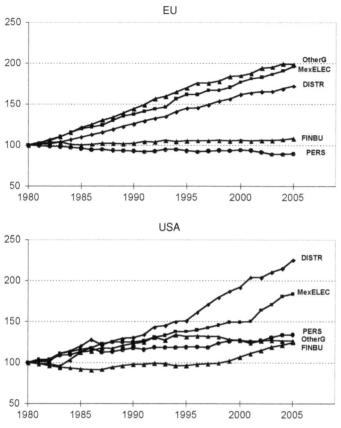

Figure 4.2. Value added per hour worked (1980=100). (*Source*: See Table 4.2.)

productivity growth dropped to 1.0 per cent. However, many of the findings on labour productivity are also valid for multi-factor productivity: growth is by far the highest in ICT production, manufacturing and distribution services and slowest in finance and business services and personal services.

The analysis so far points to a varied picture of sectoral developments in advanced nations in the past decades. There is continuing productivity growth in goods production, in particular in ICT production, and a decline in its shares in output and employment. On the other hand, finance and business services and personal services seem to be typical stagnant sectors with low or no productivity improvements but

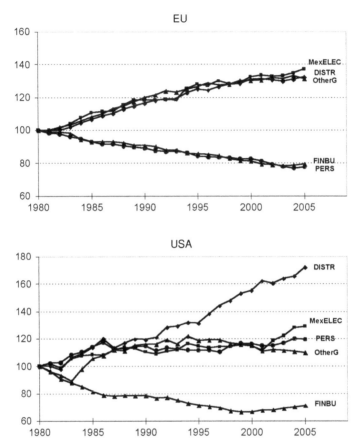

Figure 4.3. Multi-factor productivity (1980 = 100). MFP based on value added. (*Source*: See Table 4.2.)

with increasing shares in employment, as predicted by Baumol (1967) and in more recent analyses for the USA by Baumol *et al.* (1985) and Nordhaus (2008). However, distribution services do not fit the classic dichotomy between goods and services. This sector has been very dynamic with rapid labour productivity growth, while its employment share has remained more or less constant.

4.4 Growing role of skills and ICT capital

Structural change not only entails the changes in output and productivity analysed by Kuznets and Maddison, but also involves shifts in the mix of inputs used in the production process. One of Kaldor's stylised facts is the increasing use of capital per unit of labour over time (Kaldor 1963). He also found that the prices of capital relative to wages declined proportionally, so that the shares of labour and capital in the GDP remained more or less constant. These findings were based on historical evidence on US and UK growth.[10] More recently, Blanchard (1997) found that although the labour share continued to be stable in the USA and other Anglo-Saxon countries, it tended to decrease in continental Europe over the period 1980–95. He linked this difference to a stronger substitution process of capital for labour in Europe, partly due to higher wage–rental ratios.

In the past decade, attention was focused on the increasing use of inputs that are well suited to the generation, processing and diffusion of knowledge and information, namely, skilled labour and ICT equipment. Berman *et al.* (1998) document the pervasiveness of increasing use of skilled labour in manufacturing production in the OECD. As skill premia remained stable or even increased, this was seen by many economists as strong evidence for pervasive skill-biased technological change (SBTC). An alternative explanation is the complementarity between increased use of ICT and skilled labour (O'Mahony *et al.* 2008).[11] For the USA, Jorgenson *et al.* (2005) document large increases in the use of both skilled labour and ICT capital across the economy, which seems to be consistent with this idea. They also found substantial variation in the use of these inputs across detailed industries. In this section we will track the use of skilled labour and ICT capital in major sectors in Europe and the USA to see common patterns in the knowledge intensification of production and its sector-specific characteristics.

Measures of input intensity

In this chapter we use the cost measures of inputs rather than the more frequently used quantity measures. The differences between these measures will be explained below. Input measures based on the cost approach start from the standard national accounting identity that

---

[10] See Gollin (2002) for more recent evidence across a large set of countries.
[11] See Hornstein *et al.* (2005) for an overview.

value added equals the compensation for labour and capital.[12] We will distinguish between two groups of labour (skilled, *SL*, and unskilled, *UL*) and two types of capital (ICT capital, *KIT*, and non-ICT capital, *KNIT*). Let *P* and *Q* denote prices and quantities respectively, indexed for value added and various inputs, then

$$P_{VA}\,Q_{VA} = P_{SL}\,Q_{SL} + P_{UL}\,Q_{UL} + P_{KIT}\,Q_{KIT} + P_{KNIT}\,Q_{KNIT} \qquad (4.1)$$

Using identity (4.1), we will look at three cost shares as indicators, namely the labour intensity of production *I(Labour)* defined as:

$$I(Labour) = \frac{P_{UL}\,Q_{UL} + P_{SL}\,Q_{SL}}{P_{VA}\,Q_{VA}} \qquad (4.2)$$

the skill intensity of production *I(Skill)* defined as:

$$I(Skill) = \frac{P_{SL}\,Q_{SL}}{P_{VA}\,Q_{VA}} \qquad (4.3)$$

and the ICT-capital intensity of production *I(ICT)* defined as:

$$I(ICT) = \frac{P_{KIT}\,Q_{KIT}}{P_{VA}\,Q_{VA}} \qquad (4.4)$$

An increase in a cost share indicates a growing importance of the input in production. Note that this rise can be due to an increase in the price of the input, or to an increase in the quantity used, relative to the other inputs. These indicators are different from simpler measures that are often used, such as the share of high-skilled workers in total employment $Q_{SL}/(Q_{SL} + Q_{UL})$. The latter indicator is based on quantities alone and ignores price changes. If, for example, the marginal productivity of skilled labour increases more than that of unskilled labour because of skill-biased technological change, the cost shares correct for this. Under the standard assumption that differences in marginal productivity are reflected in relative prices, this is picked up in the cost share given in (4.3). Another common alternative

---

[12] Ideally, we would like to include intermediate inputs as well. However, industry measures require aggregation of outputs and inputs over firms in the same industry. This introduces problems of interpretation as part of the output is used by firms in the same industry as intermediate input. Therefore a switch should be made to the so-called sectoral output measures introduced by Domar (1961) and discussed in section 3.6. The EU KLEMS database does not contain sectoral measures of output and therefore we will use value-added based cost shares which net out all intermediate inputs.

indicator is the share of high-skilled workers in total labour compensation: $P_{SL}Q_{SL}/(P_{SL}Q_{SL} + P_{UL}Q_{UL})$. This indicator corrects for differences in productivity between various types of labour, but does not take into account other inputs. For example, if labour (both skilled and unskilled) is substituted for capital, the share of high-skilled workers in labour compensation can increase, while their importance in production actually declines. The cost share indicator defined in (4.3) takes account of substitution effects among labour types and between labour and other inputs.

The empirical implementation of (4.3) is relatively straightforward as the hours worked by skilled labour and their relative wages can be directly taken from the EU KLEMS database. We multiply total labour compensation of all workers (variable *LAB* in the database) by the share of high-skilled workers in total labour compensation (*LABHS*) and divide by nominal value added (*VA*). Labour compensation includes an imputation for self-employed workers. High-skilled workers are defined as workers with college education and above. The series are designed to track developments over time within each country. As comparability of educational attainment and qualifications across countries is still problematical, cross-country comparisons of skill shares should be interpreted with care (see the discussion in Chapter 3).

Measuring the ICT-capital intensity of production is less straightforward as quantities and prices of capital services are not directly observable. Simpler measures are often used such as the number of computers per employee, or the share of ICT assets in total investment or capital stock. Our measure of the relative importance of ICT is based on the concept of capital services introduced by Jorgenson and Griliches (1967). In this approach, capital input is measured through its delivery of services in a specific period (in this case a year) as measured by its user cost (see Chapter 3). ICT intensity is measured by multiplying capital compensation (variable *CAP* in the EU KLEMS database) by the share of ICT assets in total capital compensation (*CAPIT*) and dividing by nominal value added (*VA*).

Labour shares in value added

Figure 4.4 and Table 4.5 provide trends in the share of labour in value added over the period 1980–2005, based on (4.2). In the EU the long-run trend of substituting labour by capital as described by

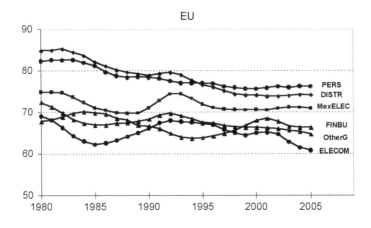

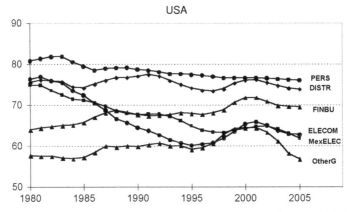

Figure 4.4. Labour compensation as a percentage of value added, including employees and self-employed persons; see equation (4.2). Three-year moving average. (*Source*: See Table 4.2.)

Blanchard (1997) continued until the mid-1990s, but has tapered off since then. The overall labour share dropped from 72 per cent in 1980 to 66 per cent in 2005, and a similar declining trend can be found in all sectors. In the USA, the overall labour share declined from 67 per cent in 1980 to 63 per cent in 2005, but this was mainly driven by the strong decreases in the returns to labour in manufacturing and ICT production. By contrast, labour shares in services remained remarkably stable over the period 1980–2005 and even increased in finance and business services. Looking across sectors a common pattern

Table 4.5 *Compensation of all workers as a percentage of value added*

| | EU | | USA | |
	1980	2005	1980	2005
Total	72.1	66.2	66.8	63.2
ICT production	69.8	61.0	77.5	62.6
Goods	73.4	68.2	68.9	58.6
Manufacturing	74.0	70.6	75.5	61.1
Other goods	72.6	64.5	58.7	55.6
Services	71.5	65.7	64.6	64.7
Market services	77.9	71.5	72.3	71.9
Distribution	83.9	74.4	75.8	73.5
Finance & business	67.1	66.9	63.6	69.5
Personal	82.0	77.5	80.0	75.9
Non-market services	64.7	58.2	56.1	55.9

Notes: Labour compensation as a percentage of value added, including employees and self-employed persons; see equation (4.2). For sector definitions, see Table 4.1.
Source: See Table 4.2.

is easily discerned across the two regions, as labour shares are highest in personal and distribution services, while lowest in ICT production and other goods. This ranking of sectors in terms of labour intensity is rather stable over time and testifies to the labour-intensive nature of the production process in services compared to other industries.

Skilled labour

In Figure 4.5 and Table 4.6, we provide the wage bill of high-skilled workers as a share of value added for each industry. The patterns are strikingly similar across industries and across regions: the importance of high-skilled labour has gradually but steadily increased over recent decades. And the rate of increase is roughly constant across all sectors in a region. This holds even when looking at detailed market services and goods industries.[13] This confirms the long-term trends

[13] Figure 4.6 should not be interpreted as evidence for the low skill level of the labour force in the EU, compared to that of the USA. The comparability of educational attainment and qualifications across countries is tenuous, since some sub-categories with relatively high wages may be classified to high skill in one country and medium skill in another.

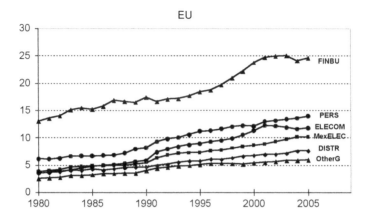

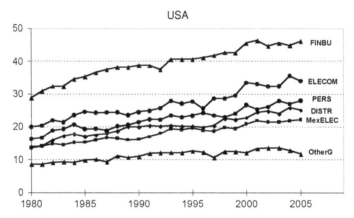

Figure 4.5. Compensation of high-skilled workers as a percentage of value added; see equation (4.3). Skill definitions differ across countries and figures can only be used for inter-temporal analysis. (*Source*: See Table 4.2.)

documented in Berman *et al.* (1998) for manufacturing in the OECD, and in Jorgenson *et al.* (2005) for the USA. Skill-upgrading of the economy is not primarily due to strong growth in a limited number of sectors, but is rather an economy-wide phenomenon. Given the fact that skill premia remained constant over 1980–2005 in the EU or increased in the USA, this is suggestive of skill-biased technological change as an important driver of increased demand for skilled workers.

Table 4.6. *Compensation of high-skilled workers as a percentage of value added*

	EU		USA	
	1980	2005	1980	2005
Total	8.3	16.0	18.5	30.4
ICT production	3.8	11.7	20.0	34.0
Goods	3.3	8.5	11.5	17.7
Manufacturing	3.8	10.1	13.5	22.2
Other goods	2.5	6.0	8.6	11.8
Services	11.2	19.0	22.2	34.1
Market services	7.1	16.3	19.0	35.5
Distribution	3.5	7.6	14.0	25.1
Finance & business	13.0	24.6	28.9	46.2
Personal	6.1	13.9	16.3	28.0
Non-market services	15.6	22.6	25.8	32.4

Notes: Compensation of high-skilled workers as a percentage of value added; see equation (4.3). Skill definitions differ across countries (see discussion in Chapter 3) and figures can only be used for inter-temporal analysis. For sector definitions, see Table 4.1.
Source: See Table 4.2.

Obviously, there are large differences between industries in the use of high-skilled labour. By far the most skill-intensive industry in the EU and the USA is finance and business services. In all regions, manufacturing and other goods production are among the least skill-intensive industries. For example, the share of high-skilled workers in value added in manufacturing is less than half of that in finance and business services. This ordering of industries is remarkably constant over time and points to persistent sectoral differences in structures of production.

ICT capital

In Figure 4.6 and Table 4.7, the shares of ICT-capital compensation in value added are given for the EU and the USA. Like skill intensity, ICT intensity is increasing over time in all sectors and regions. This is suggestive of complementarity between ICT capital and skilled labour. However, sectoral differences in the levels and their rate of increase for

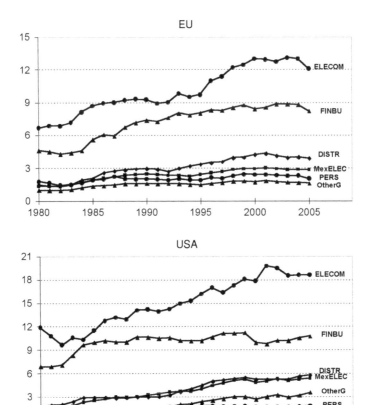

Figure 4.6. Compensation of ICT capital as a percentage of value added; see equation (4.4). ICT capital includes computers, telecommunications equipment and software. (*Source*: See Table 4.2.)

ICT capital are much more pronounced than for skills. Typically, ICT intensity of production doubled or even tripled over the period from 1980 to 2005. Perhaps surprisingly, this increase had already started in the 1980s.

ICT intensity in the market economy of the USA was 2.4 per cent in 1980, increasing to 4.2 per cent in 1990 and peaking at 5.8 per cent in 1999, but levelling off afterwards, after the bursting of the dotcom bubble. In the EU the increasing use of ICT was at least as impressive in the 1980s as it was in the 1990s (see Figure 4.6). It increased from 1.8 per cent to 3.8 per cent in the EU. The rapid increase in the share

Table 4.7. *Compensation of ICT capital as a percentage of value added*

	EU		USA	
	1980	2005	1980	2005
Total	1.8	3.8	2.4	5.6
ICT production	6.7	12.1	11.9	18.6
Goods	1.2	2.4	0.8	4.6
Manufacturing	1.4	2.9	1.0	5.4
Other goods	1.0	1.6	0.6	3.6
Services	1.7	3.7	2.1	5.1
Market services	2.6	5.5	3.4	7.6
Distribution	1.5	3.9	1.7	5.8
Finance & business	4.6	8.2	6.9	10.8
Personal	1.8	2.1	1.2	1.8
Non-market services	0.8	1.4	0.7	2.1

Notes: Compensation of ICT capital as a percentage of value added; see equation (4.4). ICT capital includes computers, telecommunications equipment and software. For sector definitions, see Table 4.1.
Source: See Table 4.2.

of ICT in value added has often been attributed to strong substitution between ICT and other forms of capital induced by the rapid decline in its price relative to non-ICT assets and labour (Jorgenson 2001). The stagnation of the ICT shares after 2000 might indicate that this substitution process has lost some of its force.

Figure 4.6 also shows that the ordering of sectors in terms of their ICT intensity is similar across regions. ICT production and finance and business services are the most intensive users of ICT, while goods production and personal services are least ICT-intensive. Distribution services was one of the least ICT-intensive sectors in the past but has recently had one of the highest growth rates. A more detailed look at the individual industries reveals considerable sectoral variation in the rate and timing of the ICT intensification process. For example, in the mid-1980s, production in US finance and business services was as ICT-intensive as it was in 2005, while the major surge in ICT intensification in distribution services came in the mid 1990s. A somewhat similar sectoral pattern can be found for the EU, albeit delayed compared to the USA. This suggests interesting hypotheses about the synchronisation of technology waves and spillovers across advanced markets, which await further sector-specific study.

4.5 Concluding remarks

In this chapter we have studied long-term trends in structural change in the EU and US economies since 1980. We found an increasing share in output and employment of services at the expense of goods production, while productivity growth in goods production was higher than in overall market services. These trends are a continuation of the earlier movements documented by Kuznets (1971) and Maddison (1980). In addition, we found some trends in the more detailed measures of output and input now available from the EU KLEMS database but which were not available to Kuznets and Maddison: a declining share of labour in value added, especially in goods production, and increasing shares of skills and ICT in value added in all sectors, in particular in services. We have argued that the classical dichotomy between goods production and services has become obsolete. In 2005, services accounted for 65–75 per cent of value added and hours worked and included various sectors with widely different characteristics and performance. Our findings suggest that the treatment of the services sector as a homogeneous and stagnant sector in contrast to dynamic manufacturing is no longer warranted. In particular we have shown that distribution services had productivity growth rates at least as high as goods production. Clearly, this sector has been cured from Baumol's cost disease, although Baumol (1967) highlighted retail trade as a prominent example of a stagnant sector. However, finance and business services still have the symptoms of the cost disease as productivity growth was low and employment shares increased. This is perhaps surprising as these sectors had the highest levels of skill and ICT use. Finally, personal services also had low productivity growth rates and increasing employment shares and seem to epitomise Baumol's stagnant sector.

These findings call for a greater attention to individual services sectors to understand the drivers of growth. This will open up a broad spectrum of research ranging from empirical to more conceptual issues. For example, there is an urgent need for improved measurement of services output volumes as discussed in section 3.7. Non-market services had increased shares in output and employment, but little can be said about the productivity performance of this sector because of unresolved measurement issues. And while much is known about the drivers of technical change in manufacturing, little is known about innovation in services. This call for more research on services is certainly not the first: Fuchs (1968) is an early example and Broadberry (2006), for example, provides a reappraisal of the role of services in historical growth episodes. This chapter has merely presented new evidence that reinforces its importance.

In addition, our findings also have a number of implications for theoretical and empirical work currently relying on the Kuznets–Maddison set of stylised facts. Recent multi-sector endogenous growth models have focused mainly on the shift from agriculture to industry or from industry to services. Given the large differences in technical progress and input structures within the services industries, reliance on an aggregate representation of the services sector is tenuous at best. A more refined treatment of services might also allow a sharper analysis in models featuring household production (Pissarides 2007; Rogerson 2008). While household activities might be a substitute for certain services activities such as housekeeping, cooking and caring, this is much less obvious for business services or public administration. Lastly, the simultaneous increase in the use of skills and ICT in all sectors is strongly suggestive of pervasive capital–skill complementarities. However, since 2000, ICT shares have been stagnant or even declining, while cost shares of skilled labour have continued to increase, suggesting skill-biased technological change. This highlights new possibilities for investigating the links among investment, education and technological change, based on international evidence at a detailed industry level as presented in this book.

5 | The industry origins of aggregate growth

5.1 Introduction

The purpose of this chapter is to examine in more detail the industry origins of growth. This involves analysing how the growth of inputs and MFP of each industry contributes to aggregate value added. Thus we not only look at which industries contribute most to productivity growth but also which industries contribute most to the increased use of ICT and skilled labour. In addition, we will provide analyses based on data for twenty-six detailed industries, rather than for broad sectors as done so far. These yield much richer information on the sources of growth than those in earlier chapters as the latter could miss sizeable within-group heterogeneity. As before, we focus on two areas: the performance of the European Union over the period 1980–2005, and a comparison of the EU with the USA for the 1995–2005 period.

The chapter is organised as follows. Section 5.2 outlines the methodology used to determine industries' contributions to aggregate growth. This is based on the direct aggregation over industries approach, outlined in Jorgenson *et al.* (2005). Section 5.3 examines labour productivity trends at the industry level and analyses contributions to aggregate productivity growth in the EU and USA. In the following sections this contribution is further dissected. In section 5.4 the contribution of input growth in industries to aggregate growth is determined for ICT capital, non-ICT capital and labour composition separately. Section 5.5 is devoted to the contributions from industry-level multifactor productivity (MFP) growth. Section 5.6 examines whether MFP growth manifests itself in yeast or mushroom patterns, based on the seminal paper by Harberger (1998). Section 5.7 concludes.

5.2 Methodology: industry contributions to growth

In this section we outline the methodology to measure the contribution of industries to aggregate growth. The method will depend crucially on the way in which aggregate volume indicators are measured. We follow the direct aggregation over industries approach, outlined in Jorgenson, *et al.* (2005). In this approach the contribution of each industry to aggregate growth is given by industry growth multiplied by industry shares of value added – this mirrors the growth accounting approach outlined in Chapter 3.

We define aggregate nominal value added (GDP) as the sum over nominal value added (Z) in all industries, *j*, as follows:

$$P_t^{GDP} GDP_t = \sum_j P_{jt}^Z Z_{jt} \tag{5.1}$$

The volume growth of GDP is defined as a Törnqvist weighted industry value added growth as follows:

$$\Delta \ln GDP_t = \sum_j \bar{v}_{Z,jt}^{GDP} \Delta \ln Z_{jt} \tag{5.2}$$

where weights are given by the period-average shares of industry *j* in aggregate value added, defined as:

$$v_{Z,jt}^{GDP} = 0.5 \times \left(\frac{P_{j,t}^Z Z_{j,t}}{\sum_j P_{j,t}^Z Z_{j,t}} + \frac{P_{j,t-1}^Z Z_{j,t-1}}{\sum_j P_{j,t-1}^Z Z_{j,t-1}} \right) \tag{5.3}$$

We define total aggregate hours worked as the sum over all industries as before. The conventional way of calculating labour productivity growth is to divide value added volume growth by the growth in total hours worked ($\Delta \ln z_t = \Delta \ln Z_t - \Delta \ln H_t$). As shown by Stiroh (2002), in this case aggregate labour productivity growth can be decomposed into industry contributions as follows:

$$\Delta \ln \frac{GDP_t}{H_t} = \sum_j \bar{v}_{Z,jt}^{GDP} \Delta \ln z_{jt} + \left(\sum_j \bar{v}_{Z,jt}^{GDP} \Delta \ln H_{jt} - \Delta \ln H \right)$$

$$= \sum_j \bar{v}_{Z,jt}^{GDP} \Delta \ln z_{jt} + R_t \tag{5.4}$$

The term in brackets in (5.4) is the reallocation of hours (R) and reflects differences in the share of an industry in aggregate value added and its share in aggregate hours worked. This term will be positive when industries with an above-average labour productivity level show positive employment growth or when industries with below-average labour productivity have declining employment shares. This decomposition allows for a calculation of the contribution of industry j to overall labour productivity growth. It is given by:

$$LPCON_j^{LP} = \overline{v}_{Z,jt}^{GDP} \Delta \ln z_{jt} \tag{5.5}$$

As outlined in Chapter 3, we can decompose labour productivity growth into the growth of inputs and multi-factor productivity growth:

$$\Delta \ln z_{jt} = \overline{v}_{ICT,jt}^{Z} \Delta \ln k_{jt}^{ICT} + \overline{v}_{N,jt}^{Z} \Delta \ln k_{jt}^{N} + \overline{v}_{L,jt}^{Z} \Delta \ln LC_{jt} + \Delta \ln A_{jt}^{Z} \tag{5.6}$$

Combining the decomposition of industry labour productivity in (5.6) with the decomposition in (5.4), the full decomposition of aggregate labour productivity growth can be written as:

$$\Delta \ln \frac{GDP_t}{H_t} = \sum_j \overline{v}_{Z,jt}^{GDP} \left(\overline{v}_{ICT,jt}^{Z} \Delta \ln k_{jt}^{ICT} + \overline{v}_{N,jt}^{Z} \Delta \ln k_{jt}^{N} \right.$$
$$\left. + \overline{v}_{L,jt}^{Z} \Delta \ln LC_{jt} + \Delta \ln A_{jt}^{Z} \right) + R_t \tag{5.7}$$

In this way, the contribution of input and MFP growth from each industry to aggregate labour productivity growth can be calculated. For example, the contribution of ICT-capital deepening in industry j to aggregate labour productivity growth is given by:

$$LPCON_j^{ICT} = \overline{v}_{Z,jt}^{GDP} \left(\overline{v}_{ICT,jt}^{Z} \Delta \ln k_{jt}^{ICT} \right) = \overline{v}_{ICT,jt}^{GDP} \Delta \ln k_{jt}^{ICT} \tag{5.8}$$

which is the growth of ICT capital per hour worked in industry j weighted by the share of ICT capital compensation in industry j in aggregate nominal value added ($\overline{v}_{ICT,jt}^{GDP}$). The weight is the product of the share of industry j in aggregate value added ($\overline{v}_{Z,jt}^{GDP}$) and the share of ICT capital compensation in industry value added ($\overline{v}_{ICT,jt}^{Z}$).

Similarly, the contribution to aggregate labour productivity growth from non-ICT capital deepening in industry j ($LPCON_j^{N}$) is given by the growth of non-ICT capital per hour worked in industry j weighted by the share of non-ICT capital compensation in industry j in aggregate nominal value added:

$$LPCON_j^{N} = \overline{v}_{Z,jt}^{GDP} \left(\overline{v}_{N,jt}^{Z} \Delta \ln k_{jt}^{N} \right) = \overline{v}_{N,jt}^{GDP} \Delta \ln k_{jt}^{N} \tag{5.9}$$

The contribution to aggregate labour productivity growth from labour quality ($LPCON_j^{LC}$) is given by:

$$LPCON_j^{LC} = \overline{v}_{Z,jt}^{GDP} \left(\overline{v}_{L,jt}^{Z} \Delta \ln LC_{jt} \right) = \overline{v}_{L,jt}^{GDP} \Delta \ln LC_{jt} \tag{5.10}$$

Table 5.1. *Industry sources of labour productivity growth, EU and USA*

	EU		USA	
	1980–95	1995–2005	1980–95	1995–2005
Aggregate labour productivity	2.52	1.52	1.94	2.93
Reallocation	0.05	−0.14	−0.28	−0.25
Industry-weighted labour productivity	2.46	1.66	2.22	3.19
Contribution of industry-weighted:				
Labour composition	0.30	0.21	0.23	0.30
ICT capital per hour	0.39	0.53	0.78	1.02
Non-ICT capital per hour	0.77	0.54	0.44	0.53
Multi-factor productivity	1.00	0.39	0.78	1.33

Note: The table gives the contributions of industry-level inputs per hour worked and MFP to aggregate market economy labour productivity growth. These contributions are aggregated over industries as given in Tables 5.4 to 5.7.
Source: Calculations based on EU KLEMS database, March 2008; see Chapter 3.

which is the growth of labour services per hour worked in industry j weighted by the share of labour compensation in industry j in aggregate nominal value added. The weight is the product of the share of industry j in aggregate value added and the share of labour compensation in industry value added. Finally, the contribution to aggregate labour productivity growth from MFP growth ($LPCON_j^{MFP}$) is given by:

$$LPCON_j^{MFP} = \bar{v}_{Z,jt}^{GDP} \Delta \ln MFP_{jt}^Z \qquad (5.11)$$

which is the growth of MFP in industry j weighted by the share of industry j in aggregate value added.[1]

In Table 5.1 the basic decomposition of aggregate labour productivity growth is given. The first three rows indicate the breakdown of labour productivity growth in the market economy into the weighted

---

[1] In a more general setting, MFP is derived for gross output rather than value added (see Chapter 3). In this case, the industry weights will be different, and are often referred to as Domar-weights; see, for example, Jorgenson, Gollop and Fraumeni (1987). Aulin-Ahmavaara and Pakarinen (2007) provide an alternative aggregation scheme based on weaker assumptions.

growth of industry-level labour productivity growth and the reallocation term as in (5.4). The second row shows that the reallocation of labour between industries had a negative impact on aggregate growth in the USA as hours worked were reallocated to industries with lower levels of labour productivity, mainly in trade and hotels and restaurants. This also took place in the EU in the period 1995–2005. Overall though, this term is relatively small.[2] The weighted industry contribution as given in the third row is further decomposed into industry-weighted contributions of ICT and non-ICT capital, labour services per hour worked and multi-factor productivity as in (5.7). In the following sections these aggregate contributions are broken down by industry to investigate the industry sources of growth. We first analyse aggregate contributions of labour productivity growth in industries in section 5.3, and then decompose this further into the industry origins of input and multi-factor productivity growth in section 5.4. In Table 5A.1 one can find the growth accounting results for each industry separately that are the basis for these decompositions of aggregate growth.

5.3 Labour productivity growth

In Chapter 2 it was shown that the industry sources of productivity growth differed considerably between Europe and the USA. In the USA, ICT production and market services appeared to be much more important drivers of aggregate growth than in the EU. In this section we provide a more detailed industry perspective on the transatlantic growth divide. In addition, we locate the industries mainly responsible for the productivity slowdown in Europe since the mid 1990s. In Figure 5.1, labour productivity growth rates for detailed market industries in the EU are shown for the periods 1980–95 and 1995–2005. Industries are ranked on growth in the earlier period. Labour productivity growth rates varied widely across the twenty-six industries. In the early period the highest growth took place in agriculture, post and telecommunications and various manufacturing industries such

---

[2] The size of the reallocation term depends on the level of industry detail at which the decomposition is made. The reallocation term in this table is based on twenty-six industries, while, for example, the decomposition shown in Table 2.2 is based on six sectors only.

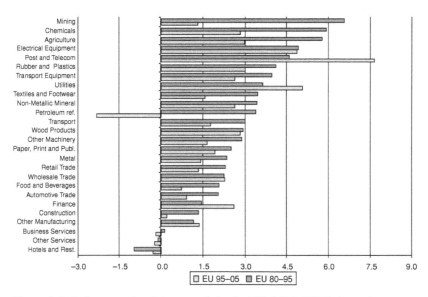

Figure 5.1. Labour productivity growth in the EU, 1980–2005. Annual compound growth rates of value added per hour worked. Industries ranked on EU, 1980–95. (*Source*: See Table 5.1.)

as chemicals, electrical equipment, rubber and plastics and transport equipment. In contrast, productivity growth was small or even negative in business services, hotels and restaurants and other personal services. This ranking did not change much after 1995 as more or less the same industries were ranked at the top and bottom, but productivity growth rates declined over the two periods in most industries. Out of twenty-six industries, only six increased growth. This is in stark contrast with developments in the USA. In Figure 5.2 trends in the EU and the USA in the period 1995–2005 are compared. In this figure, industries are ranked on growth rates in the EU. The correlation with the ranking in the USA is only weak. By far the fastest growing sector in the USA is electrical equipment manufacturing with annual labour productivity growth of more than 15 per cent, followed by wholesale trade. In the EU, post and telecommunications and utilities topped the ranking, followed by electrical equipment. During this period labour productivity growth in the USA was higher than in the EU in nineteen out of twenty-six industries. European growth was only faster in

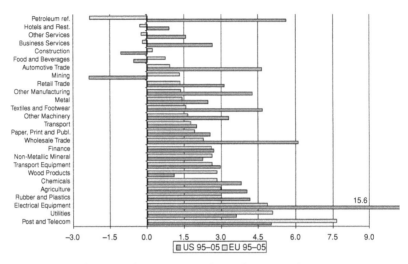

Figure 5.2. Labour productivity growth in the EU and USA, 1995–2005. Annual compound growth rates of value added per hour worked. Industries ranked on EU. (*Source*: See Table 5.1.)

industries like mining, post and telecommunications, wood manufacturing and utilities.

The importance of an industry in explaining differences in aggregate productivity growth does not only depend on its productivity growth rate, but also on its share in value added. We use (5.5) to measure the contribution of each sector to aggregate productivity growth. In Table 5.2 the basic data for this calculation is given for six broad sectors, together covering the market economy. Based on the average share in value added and the growth in labour productivity, the contribution of each sector to aggregate labour productivity growth is derived and shown in the lowest section of Table 5.2. For example, during 1995–2005, finance and business services contributed 0.7 percentage points to aggregate labour productivity growth in the USA. This is not because growth in this sector was particularly high. Growth was below average (2.6 per cent), but due to its large share in the economy (27 per cent), its contribution was substantial. On the other hand, labour productivity growth in ICT production was much higher (10 per cent), but as its share in value added was only small (8 per cent), its

Table 5.2. *Industry contributions to aggregate labour productivity, EU and USA*

	EU		USA	
	1980–95	1995–2005	1980–95	1995–2005
Average share in aggregate value added (percentage)				
ICT production	6.7	6.6	8.9	8.1
Manufacturing	27.8	24.3	24.6	20.0
Other goods	19.1	16.0	15.3	14.1
Distribution	21.5	21.5	23.2	22.1
Finance & business	17.4	22.8	20.3	26.9
Personal	7.5	8.8	7.7	8.9
Market economy	100.0	100.0	100.0	100.0
Growth in labour productivity (annual growth)				
ICT production	4.9	6.5	5.9	10.0
Manufacturing	3.2	2.0	2.1	2.9
Other goods	3.5	1.6	1.8	−0.4
Distribution	2.5	1.7	2.7	4.0
Finance & business	0.3	0.3	0.3	2.6
Personal	0.5	0.4	1.1	1.2
Market economy	2.5	1.5	1.9	2.9
Contribution to market economy labour productivity growth (percentage points)				
ICT production	0.33	0.42	0.52	0.81
Manufacturing	0.89	0.48	0.52	0.58
Other goods	0.67	0.25	0.28	0.05
Distribution	0.53	0.37	0.64	0.88
Finance & business	0.05	0.07	0.05	0.69
Personal	0.04	0.03	0.09	0.11
Reallocation effect	0.08	−0.03	−0.05	−0.08
Market economy	2.52	1.52	1.94	2.93

Source: See Table 5.1.

contribution to aggregate labour productivity growth was only slightly higher at 0.8 percentage points. Figures 5.3 and 5.4 provide a more detailed analysis of the industry sources of productivity growth at the level of twenty-six industries. Each bar indicates the percentage contribution of an industry to aggregate labour productivity growth.

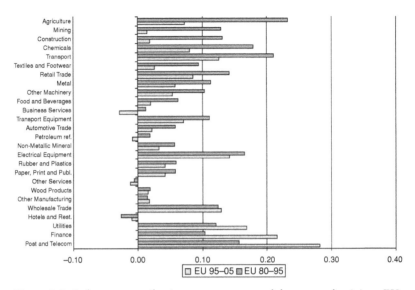

Figure 5.3. Industry contributions to aggregate labour productivity, EU, 1980–2005. Contributions in percentage points to annual growth rates of value added per hour worked. Industries ranked on difference between two periods. (*Source*: See Table 5.1.)

Industries are ranked on the difference in growth rates between the two periods (Figure 5.3) and between the EU and USA (Figure 5.4).

Table 5.2 shows that the labour productivity growth decrease in Europe was mainly due to the weaker performance in manufacturing and other goods production after 1995. Decreases in the contribution from agriculture, mining and construction were as important as the decreases in manufacturing. This was one of the main findings in Chapter 2. The decrease was not concentrated in a limited set of industries. Rather, the contribution of almost all manufacturing and other goods-producing industries decreased substantially. This can be seen in Figure 5.3 which provides additional industry detail. In fact, the pattern of industry contributions to growth in Europe during 1995–2005 looked quite similar to the pattern in the USA in the previous period (1980–1995). After this point the engines of growth in the USA shifted towards market services with large contributions from distribution and finance and business services (Table 5.2). Compared to Europe, the contributions of electrical equipment manufacturing, wholesale

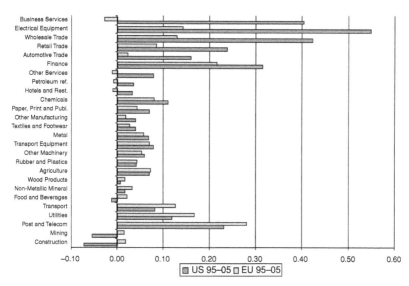

Figure 5.4. Industry contributions to aggregate labour productivity, EU and USA, 1995–2005. Contributions in percentage points to annual growth rates of value added per hour worked. Industries ranked on difference between EU and USA. (*Source*: See Table 5.1.)

and business services clearly stand out (Figure 5.4). But other trade sectors (retail and automotive trade) also contributed significantly to the difference in performance. Finance and post and telecommunications appeared to be important sources of growth in both Europe and the USA, contributing similarly in the two regions.

5.4 Capital and labour input growth

In this section we investigate the contribution of capital and labour input growth in industries to aggregate labour productivity growth. We first focus on the contribution of ICT capital, then non-ICT capital and finally the changing composition of labour.

ICT capital

In Table 5.1, it was shown that the overall contribution of ICT capital to labour productivity growth has increased in both the EU and the

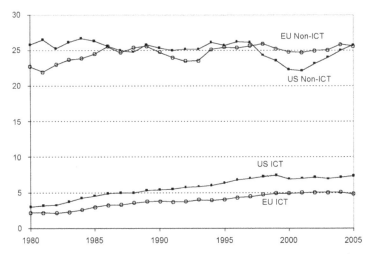

Figure 5.5. Share of ICT and non-ICT capital compensation in value added, market economy, EU and USA, 1980–2005. (*Source*: See Table 5.1.)

USA over the past decades. In Figure 5.5 we show that the rapidly increasing role of ICT capital in the economy in the past decades levelled off from about 2000. The figure shows the share of ICT-capital compensation in value added in the period from 1980 to 2005 for the market economy in the EU and the USA. This share increased strongly in the USA from 3 per cent in 1980 to over 7 per cent in 1999, but after that the share stalled and remained more or less flat. This is most likely related to the burst of the New Economy bubble in 2000, but might also indicate that the diffusion of ICT assets in the economy had reached a certain saturation point. In the EU a similar trend can be seen as the share of ICT increased from around 2 per cent in 1980 to around 5 per cent in 1999 and levelled off afterwards. However, in 2005 the EU level was well below the USA and was comparable to the US level at the end of the 1980s. This suggests ample opportunities for catch-up in the use of ICT capital in the EU, although this did not happen in the early 2000s. In 2005, the level of ICT capital services per hour worked in the EU was only about 50 per cent of the US level (see section 6.5).

In Table 5.1, it was shown that the overall contribution of ICT capital has increased in both the EU and the USA. It contributed 0.5 percentage points to aggregate labour productivity growth in the EU

Table 5.3. *Growth of ICT-capital deepening and ICT shares,*
EU and USA

	EU		USA	
	1980–95	1995–2005	1980–95	1995–2005
Average ICT share in aggregate value added (percentage)				
ICT production	0.55	0.72	1.25	1.39
Manufacturing	0.52	0.64	0.58	0.93
Other goods	0.23	0.25	0.21	0.43
Distribution	0.52	0.78	0.70	1.13
Finance & business	1.15	1.86	1.81	2.83
Personal	0.14	0.18	0.12	0.16
Market economy	3.12	4.42	4.67	6.86
Growth in ICT-capital deepening (annual growth)				
ICT production	10.0	9.9	7.6	9.3
Manufacturing	10.7	9.1	17.6	11.4
Other goods	9.0	8.2	19.6	15.0
Distribution	12.5	11.3	20.0	15.5
Finance & business	15.5	14.5	21.0	18.8
Personal	11.8	13.0	15.2	12.0
Market economy	12.6	12.0	16.6	14.9

Source: See Table 5.1.

and even a full percentage point in the USA during the period 1995–
2005. In Tables 5.3 and 5.4, this contribution is broken down to the
industry level to investigate the underlying sources by industry. As
shown in (5.8), the contribution of ICT capital depends on its share in
aggregate value added and its growth rate. These separate component
parts convey interesting information about the changing role of ICT in
economic growth. In the lower part of Table 5.3 we show growth rates
of ICT capital services per hour worked for our six major sectors and
the market economy. In the upper part of the table the share of ICT
compensation in market economy value added is given. These shares
indicate the importance of ICT capital in a sector for the overall market
economy. In Table 5.4 we bring together the results in the previous
table to show the contribution of growth in ICT capital in each sector
to aggregate labour productivity growth.

Table 5.4. *Contribution of industry ICT-capital deepening,*
EU and USA

	EU		USA	
	1980–95	1995–2005	1980–95	1995–2005
Market economy	0.39	0.53	0.78	1.02
Contribution of:				
ICT production	0.06	0.07	0.10	0.13
Manufacturing	0.06	0.06	0.10	0.11
Other goods	0.02	0.02	0.04	0.06
Distribution	0.06	0.09	0.14	0.17
Finance & business	0.18	0.27	0.38	0.53
Personal	0.02	0.02	0.02	0.02

Note: The table gives the contribution of ICT-capital deepening in an industry to aggregate market economy labour productivity growth. This is calculated as the industry growth in ICT capital per hour worked weighted by its share of ICT-capital compensation in aggregate value added given in Table 5.3 (see equation 5.8).
Source: See Table 5.1.

Looking at Table 5.3, it is striking to see that the figures for the EU and USA do not differ by much: ICT-capital deepening has progressed at double-digit growth rates since 1980 in both regions. Although growth has been faster in the USA, the differences are relatively minor. This picture extends quite well to each of the sectors. The fact that ICT-capital service growth is high in both the EU and the USA does not contradict our earlier finding in Table 5.2 that ICT-capital deepening makes a much larger contribution to aggregate labour productivity growth in the USA than it does in the EU. The larger contribution is due to the fact that ICT-capital compensation makes up a much larger share of value added in the USA than in the EU, as shown in Table 5.3. The higher share is due to the fact that the levels of ICT investment in the EU were much lower than in the USA in the period under consideration, although growth rates were high in both regions. Consequently, the absolute gap in ICT-capital intensity increased steadily. Table 5.3 shows that this is true for all sectors except personal services. On average between 1980 and 1995, ICT capital made up only 3.1 per cent of aggregate value added in the EU but 4.7 per cent in the USA. For the 1995–2005 period, the gap grew to more than two percentage points.

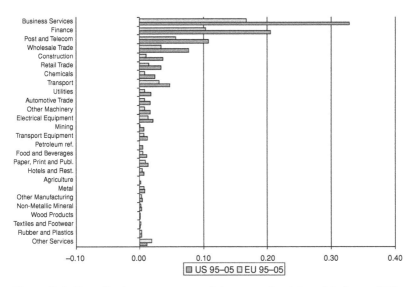

Figure 5.6. Contribution to aggregate labour productivity of industry ICT-capital deepening, EU and USA, 1995–2005. Contributions in percentage points to annual growth rates of value added per hour worked. Industries ranked on difference between EU and USA. (*Source*: See Table 5.1.)

This gap can be found in all of the industry groups and is largest in ICT-producing industries and finance and business services.

By combining ICT-capital deepening with the ICT shares in Table 5.3 as in (5.8), the contribution of ICT-capital deepening in each industry to aggregate labour productivity growth can be derived. The results are shown in Table 5.4. The first row shows the contribution to aggregate labour productivity growth of ICT-capital deepening in all industries. This row is reproduced from the corresponding row in Table 5.1. Subsequent rows decompose the contributions given in the first row by sector. So, for example, the entry 0.27 for financial and business services in the EU for the 1995–2005 period indicates that ICT-capital deepening in this sector contributed 0.27 percentage points to aggregate labour productivity growth in this period. In contrast, ICT-capital deepening in ICT-producing industries contributed only 0.07 percentage points.

In Figure 5.6 the contribution of the twenty-six detailed industries to aggregate growth in the EU and USA during 1995–2005 is given.

Industries are ranked on the difference in EU and US growth rates. This figure shows that only a few industries are responsible for the EU–US gap in the growth contribution from ICT. Together, financial and business services are responsible for more than half of the difference in the contribution of ICT capital to labour productivity growth between the EU and the USA (0.26 percentage points out of 0.49 percentage points difference). The rest is accounted for by the remaining industries. In twenty-three out of twenty-six industries, the contribution of ICT is higher in the USA than in the EU. Nevertheless, the ranking of industries in terms of their contribution is rather similar in both regions. All industries that are near the top of the distribution in the USA are also near the top in the EU. The role of ICT in driving productivity growth is clearly concentrated in market services.

Non-ICT capital

The contribution of ICT capital to aggregate productivity growth has steadily increased over time as indicated above. However, this does not imply that the role of non-ICT assets in production is only minor or eclipsed by the increasing use of ICT assets. On the contrary, the share of non-ICT capital in value added is much higher than that of ICT assets and has been rather stable, hovering around 25 per cent of market economy value added in both the EU and USA since the 1980s (see Figure 5.5). In Table 5.1 it was shown that the contribution of non-ICT to European productivity growth during 1995–2005 was still as high as that of ICT-capital deepening. Rather, the growth in non-ICT assets per hour worked declined in the EU and this provides an important reason for the European growth deceleration. Therefore, we now turn to a discussion of the industry sources of trends in non-ICT assets.

The contribution of non-ICT capital deepening in an industry to aggregate labour productivity growth can be calculated as the growth of non-ICT capital per hour worked in the industry weighted by its share of non-ICT capital compensation in aggregate nominal value added (see equation 5.9). The results are given in Table 5.5 and should be interpreted analogously to the results in Table 5.4 for ICT capital. The first row shows the contribution to aggregate labour productivity growth by non-ICT capital deepening aggregated over all industries. It corresponds to the row 'contribution from non-ICT capital

Table 5.5. *Contribution of industry non-ICT capital deepening,*
EU and USA

	EU		USA	
	1980–95	1995–2005	1980–95	1995–2005
Market economy	0.77	0.54	0.44	0.53
Contribution of:				
ICT production	0.06	0.05	0.06	0.07
Manufacturing	0.27	0.14	0.10	0.11
Other goods	0.23	0.17	0.09	0.11
Distribution	0.11	0.11	0.06	0.07
Finance & business	0.08	0.05	0.13	0.16
Personal	0.02	0.02	0.00	0.01

Note: The table gives the contribution of non-ICT capital deepening in an industry
to aggregate market economy labour productivity growth. This is calculated as the
industry growth in non-ICT capital per hour worked weighted by its share of non-ICT
capital compensation in aggregate value added (see equation 5.9).
Source: See Table 5.1.

deepening' in Table 5.1. Subsequent rows decompose the contributions given in the first row by sector. The results for detailed industries
for the EU are given in Figure 5.7, comparing contributions in the periods 1980–1995 and 1995–2005. Industries are ranked on differences
in growth between the two periods. The striking finding in Figure 5.7
is that the deceleration in non-ICT capital deepening in the EU was
rather pervasive, as contributions after 1995 declined in nineteen out
of twenty-six industries. The contribution of the mining sector, the
most important contributor during the early period, declined dramatically. But also the contribution of business services, another heavy user
of non-ICT capital, diminished. The manufacturing sector was responsible for more than half of the aggregate deceleration and this decline
was widespread across all manufacturing sectors. Only construction
and retailing showed increased contributions.

One interpretation of the decline in contributions after 1995 is that
the possibilities for European catch-up were mostly exhausted by 1995
and that growth had slowed down to a pace more comparable to the
productivity leader. To investigate this hypothesis, relative levels of
capital inputs would be required. These are provided in Chapter 6 and

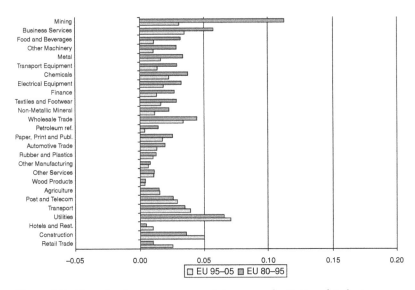

Figure 5.7. Contribution to aggregate labour productivity of industry non-ICT capital deepening, EU, 1980–2005. Contributions in percentage points to annual growth rates of value added per hour worked. Industries ranked on difference between two periods. (*Source*: See Table 5.1.)

indicate that non-ICT capital services per hour worked in the EU rose rapidly during the 1980s and were indeed already above the level in the USA during the early 1990s. This has generally been attributed to higher wages in Europe relative to the USA, leading to a greater degree of substitution capital for labour. As discussed in Chapter 2, moderation in the growth in wages in Europe since the mid 1990s, driving up the relative price of capital, contributed to the cessation of this substitution process. Since the mid 1990s relative levels were more or less stable. In 2005, non-ICT capital services per hour in the EU market economy were about 7 per cent higher than in the USA. This is not true for all sectors. While levels in manufacturing, transport and business services were higher than in the USA, gaps continued to exist in other goods production and in finance and business (see Chapter 6).

In focusing on the slowdown in non-ICT capital deepening in the EU we should not lose sight of the fact that before 1995, non-ICT capital deepening progressed at a much faster pace than in the USA

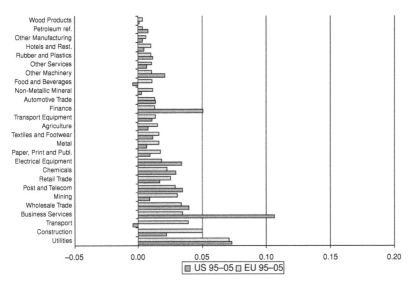

Figure 5.8. Contribution to aggregate labour productivity of industry non-ICT capital deepening, EU and USA, 1995–2005. Contributions in percentage points to annual growth rates of value added per hour worked. Industries ranked on EU. (*Source*: See Table 5.1.)

in most industries. After 1995 the contributions in the EU and USA are much more similar. This becomes especially clear in Figure 5.8, which ranks the contributions to aggregate labour productivity from non-ICT capital deepening for the 1995–2005 period for both regions. While the ranking of industries differs in some cases, contributions in many industries are remarkably close. Utilities, construction, transport services, business services and wholesale trade dominated in both regions.

Changes in the composition of labour

Changes in the composition of labour force are relatively unimportant in terms of explaining the aggregate labour productivity growth differential between the EU and the USA. However, the results at the industry level do point to some noticeable differences between the two regions. The contribution to aggregate labour productivity growth can be calculated as the change in labour services per hour worked in

Table 5.6. *Contribution of change in industry labour composition, EU and USA*

	EU		USA	
	1980–95	1995–2005	1980–95	1995–2005
Market economy	0.30	0.21	0.23	0.30
Contribution of:				
ICT production	0.02	0.01	0.03	0.03
Manufacturing	0.09	0.07	0.07	0.06
Other goods	0.04	0.03	0.04	0.01
Distribution	0.05	0.03	0.04	0.06
Finance & business	0.08	0.06	0.04	0.10
Personal	0.02	0.01	0.00	0.02

Note: The table gives the contribution of change in labour composition in an industry to aggregate market economy labour productivity growth. This is calculated as the industry growth in labour services per hour worked weighted by its share of labour compensation in aggregate value added (see equation 5.10).
Source: See Table 5.1.

an industry weighted by its share of labour compensation in aggregate nominal value added (see equation 5.10). The results are given in Table 5.6 and should be interpreted analogously to the results in Tables 5.4 and 5.5. The first row corresponds to the row 'labour composition' in Table 5.1. Subsequent rows decompose the contributions given in the first row by sector.

Table 5.6 shows that after 1995 the contribution of labour services to aggregate labour productivity growth slowed down in the EU, but increased in the USA. Throughout this period contributions were generally close around 0.3 percentage points. The table shows that between 1980 and 1995, manufacturing in the EU showed particularly large contributions. These are sectors that intensively use craft-level skills, a traditional area of focus of European upskilling. Figure 5.9 provides the contributions of detailed industries for the period 1995–2005, ranked on the contributions in the EU. Business and financial services top the ranking in both regions. In the USA, the contribution of these industries was noticeably higher than in the EU. These industries intensively use university graduates, which has long been an area of strength of the US skill acquisition system.

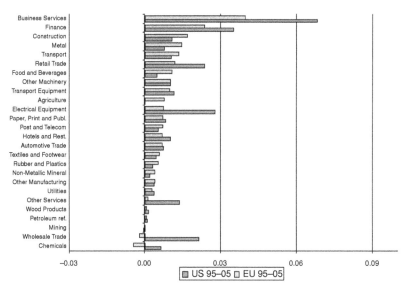

Figure 5.9. Contribution to aggregate labour productivity of industry changes in labour composition, EU and USA, 1995–2005. Contributions in percentage points to annual growth rates of value added per hour worked. Industries ranked on EU. (*Source*: See Table 5.1.)

The earlier lead of the USA in these industries points to possible ICT–skill complementarities as the USA also leads in the use of ICT in these sectors. Indeed, there is ample evidence for the USA to suggest that new technology, and ICT in particular, is complementary (Autor *et al.* 1998; Chun 2003) and recent evidence suggests that some European countries lag behind the USA in this respect (O'Mahony *et al.* 2008). The issue of factor complementarities, which requires factor demand analysis, cannot be handled in a growth accounting framework and so is not pursued further in this chapter.

Beneath these aggregate figures there are other compositional changes that appear to impact on all industries, such as the increasing employment of women and older workers, the latter driven by an aging population, especially in Europe. However, in terms of aggregate labour composition, the impact of age, leading to greater deployment of higher wage workers, and the increasing use of females, who typically earn less than males, tend to counterbalance each other. Hence the trends, and cross-industry variation, tend to be dominated by changes in skill composition. Nevertheless, these worker characteristics are important and there is some evidence that ICT is age-biased against older workers in the 50-plus age groups (O'Mahony and Peng 2008). Daveri and Maliranta (2007) consider Finnish firms located in three distinct sectors, forestry, industrial machinery and electronics. They show that the electronics sector shows a productivity profile that first increases with age but turns negative beyond a certain level of seniority. However, similar profiles are not observed in the other two sectors. They argue that rapid technical progress can accelerate the depreciation of skills that occurs naturally as workers age. Hence there may be variations across industries in the use of older workers that correlate with technology use. Further work is required to gauge the extent of this.

5.5 Multi-factor productivity growth

Although the differences in ICT investment play a major role in explaining the aggregate labour productivity growth differential between the EU and the USA, trends in MFP growth are most important, as shown in Table 5.1. In the period 1980–95, the contribution of MFP was comparable in both regions. But while aggregate MFP growth in the EU strongly decreased after 1995, US growth accelerated. As such, trends in MFP can provide an explanation for both the European slowdown and the US growth resurgence. Which industries were responsible for these trends? To answer this question we first provide an overview of the MFP growth rates by industry before we turn to the contribution of each sector to the aggregate. We start with a focus on the European slowdown. In Figure 5.10, MFP growth rates for detailed market industries in the EU are shown for the periods 1980–95 and 1995–2005. Industries are ranked on growth rates in the early period. MFP growth rates varied widely across the twenty-six industries and closely reflect the patterns in labour productivity shown in Figure 5.1. In the early period the highest growth took place in agriculture, post and telecommunications and various manufacturing industries such as chemicals, electrical equipment and rubber and plastics. In contrast, productivity growth was small or even negative in business services, hotels and restaurants and other personal services. This ranking did change somewhat after 1995 but more or less the same industries were ranked at the top and bottom, except for utilities,

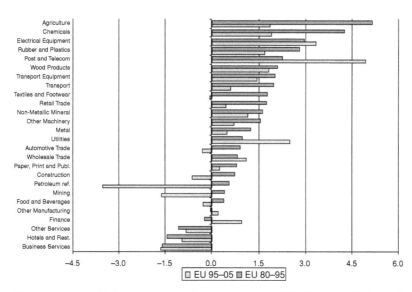

Figure 5.10. Multi-factor productivity growth in the EU, 1980–2005. Annual compound growth rates of multi-factor productivity (value-added based). Industries ranked on differences between growth in two periods. (*Source*: See Table 5.1.)

which improved remarkably, and petroleum refining and mining, in which performance deteriorated strongly. Overall MFP growth rates declined over the two periods in nineteen out of twenty-six industries.

The low MFP growth rates in European industries after 1995 are in stark contrast with developments in the USA. In Figure 5.11 average annual MFP growth rates in the EU and USA for 1995–2005 are compared for detailed industries. In this figure, industries are ranked on growth rates in the EU. The correlation with the ranking in the USA is only weak. In the EU post and telecommunications, electrical equipment manufacturing and utilities topped the ranking. By far, the fastest growing sector in the USA was electrical equipment manufacturing with annual MFP growth of more than 13 per cent, followed by wholesale trade, automotive trade and agriculture. In the EU, various industries had strong negative MFP growth rates, including business services, hotels and restaurants, construction and mining. Construction and mining also showed MFP declines in the USA, but this was not the case in the other industries. During this period, MFP growth

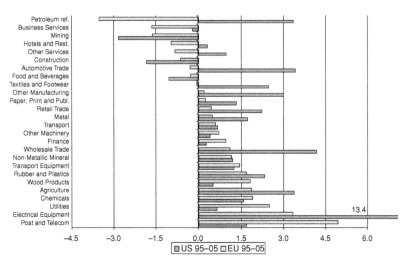

Figure 5.11. Multi-factor productivity growth in the EU and USA, 1995–2005. Annual compound growth rates of multi-factor productivity (value-added based). Industries ranked on growth in EU. (*Source*: See Table 5.1.)

in the EU was higher than in the USA in only ten out of twenty-six industries, including some high-tech manufacturing industries such as chemicals, transport equipment and other machinery.

The impact of MFP growth in an industry on aggregate growth can be determined on the basis of (5.11). The contribution to aggregate labour productivity growth can be calculated as the growth of MFP in an industry weighted by its share in aggregate value added. The results are given in Table 5.7 and should be interpreted analogously to the results in the previous tables. The first row shows the contribution to aggregate labour productivity of MFP growth, aggregated over all industries. It corresponds to the row 'multi-factor productivity' in Table 5.1. Subsequent rows decompose the contributions given in the first row by sector.

Table 5.7 indicates that the slowdown in European multi-factor productivity is not only located in goods-producing sectors, but is also due to a slowdown in efficiency improvements in distribution and transport services. A more detailed analysis reveals that the declining trend was widespread over goods and services industries. In Figure 5.12,

Table 5.7. *Contribution of industry MFP growth, EU and USA*

	EU		USA	
	1980–95	1995–2005	1980–95	1995–2005
Market economy	1.00	0.39	0.78	1.33
Contribution of:				
ICT production	0.18	0.28	0.33	0.54
Manufacturing	0.46	0.17	0.24	0.25
Other goods	0.32	0.05	0.18	−0.11
Distribution	0.31	0.13	0.42	0.60
Finance & business	−0.18	−0.16	−0.46	0.00
Personal	−0.08	−0.07	0.06	0.06

Note: The table gives the contribution of MFP growth in an industry to aggregate market economy labour productivity growth. This is calculated as the industry value-added based MFP growth weighted by its share of value added in aggregate value added (see equation 5.11).
Source: See Table 5.1.

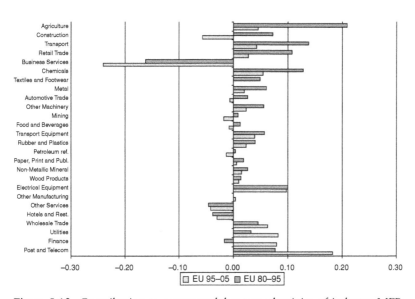

Figure 5.12. Contribution to aggregate labour productivity of industry MFP growth, EU, 1980–2005. Contributions in percentage points to annual growth rates of value added per hour worked. Industries ranked on difference between two periods. (*Source*: See Table 5.1.)

industries are ranked on the difference in their contribution between 1980–95 and 1995–2005. The biggest contributors to the decline are other-goods producing industries (agriculture and construction, but not mining). During 1980–95, these industries were strong drivers of aggregate MFP growth, contributing 0.8 percentage points, but during 1995–2005 their contribution was a mere 0.2 percentage points. The next three biggest contributors to the decline were services industries (transport, retail and business services). There was also a declining trend in most manufacturing industries, especially in chemicals, textiles and metals. Only the contribution of the post and telecommunications sector improved significantly over time. As discussed in Chapter 2, this broad-based decline might be due to a combination of exhausted potential for catch-up growth in traditional goods industries and increasing global competition in low- and medium-tech manufacturing.

In contrast to Europe, MFP growth in the USA accelerated in many industries, especially in market services. Whereas their combined contribution was about nil in the early period, market services contributed half of US MFP growth in the later period. This was mainly concentrated in the distribution sector as wholesale, retail and automotive trade ranked second, third and fourth during 1995–2005, together contributing 0.58 percentage points. Compared to Europe, their contribution to aggregate growth was 0.50 points higher, explaining more than half of the EU–US difference in MFP growth. In addition, the contribution from the largest single driver of MFP growth, electrical equipment manufacturing, increased even further to 0.54 percentage points in the USA, while only contributing 0.10 points in the EU. Together with the trade industries, superior performance in this sector can fully explain the EU–US MFP growth gap during 1995–2005. Figure 5.13 provides a detailed analysis for the period 1995–2005, ranking industries on the basis of the difference in growth between the EU and the USA. Interestingly, financial and business services combined did not contribute to aggregate MFP growth in either region. But while this sector was a large drag on aggregate MFP growth in the USA in the early period, this was no longer true in the later period. In contrast, this sector continued to contribute negatively to European productivity growth after 1995, adding another 0.16 percentage points to the EU–US growth gap. This was overridingly due to weak performance in European business services. The decline in MFP levels in this sector in

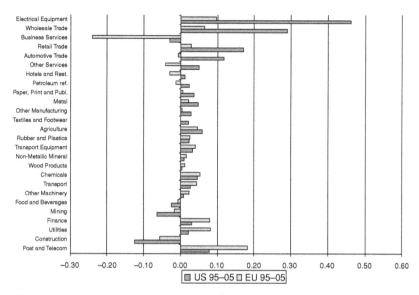

Figure 5.13. Contribution to aggregate labour productivity of industry MFP growth, EU and USA, 1995–2005. Contributions in percentage points to annual growth rates of value added per hour worked. Industries ranked on difference between EU and USA. (*Source*: See Table 5.1.)

the 1980s even accelerated after 1995. Measured MFP growth in the finance sector was only small in both regions and did not contribute much to aggregate growth, although the sector had grown rapidly in size.

5.6 Patterns of growth: yeast versus mushrooms

With the availability of more industry-level data, an increasingly detailed picture of the patterns and sources of growth has become feasible. At the same time, there is a need to find insightful ways to summarise the wealth of industry detail. The most straightforward approach is to aggregate industries into larger groups and analyse the performance of these groups as a whole. However, by doing this we run the risk of missing possibly sizeable within-group heterogeneity. Alternatively, one can provide graphs with detailed industry data, as we have also done in the first part of this chapter. But these graphs do not provide a clear interpretation of the overall growth process. So to complement our discussion we use, in this section, the Harberger diagram as a way to characterise the growth pattern of all industries (Harberger 1998). Specifically, we use these diagrams and a number of summary statistics to characterise how widespread (yeast-like) or localised (mushroom-like) are capital deepening and productivity growth.

These Harberger diagrams can be used to shed light on some of the hypotheses about productivity growth in the USA and other countries that have circulated in recent years. At various points, it has been suggested that the acceleration of US labour productivity growth and/or the difference with other countries can be traced mostly to ICT production, the strong performance of a small number of ICT-using industries or a broad set of services industries. Harberger diagrams provide an intuitive and standardised way to determine how widespread growth and changes in growth are within an economy. They can also be used to determine how evenly new technology spreads across an economy. For instance, below we use Harberger diagrams to analyse whether ICT capital is growing at similar or very different rates across industries.

The Harberger diagram provides a convenient graphical summary of the industry pattern of growth. The diagram shows the cumulative contribution of the industries to aggregate growth on the y-axis and the cumulative share of these industries on the x-axis. It is based on a dataset of industries and their contributions to aggregate growth, calculated as outlined in section 5.2. The industries are first ranked by growth rate to ensure a concave diagram, so the fastest growing industries are to be found near the origin. The resulting pattern can have a more yeasty or more mushroom-like character, depending on the number of industries contributing positively to aggregate growth and the distribution of growth rates. Growth is yeasty when it is broad-based and takes place in many industries or firms. Mushroom-like growth indicates a pattern in which only a limited number of industries contribute positively to aggregate growth.[3]

For illustration purposes, Figure 5.14 shows two examples of Harberger diagrams. For easy comparison, the sum of the industry contributions is the same for both diagrams, implying equal aggregate

---

[3] The analogy with yeast and mushrooms comes from the fact that yeast causes bread to expand slowly and evenly, while mushrooms are scattered and pop up almost overnight, in a fashion that is not easy to predict (Harberger 1998).

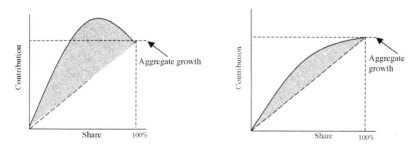

Figure 5.14. Examples of Harberger diagrams.

growth. The diagram on the left is an example of mushroom-type growth. Not all industries have positive growth, as the downward-sloping part of the diagram implies some industries have negative growth. The diagram on the right is an example of more yeasty, balanced growth. It is closer to the straight diagonal line, so the growth rates of the industries are relatively close to each other and, in addition, all industries have positive growth.

Diagrams such as these can be useful in quickly identifying how important certain industries are in achieving growth. To compare diagrams of different shapes and with different levels of aggregate growth, Inklaar and Timmer (2007a) devised some useful summary statistics of the Harberger diagram. Figure 5.14 illustrates that the general shape of the diagram can be summarised by three statistics, namely:

(1) aggregate growth, which is the sum of industry contributions
(2) the cumulative share of industries with positive contributions, as an indicator of the pervasiveness of growth[4]
(3) the curvature as measured by the area between the diagram and the diagonal line (the shaded areas in Figure 5.14) divided by the total area beneath the diagram; this relative area measure lies between 0 and 1; it is 0 when all industries have equal growth; when

---

[4] Harberger (1998) stresses the importance of the shares of industries that together make up aggregate growth. In other words, he focuses on the crossing of the aggregate growth line in Figure 5.14. We feel that a split between industries with positive growth and those with negative growth is a more natural distinction.

Table 5.8. *Patterns of market economy MFP growth, 1980–2005*

	Aggregate MFP growth		Percentage of industries with positive MFP growth		Relative area under Harberger	
	1980–95	1995–2005	1980–95	1995–2005	1980–95	1995–2005
Austria	1.3	1.1	81	74	0.41	0.53
Belgium	0.7	0.0	63	39	0.61	0.99
Denmark	1.1	0.1	73	53	0.54	0.93
Finland	1.4	2.6	73	91	0.43	0.39
France	1.3	0.8	68	56	0.55	0.58
Germany	0.8	0.3	73	59	0.50	0.81
Italy	0.8	−0.7	65	29	0.62	0.56
Netherlands	0.4	1.0	64	63	0.75	0.53
Spain	0.6	−0.9	63	23	0.71	0.49
Sweden	1.7	1.6	68	59	0.64	0.51
United Kingdom	1.6	0.9	74	78	0.40	0.44
European Union	1.0	0.4	73	59	0.47	0.69
USA	0.7	1.3	61	73	0.63	0.48

Note: Harberger summary statistics; see main text.
Source: See Table 5.1.

industry growth rates start to diverge, the relative area increases to a maximum of 1.[5]

In Table 5.8 we report aggregate MFP growth, the share of industries with positive MFP growth and the relative area underneath the Harberger diagram for European countries and the USA before and after 1995. The column with aggregate MFP growth shows the familiar picture of a decline in MFP growth in most European countries and an increase in the United States. What is novel is that in many cases the decline in aggregate MFP growth coincides with an increase in the number of industries showing declines in MFP. To illustrate:

---

[5] In practice, the diagrams are not smooth as in Figure 5.15, as we have a discrete number of industries. Instead, they consist of piecewise linear plots. This means that the area underneath the diagram can be calculated as the sum of triangles and squares.

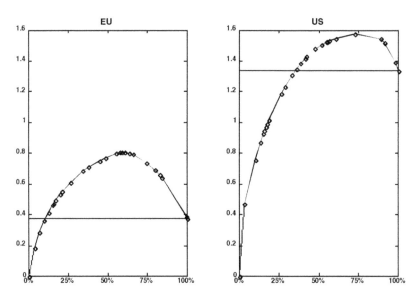

Figure 5.15. Harberger diagrams of market economy MFP growth in the EU and USA, 1995–2005. (*Source*: See Table 5.1.)

before 1995, almost three-quarters of the industries in Europe had positive MFP growth, while after 1995 this share had dropped below 60 per cent. Furthermore, the relative-area statistic increased from 0.5 to 0.7, implying that growth had become more concentrated among a few industries, i.e. had become more mushroom-like. MFP growth in the USA is marked by the reverse pattern: increasing aggregate growth, a larger share of industries with positive MFP growth and a more yeast-like pattern as evidenced by the decline in relative area. This is not a uniform relationship though. For instance, in Spain, MFP growth declined (and even became negative), but the relative area declined as well, implying a broad-based decline. MFP growth in Belgium after 1995 also stands out: while aggregate growth is zero, almost 40 per cent of industries had positive MFP growth. This is also an illustration of extremely mushroom-like growth as the relative area is almost 1. In other words, each of these three statistics conveys distinct information about the patterns of growth across industries.

Figure 5.15 shows the MFP Harberger diagrams for the period 1995–2005 for Europe and the USA. European growth is characterised

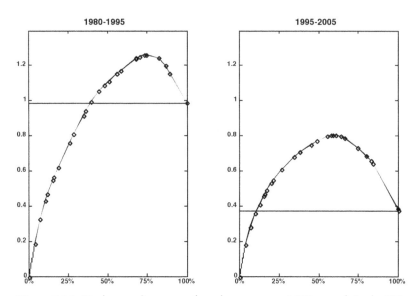

Figure 5.16. Harberger diagrams of market economy MFP growth in the EU, 1980–95 and 1995–2005. (*Source*: See Table 5.1.)

by a mix of industries contributing positively and negatively to aggregate growth. In the USA, the MFP growth process is clearly more yeast-like with only a few industries showing negative growth and the positive contributions adding up to almost 1.6 per cent. These diagrams therefore suggest that the growth gap between Europe and the USA is broad-based: numerous industries show positive growth in the USA and negative growth in Europe. The alternative would have been a more mushroom-like pattern, for instance if the growth gap could have been fully attributed to a larger contribution from a limited set of industries like ICT production and retail trade.

Figure 5.16 shows the pattern of the European MFP slowdown after 1995 in Harberger diagrams for both periods. A common factor in both periods is the large negative contribution from business services (the rightmost industry in the diagram in both periods). However, for the 1980–95 period, the contribution was smaller since the average value added share of business services was only 10 per cent rather than the 15 per cent for 1995–2005. In addition though, the 1995–2005 period shows considerably more industries with MFP declines.

These declines show up in some manufacturing industries but also in construction and motor vehicle trade. In contrast, growth held up well in some industries, such as ICT manufacturing, telecommunication services and utilities. The result of this is a more mushroom-like MFP growth process.

The Harberger tool can be used in analysing more than just the industry pattern of MFP growth. Indeed, another useful application is analysing industry investment patterns. The theory of general-purpose technologies (for example, Bresnahan and Trajtenberg 1995) suggests that a new technology spreads across the economy as the new technology becomes cheaper and more industries have invested in the complementary assets. During this initial adoption phase, it might be expected that the industry pattern of ICT-capital growth would be mushroom-like, as some industries are new and rapidly adopting the new technology, while other industries, which have already been through this phase, are on a more gradual expansion path for their ICT-capital stock, based on the continued cost declines of those assets. On the other hand, once all industries have started using ICT and are past the initial adoption phase, we would expect a very yeast-like process. Figure 5.17 shows the Harberger diagrams for ICT-capital growth in Europe and the USA, for the period 1995–2005. In both regions, growth in ICT capital is very yeast-like. Indeed, the relative-area statistic is 0.13 in Europe and 0.14 in the USA. Also, all industries in the USA have positive ICT-capital growth and all but one have positive growth in Europe. In other words, all industries have gone through an initial adoption period and are now steadily expanding their ICT-capital stocks. This does not mean that ICT is equally important in all industries, but it does mean that given differences in investment rates, the growth rates are very similar.

In summary we would argue that the Harberger diagram provides a useful additional tool to explore growth of productivity or other variables and provides an illuminating summary description of the growth process.

5.7 Concluding remarks

In this chapter we considered the contribution of industries to aggregate growth based on an in-depth analysis of data for twenty-six industries. Rather than looking at broad industry groups, we have analysed

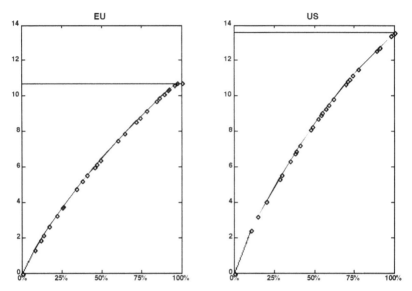

Figure 5.17. Harberger diagrams of market economy ICT capital growth in the EU and USA, 1995–2005. (*Source*: See Table 5.1.)

trends in input use and productivity growth across all industries to get a more precise insight into the reasons for the European slowdown since the mid 1990s and for the growth gap with the USA that has opened up since then.

In line with our findings in Chapter 4, we find a pervasive trend of increasing use of ICT capital and skilled labour over time in all industries, both the EU and the USA. Europe lags the USA in this respect, as in twenty-four out of twenty-six industries, the contribution of ICT was higher in the USA than in the EU during the period 1995–2005. This is driven by differences between the two regions in the shares of ICT in output, rather than by differences in growth rates. This in turn reflects the earlier adoption of this technology in the USA. Nevertheless, the ranking of industries in terms of their contribution is rather similar in the two regions. Changes in labour composition in the period from 1995 are highest in industries that intensively use high-skilled labour, such as business and financial services, and the contribution from this source of growth is noticeably higher in the USA than in Europe. These findings are consistent with a large literature that emphasises the complementarity between ICT and skilled labour.

At the same time, by sharpening the picture we also find that aggregate trends conceal much heterogeneity among the industries. The European labour productivity growth slowdown after 1995 was widespread and took place in twenty out of twenty-six industries. Growth rates only increased substantially in post and telecommunications, utilities and finance. All manufacturing industries (except other manufacturing) experienced a strong slowdown in labour productivity growth due to slower increases in capital intensity and MFP. While in the past, increases in the use of capital per hour worked were a major driver of growth, this was no longer the case as contributions declined strongly in all manufacturing industries. In addition to lacklustre investment, improvements in the efficiency with which labour and capital were used also faltered as MFP growth rates declined in almost all manufacturing industries. Declines were especially strong in technologically less sophisticated industries such as textiles, paper and food manufacturing, but also took place in more high-tech industries such as chemicals and transport equipment. Only in electrical equipment manufacturing did MFP growth rates improve. The pervasive nature of the manufacturing slowdown suggests that economy-wide factors may be important, especially the moderation of wage growth in Europe following the implementation of policies to raise the employment rate and the consequent reduction in incentives to substitute capital for labour.[6] Low- and medium-tech manufacturing also suffered from global competition from new EU member states and the emerging economies, especially India and China.

In addition to manufacturing, agriculture, mining and construction were important sources of growth in Europe before 1995, but growth also faltered in these sectors. In mining the declining contribution is related to a sharp downfall in the contribution of capital. Lower contributions from agriculture are an echo of the end of the rationalisation process and depletion of catch-up potential in most European countries as indicated by faltering MFP growth. Construction was one of the few goods-producing industries in which employment actually increased in the 1990s and this building boom led to a decline in efficiency as MFP growth even became negative.

[6] See Dew-Becker and Gordon (2008) for more evidence on this.

As discussed before, the European slowdown is all the more surprising given the acceleration in the US economy. During the period 1995–2005, labour productivity growth was higher in the USA in nineteen out of twenty-six industries and this was mainly due to higher contributions from ICT capital (twenty-three industries) and from MFP (sixteen industries). The analysis using Harberger diagrams highlights the different industry patterns of growth in the two regions. While MFP growth in the EU manifests as a mushroom pattern with positive contributions concentrated in a few sectors, positive MFP growth in the USA was more widespread across industries, showing a more yeast-like pattern. Weighted by shares in value added, the EU–US aggregate growth difference is mainly due to smaller contributions from electrical equipment manufacturing, business services and automotive, wholesale and retail trade services. The gap in electrical equipment manufacturing is fully due to much higher rates of innovation in the USA as indicated by superior MFP growth. Higher growth contributions from trade industries in the USA are related to higher use of ICT and in particular faster technological change than in the EU. Business services in the EU experienced strong increases in employment and high levels of investment, but the efficiency with which they were being used declined, as indicated by negative MFP growth. In contrast, rapid investment in both ICT and non-ICT capital in the USA took place while efficiency was maintained.

All in all, this chapter has demonstrated that a detailed industry analysis is an important first step in understanding sources of comparative growth. The subsequent chapters provide additional analysis of the determinants of slow productivity growth in Europe.

Appendix

Table 5A.1. *Growth accounts by industry, EU, 1980–2005*

Industry	EU KLEMS code	1980–1995					1995–2005				
				Contributions from					Contributions from		
		Labour productivity	Labour composition	ICT capital per hour	Non-ICT capital per hour	Multi-factor productivity per hour	Labour productivity	Labour composition	ICT capital per hour	Non-ICT capital per hour	Multi-factor productivity per hour
Agriculture	A–B	5.8	0.3	0.0	0.5	5.2	3.0	0.3	0.0	0.6	1.8
Mining	C	6.6	0.3	0.2	5.7	0.4	1.3	0.0	0.2	2.8	−1.6
Food and beverages	15–16	2.1	0.3	0.3	1.1	0.4	0.7	0.4	0.2	0.4	−0.3
Textiles and footwear	17–19	3.4	0.4	0.2	1.1	1.8	1.6	0.4	0.2	0.9	−0.1
Wood products	20	2.9	0.1	0.1	0.6	2.1	2.8	0.1	0.2	0.6	1.8
Paper, print and publ.	21–22	2.5	0.1	0.4	1.1	0.8	1.9	0.3	0.5	0.8	0.3
Petroleum ref.	23	3.4	0.1	0.5	2.4	0.6	−2.3	0.2	0.1	1.0	−3.5
Chemicals	24	5.9	0.2	0.3	1.2	4.2	2.8	−0.2	0.3	0.8	1.9
Rubber and plastics	25	4.1	0.3	0.2	0.9	2.8	3.0	0.4	0.3	0.7	1.7
Non-metallic mineral	26	3.4	0.3	0.2	1.4	1.6	2.6	0.3	0.2	0.9	1.1
Metal	27–28	2.3	0.3	0.1	0.7	1.2	1.4	0.4	0.2	0.4	0.5
Other machinery	29	2.9	0.4	0.3	0.8	1.5	1.7	0.3	0.3	0.3	0.7
Electrical Equipment	30–33	4.9	0.4	0.4	1.0	3.0	4.9	0.3	0.6	0.6	3.3

(*cont.*)

Table 5A.1. (*cont.*)

Industry	EU KLEMS code	1980–1995 Labour productivity	1980–1995 Contributions from: Labour composition	1980–1995 ICT capital per hour	1980–1995 Non-ICT capital per hour	1980–1995 Multi-factor productivity	1995–2005 Labour productivity	1995–2005 Contributions from: Labour composition	1995–2005 ICT capital per hour	1995–2005 Non-ICT capital per hour	1995–2005 Multi-factor productivity
Transport equipment	34–35	4.0	0.6	0.2	1.0	2.0	2.6	0.4	0.3	0.5	1.4
Other manufacturing	36–37	1.2	0.4	0.2	0.6	0.0	1.4	0.3	0.3	0.5	0.2
Utilities	E	3.6	0.3	0.4	2.0	1.0	5.1	0.1	0.3	2.2	2.5
Construction	F	1.3	0.1	0.1	0.4	0.7	0.2	0.2	0.1	0.5	−0.6
Automotive trade	50	2.0	0.2	0.2	0.7	0.9	0.9	0.3	0.3	0.5	−0.3
Wholesale trade	51	2.2	0.1	0.5	0.8	0.8	2.3	0.0	0.6	0.6	1.1
Retail trade	52	2.3	0.3	0.1	0.2	1.7	1.3	0.2	0.2	0.4	0.4
Hotels and rest.	H	−1.0	0.3	0.1	0.2	−1.4	−0.3	0.2	0.1	0.3	−1.0
Transport	60–63	3.0	0.3	0.3	0.5	2.0	1.8	0.2	0.4	0.6	0.6
Post and telecom.	64	4.6	0.2	1.3	0.8	2.2	7.6	0.2	1.6	0.8	4.9
Finance	J	1.4	0.3	1.1	0.4	−0.2	2.6	0.3	1.2	0.2	1.0
Business services	71–74	0.1	0.5	0.6	0.6	−1.6	−0.2	0.3	0.9	0.2	−1.7
Other services	O	−0.1	0.4	0.3	0.3	−1.1	−0.2	0.0	0.3	0.2	−0.8

Notes: Growth accounting decomposition of labour productivity growth (annual compound growth rates) by industry. Numbers may not sum exactly because of rounding.
Source: See Table 5.1.

6 | *Productivity levels and convergence*

6.1 Introduction

When analysing cross-country patterns, growth accounts provide only a partial analysis. It is now widely accepted that understanding the pattern of cross-country growth and productivity requires estimates of relative levels. Models in the technology-gap tradition consider technological effort as the main determinant of income differences between countries and international technology diffusion as the driving force for catch-up. The rate of catch-up of one country with another depends upon the two forces of innovation and imitation. Innovation refers to the creation of new technologies unknown to the world and imitation refers to the spillover of existing technologies from leading to following countries. The larger the distance from the world technology frontier, the higher the rate of diffusion to a follower might be. But the cost of imitation rises as the pool of non-copied ideas becomes smaller and the potential for growth decreases. The effectiveness of educational systems, technology policies and market regulation might thus crucially depend on the distance to the technology frontier (Fagerberg 1994).[1] In the same vein, Aghion and Howitt (2006) suggest that the post-World War II catch-up of European economies to the USA has slowed down as the technology gap with the USA has narrowed. Policies and institutions which facilitated imitation of technologies in the past are not well suited for growth close to the technology frontier. The latter should be based on innovation in a competitive market environment and rooted in a country's own resources such as skilled labour and research and development. Studies on the impact of these drivers of

---

[1] This advantage of backwardness was first formulated by Gerschenkron (1962), referring to Veblen. Abramovitz (1989) provides a broader discussion of the conditions for catch-up and Fagerberg (1994) provides an overview of the early literature.

economic growth rely heavily on level measures of multi-factor productivity to indicate the distance of a country to the technology frontier.[2]

Comparisons of input and productivity levels also provide new insights into the differences in production structures across countries, such as in the use of ICT capital or energy inputs. For example, it is often hypothesised that capital–labour ratios in Europe were much higher than in the USA because of higher wage–rental ratios (see Chapter 2). They also figure prominently in cross-country studies of technology spillovers, multi-sector growth and dynamic models of trade.[3] Inklaar and Timmer (2008b) provided the first comprehensive set of comparative productivity levels at the industry level for a large set of OECD countries that allow such analyses, in the form of the GGDC Productivity Level database. It is based on a new set of purchasing power parities (PPPs) for both output and intermediate inputs at the detailed industry level. In addition, novel measures of labour and capital inputs are used that take account of differences in the composition of each input, such as different levels of skills or types of capital goods such as ICT and other assets. We drew extensively on this database in our analysis of comparative EU–US performance in Chapter 2 and again use it extensively here.

In this chapter we describe the main features of the level accounting methodology and data sources employed by Inklaar and Timmer (2008b) to construct the GGDC Productivity Level database. We also provide various applications to illustrate its usefulness and the importance of having industry-specific measures of productivity and prices that are rooted in neo-classical theory. Section 6.2 describes the methodology for comparing levels of output, input and productivity across countries. The basic methodology, grounded in neo-classical production theory, has a long history but has never been comprehensively applied in a large cross-country setting, mainly because of a lack of suitable data. In section 6.3 we describe the basic data sources used to implement this methodology and discuss the concepts of sectoral output and input and purchasing power parities that play a pivotal role. Section 6.4 provides a comparison of the crude productivity level

---

[2] See, for example, Nicoletti and Scarpetta (2003), Griffith *et al.* (2004), Cameron *et al.* (2005), Vandenbussche *et al.* (2006) and Inklaar *et al.* (2008).
[3] See, for example, Keller (2002), Aghion and Howitt (2006) and Restuccia *et al.* (2008).

measures, previously used in the literature, and the new more data-intensive measures. The reliability of the new estimates is discussed in section 6.5. In section 6.6 we present productivity level comparisons for 2005 between the EU and the USA, and a breakdown of the gaps in labour productivity at a detailed industry level. Section 6.7 provides a convergence analysis and illustrates the importance of having industry-level measures of productivity. Based on technology-gap models we investigate possible determinants of productivity growth in section 6.8. Section 6.9 concludes.

6.2 Level accounting methodology

In this section we present our methodology for comparing levels of output, input and productivity across countries, so-called 'level accounting'. The methodology for level accounting is akin to the methodology for growth accounting discussed in Chapter 3. Instead of comparing two points in time, as in growth accounting, we compare two countries at a similar point in time (Caves *et al.* 1982a).[4] Jorgenson and Nishimizu (1978) were the first to apply bilateral production models to cross-country comparisons based on value added. The bilateral gross output model was first used by Jorgenson, Kuroda and Nishimizu (1987). Caves *et al.* (1982b) provide an index procedure for making transitive multilateral productivity comparisons. Empirical applications in a large cross-country setting have been scarce, mainly because of a lack of suitable data. Christensen *et al.* (1981) is an early example, providing relative MFP levels at the aggregate level for the G7 countries (updated in Jorgenson and Yip 2001), and Schreyer (2008) is a more recent one. At the industry level, applications of this methodology to small sets of countries can be found in, for example, van Ark and Pilat (1993), O'Mahony (1999), Lee and Tang (2000), Inklaar and Timmer (2007b) and Jorgenson and Nomura (2007).

As we are trying to construct a consistent set of productivity measures for a large number of countries and industries at the same time, various choices have to be made not only concerning the use of particular index number formulas, but also about their actual

---

[4] Level accounting is also known as development accounting (see, for example, Caselli 2005). We keep to the term 'level accounting' as it most clearly indicates both the difference from and the similarity with growth accounting.

implementation. In this section the basic methodology is laid out. This essentially consists of two steps. In the first step, PPPs for output, capital, labour and intermediate inputs for twenty-nine industries are derived based on data for forty-five sub-industries. This is done with the price variant of the multilateral index number approach introduced by Caves *et al.* (1982b) (and also known as the CCD method). These PPPs are used to implicitly derive quantities of all inputs (capital, labour and intermediate inputs) and output. In the second step, productivity comparisons are made for each industry on the basis of input and output quantities in a bilateral Törnqvist model following Diewert (1976) and Jorgenson and Nishimizu (1978). This approach is also known as primal level accounting.[5] In this section we first outline our basic methodology for measuring productivity; this is followed by our approach to deriving PPPs for outputs and inputs. Our general notation is as follows. Variable *V* indicates values in current national prices and *PPP* indicates a relative price index across two countries. Superscripts indicate the type of output or inputs, and subscripts indicate industry *j*, country *c* and time *t*. However, wherever possible we leave out the subscripts for industry and time to avoid notational cluttering.

Multi-factor productivity

As in Chapter 3, we assume a gross output production function where output *Y* is given as a function of intermediate inputs *X*, capital services *K*, labour services *L* and technology *T* as before. Following Jorgenson Kuroda and Nishimizu (1987), we define a bilateral translog index of difference in multi-factor productivity between two

---

[5] Comparisons of multi-factor productivity can be made using the so-called 'primal' and 'dual' approaches. In the primal approach, relative MFP levels are based on comparisons of quantities as is also the case here. Alternatively, in the dual approach they are based on comparisons of prices. Usually, productivity measures are expressed in terms of relative quantities, as this is most closely related to the notion of production as a physical process in which quantities of inputs are converted into quantities of outputs. In theory, the two different estimates should be close, but in practice this is not always the case, in particular when production structures differ considerably between the two countries being compared. We opt for the primal approach as we are interested in a full and consistent decomposition of output quantities, rather than output prices.

countries.[6] Under the assumptions of competitive factor markets, full input utilisation and constant returns to scale and using the translog functional form common in such analyses, we can define the level of multi-factor productivity in country c relative to the USA (A_c^Y) as follows:

$$\ln A_c^Y \equiv \ln \frac{Y_c}{Y_{US}} - \overline{w}_X^Y \ln \frac{X_c}{X_{US}} - \overline{w}_K^Y \ln \frac{K_c}{K_{US}} - \overline{w}_L^Y \ln \frac{L_c}{L_{US}} \qquad (6.1)$$

where the weights $\overline{w}$ are defined as the share of each input in nominal gross output averaged over the two countries. The value share of each input is defined as

$$w_{X,c}^Y = \frac{p_c^X X_c}{p_c^Y Y_c}$$

$$w_{K,c}^Y = \frac{p_c^K K_c}{p_c^Y Y_c} \qquad (6.2)$$

$$w_{L,c}^Y = \frac{p_c^L L_c}{p_c^Y Y_c}$$

and the country average shares as

$$\overline{w}_X^Y = 0.5^*\left(w_{X,c}^Y + w_{X,US}^Y\right)$$
$$\overline{w}_K^Y = 0.5^*\left(w_{K,c}^Y + w_{K,US}^Y\right) \qquad (6.3)$$
$$\overline{w}_L^Y = 0.5^*\left(w_{L,c}^Y + w_{L,US}^Y\right)$$

such that they sum to unity. The measure of multi-factor productivity defined in (6.1) is an indicator of the difference in the level of technology between country c and the USA. As it is based on the gross output concept, it treats all inputs symmetrically and does not put additional restrictions on the nature of the technology difference. Our models of production are bilateral and involve comparisons of a country c with the USA as base. We chose the USA as the base country as these comparisons generally generate the highest interest, the USA being the overall productivity leader. Alternative bilateral comparisons, with other countries as the base, can be made using the same

---

[6] Jorgenson and Nishimizu (1978) were the first to apply bilateral production models to cross-country comparisons based on value added. The gross output model was first used by Jorgenson, Kuroda and Nishimizu (1987).

approach by simply replacing the USA by another base country in the formulas given above.[7]

In many applications, multi-factor productivity is measured on the basis of a more restrictive value-added function (A_c^Z). Under the necessary conditions for producer equilibrium in each country, this index is defined for a country c as follows:

$$\ln A_c^Z \equiv \ln \frac{Z_c}{Z_{US}} - \overline{w}_K^Z \ln \frac{K_c}{K_{US}} - \overline{w}_L^Z \ln \frac{L_c}{L_{US}} \tag{6.4}$$

where the weights $\overline{w}^Z$ are defined as the share of each factor input in nominal value added averaged over the two countries. The value share of each input is defined as

$$
\begin{aligned}
w_{K,c}^Z &= \frac{p_c^K K_c}{p_c^Z Z_c} \\
w_{L,c}^Z &= \frac{p_c^L L_c}{p_c^Z Z_c}
\end{aligned}
\tag{6.5}
$$

and the country average shares as

$$
\begin{aligned}
\overline{w}_K^Z &= 0.5^*\left(w_{K,c}^Z + w_{K,US}^Z\right) \\
\overline{w}_L^Z &= 0.5^*\left(w_{L,c}^Z + w_{L,US}^Z\right)
\end{aligned}
\tag{6.6}
$$

Since we assume constant returns to scale, the shares of labour and capital compensation in value added sum to unity.

The formulas indicate that comparable volume measures of output and inputs for the countries are needed. When a single output or input is compared, physical measures, such as numbers of cars produced or hours worked, are possible. However, comparisons at the industry or aggregate level require quantity indices to be calculated implicitly by the ratio of the nominal values and the relevant price indices. This is usually done with a purchasing power parity (PPP) that indicates the

---

[7] The disadvantage of using bilateral models is that the level comparisons do not satisfy transitivity. Alternatively, one can use the multilateral approach advocated by Caves *et al.* (1982b), who derive translog multilateral productivity indices that satisfy the transitivity requirement. The main reason not to opt for a multilateral approach is that this does not provide a consistent decomposition of relative output in terms of relative inputs and MFP levels. This is an important disadvantage given our interest in such decompositions; see the discussion later in this chapter.

price of output or input in one country relative to another country. The value-added volume index for country c is given by

$$Z_c = \frac{V_c^Z}{PPP_c^Z} \qquad (6.7)$$

where V_c^Z is nominal value added in country c at national prices and PPP_c^Z the price of value added in country c relative to that in the USA. A volume index of labour services is given by

$$L_c = \frac{V_c^L}{PPP_c^L} \qquad (6.8)$$

with V_c^L the value of labour compensation in country c (at current national prices) and PPP_c^L the price of labour services in country c relative to that in the USA. And similarly for aggregate capital input in country c:

$$K_c = \frac{V_c^K}{PPP_c^K} \qquad (6.9)$$

with V_c^K the nominal value of capital compensation in country c and PPP_c^K the relative price of capital services in country c. It is important to note here that the measure of K will crucially depend on the approach taken to measuring capital services. In the ex-post approach it will be the same measure as used as the weight in (6.4). In the so-called hybrid approach followed by Inklaar and Timmer (2008b), V_c^K will be based on ex-ante measures of rates of return and be different from this weight (see section 6.4 for further discussion).

The PPPs for outputs and inputs required in (6.7)–(6.9) are derived on the basis of detailed sets of output and input prices.[8] Prices are aggregated using the multilateral translog price indices introduced by Caves *et al.* (1982b) (CCD indices). In this methodology an artificial country is created by averaging over all countries in the dataset, and this constructed country is used as a bridge when making binary comparisons between two countries. This creates so-called transitive PPPs that are base-country independent. As with our MFP indices, the PPPs

---

[8] We aggregate over prices rather than over quantities as variation in prices across countries is much less than variation in quantities (see also Allen and Diewert 1981).

are normalised with the USA at unity. This is further discussed in section 6.3.

Labour and capital volume indices grounded in production theory should take into account the composition of each factor input, such as different levels of skills or types of capital goods, in particular ICT versus non-ICT assets. For labour, this can be achieved by deflation with an appropriate PPP (PPP_c^L) based on relative wages of each labour type l, as follows:

$$\ln PPP_c^L = \sum_l \overline{w}_l^L \left[\ln PPP_{l,c}^L - \overline{\ln PPP_l^L} \right] \tag{6.10}$$

where the bar in the last term indicates a geometric average over all countries indexed by c running from 1 to N, and N is the number of countries. $\overline{\ln PPP_l^L} = 1/N \sum_c \ln PPP_{l,c}^L$ and $\overline{w}_l^L$ is the average weight of labour type l defined as $\overline{w}_l^L = \frac{1}{2}[w_{l,c}^L + \Sigma_c(w_{l,c}^L/N)]$ with $w_{l,c}^L$ the share of labour type l in total labour compensation in country c: $w_{l,c}^L = V_{l,c}^L/V_c^L$. The PPP for each labour type is derived on the basis of relative wages as described in section 6.3.

The derivation of an appropriate capital PPP is similar to that of a labour PPP. Suppose one has a PPP for each capital asset type k, then the aggregate capital PPP is given by:

$$\ln PPP_c^K = \sum_k \overline{w}_k^K \left[\ln PPP_{k,c}^K - \overline{\ln PPP_k^K} \right] \tag{6.11}$$

with weights and averages defined analogously as for labour.

For the deflation of value added, a double-deflation procedure is used based on separate PPPs for gross output and intermediate inputs as required (Jorgenson, Kuroda and Nishimizu 1987). We follow a CCD-like approach by taking a geometric mean of all possible binary Törnqvist indices for a particular country c. First, we calculate the binary value-added PPP for each country pair (c,d) as follows:

$$\left[\ln PPP_c^Z - \ln PPP_d^Z \right]$$
$$= \frac{1}{1 - \overline{w}_X^Y} \left[(\ln PPP_c^Y - \ln PPP_d^Y) - \overline{w}_X^Y (\ln PPP_c^X - \ln PPP_d^X) \right] \tag{6.12}$$

The weight $\overline{w}_X^Y$ is the share of intermediate inputs in gross output, averaged over the two countries. PPP_c^Y is the multilateral index for output for country c and derived analogously to the derivation of labour PPPs, but now using shares of output types in total output value as weights, and similarly for PPP_c^X, which is the multilateral index for intermediate input. Finally, a Gini-EKS procedure is applied to multilateralise the set of value-added binaries given in (6.12), as in Caves *et al.* (1982b). Together, these equations provide the system used to derive MFP measures consistent with neo-classical production theory.

Level accounting

One of the main applications in productivity comparisons is level accounting. In this approach, differences in output across countries are decomposed into differences in the weighted level of inputs and differences in productivity. Below we discuss the decomposition of differences in value added and in labour productivity. We split the contribution of capital into ICT and non-ICT assets and the contribution of labour into total hours worked (H) and differences in labour composition (LC). Rearranging (6.4):

$$
\ln \frac{Z_c}{Z_{US}} = \overline{w}_{ICT}^Z \ln \frac{K_c^{ICT}}{K_{US}^{ICT}} + \overline{w}_N^Z \ln \frac{K_c^N}{K_{US}^N}
$$

$$
+ \overline{w}_L^Z \ln \frac{LC_c}{LC_{US}} + \overline{w}_L^Z \ln \frac{H_c}{H_{US}} + \ln A_c^Z \tag{6.13}
$$

where $\overline{w}_{ICT}^Z$ is the share of ICT-capital compensation in value added, averaged over the two countries, and similarly for non-ICT. Various applications of the level-accounting methodology rely on a decomposition of labour productivity (value added per hour worked). This decomposition can be derived by subtracting hours worked from the left- and right-hand sides of (6.13). Let z be labour productivity defined as the ratio of value added to hours worked, $z = Z/H$ and k the ratio of capital services to hours worked, $k = K/H$; then

$$
\ln \frac{z_c}{z_{US}} = \overline{w}_{ICT}^Z \ln \frac{k_c^{ICT}}{k_{US}^{ICT}} + \overline{w}_N^Z \ln \frac{k_c^N}{k_{US}^N} + \overline{w}_L^Z \ln \frac{LC_c}{LC_{US}} + \ln A_c^Z \tag{6.14}
$$

This equation shows the four different sources of differences in labour productivity levels across countries, namely differences in labour

Table 6.1. *Example of input and output comparison, transport equipment manufacturing, Germany and USA, 1997*

	Nominal values			Relative volume (Germany/USA)
	Germany (€ billion)	US ($ billion)	PPP (€/$)	
Sectoral output	141.8	454.8	1.25	0.25
Sectoral intermediate inputs	87.2	291.5	0.96	0.31
Energy	2.7	3.7	1.32	0.55
Materials	63.0	180.1	0.94	0.37
Services	21.5	107.8	1.02	0.20
Gross value added	54.7	163.2	2.04	0.16
Labour	43.1	122.6	1.36	0.26
High-skilled	10.4	34.9	1.32	0.23
Non-high-skilled	32.8	87.7	1.37	0.27
Capital	11.6	40.6	1.13	0.42
ICT capital	1.3	10.5	0.94	0.22
Non-ICT capital	10.2	30.1	1.16	0.48

Notes: Relative volumes are derived as nominal value of Germany divided by the corresponding PPP over the nominal value of the USA, except for capital. Relative volumes for capital are determined based on the ex-ante approach to capital measurement; see main text.

composition, ICT capital per hour worked, non-ICT capital per hour worked and MFP. The calculation of productivity measures and the decomposition are defined according to the formulas above at each level of industry aggregation. As such it follows the approach in the EU KLEMS Growth Accounts described in Chapter 3.

It is useful at this stage to present an example of the level accounting method to give a flavour of the type of results that can be derived. We use a comparison of output, inputs and productivity in transport equipment manufacturing between Germany and the USA in 1997. In Table 6.1 we give an overview of the nominal output and inputs in each country and the corresponding PPPs. The values in the first two columns are at national prices and given in euro for Germany and dollars for the USA. The PPPs in the third column are given in euro per dollar. These PPPs are based on industry-specific prices of outputs and detailed inputs. They show that energy inputs and, particularly, labour are more expensive in Germany than in the USA, while materials and ICT capital are relatively cheap. In the final column we give relative volumes derived as nominal value for Germany divided by the corresponding PPP over the nominal value for the USA, except for capital. Relative volumes for capital are determined based on the ex-ante approach to capital measurement (see section 6.3). The final column shows that US transport equipment output is four times greater than in Germany. The production in the USA uses relatively less energy and non-ICT capital, but more services inputs and ICT capital than in Germany.

Table 6.2 builds upon these results and provides a decomposition of value added and labour productivity (value added per hour worked) levels in Germany compared to the USA. The contributions of inputs to the output gap with the USA are based on multiplying the relative input levels by their share in value added as in (6.13). The residual is the difference in multi-factor productivity (MFP). The table shows that MFP in German transport equipment manufacturing in 1997 was only 57 per cent of the US level. The final columns provide the decomposition of value added per hour worked based on (6.14). The labour productivity level in Germany was only 60 per cent of the US level and this gap is clearly due to the gap in MFP. There is less use of skilled labour in Germany but this is more than compensated for by the higher use of non-ICT capital. Instead, it is the efficiency with which labour and capital is used that drove the gap between Germany and the USA in 1997.

Extrapolation

Level estimates are typically made for a benchmark year. There are two basic ways to extend the benchmark over time, say from 1997 to 2005. One approach is to use volume growth rates of output and inputs for the period 1997–2005 and apply these to the benchmark. The alternative is to derive a new set of PPPs for 2005 and apply those to nominal values for the same year. Unfortunately, the two approaches typically do not deliver the same result. The second approach is theoretically preferable as it takes into account the prices and quantity structures of the year under consideration. It provides a snapshot of the comparative performance in year 2005. This is also known as current-PPP comparisons, indicating that for the comparisons, PPPs from the

Table 6.2. *Example of level accounting, transport equipment manufacturing, Germany and USA, 1997*

	Average share in value added	Relative level (Ger./USA)	Contribution to log value-added gap	Relative level per hour (Ger./USA)	Contribution to log value-added per hour gap
Value added	100.0	0.16	−1.81	0.59	−0.52
Labour input	77.0	0.26	−1.04	0.00	−0.05
Hours worked	77.0	0.28	−0.99	0.00	0.00
Labour composition	77.0	0.94	−0.05	0.94	−0.05
Capital input	23.0	0.42	−0.20	1.51	0.09
ICT	4.4	0.22	−0.07	0.81	−0.01
Non-ICT	18.6	0.48	−0.13	1.75	0.10
MFP (value-added based)		−0.57	0.57	−0.57	

Notes: Level accounting example of difference in value added and labour productivity (value added per hour worked) between Germany and the USA, based on (6.13) and (6.14). Relative volumes taken from Table 6.1.

current year are used. On account of the heavy data requirements of new benchmarks, the benchmark extrapolation alternative is widely used instead. It is known as the constant-PPP approach, indicating that PPPs from a benchmark year are used to make comparisons outside that year. Constant- and current-PPP comparisons will differ on account of standard substitution biases well-known in the price index number literature. In an international context, they are referred to as time–space inconsistencies or the 'tableau effect'.[9] The inconsistency can be significant when relative price and quantity structures between countries and over time differ considerably, for example if there is a wide gap between successive benchmark comparisons, or when growth and structural change in a country is rapid. Typically, these biases will be greater the further one moves away from the benchmark year.

6.3 Basic data for productivity level comparisons

In this section we provide a short discussion of the underlying sources of the GGDC Productivity Level database.[10] This database provides productivity level comparisons for thirty OECD countries at a detailed industry level using the methodology outlined in section 6.2. These comparisons are made only for a benchmark year, 1997. The database is based on two main sets of data: a set of national input-output tables for the nominal values of output and inputs, and a set of PPPs for deflation. We discuss each in turn.

Sectoral output and inputs

An important consideration when making cross-country comparisons is the effect of differences in the degree of integration of firms within an economy. In some countries, an industry may be made up of many

---

[9] Summers and Heston (1991, p. 340) coined the term 'tableau effect' and provided a discussion in the context of the International Comparisons Project. Various smoothing methods can be used to straighten out these differences (see, for example, Krijnse-Locker and Faerber 1984), but this implies that, in the process, benchmark PPPs and/or national price series are modified compared to the original estimates. This is discussed in detail in Appendix 2 of Inklaar and Timmer (2008b). See Feenstra, Ma and Rao (2009) for an original attempt based on econometric smoothing techniques.

[10] See Inklaar and Timmer (2008b) for more details.

small firms that only handle part of the production process, while in other countries, firms may be more integrated. In the former case, there will be more intra-industry trade of intermediate products, and the industry will use more of its own production. This has consequences for comparisons of output and input levels across countries. In this study we make use of the so-called sectoral output and input concepts, as introduced by Domar (1961), in which intra-industry deliveries are netted out. Essentially, each industry is considered to be completely integrated, i.e. all individual production units in an industry are combined into a single unit. This assumption is made at all levels of aggregation. Sectoral output measures will be identical to gross output at the firm level, but as these move up the hierarchy of industries, they move closer and closer to value added. Similarly, sectoral intermediate input measures approach total imports at higher aggregation levels. Indeed, at the level of the total economy sectoral output is equal to gross domestic product (GDP) plus imports and sectoral intermediate input is equal to imports, as all domestic inter-industry deliveries have been netted out.[11] Using the terminology of Durand (1996), this approach can be called aggregation with integration, as opposed to aggregation without integration. The main advantage of the aggregation with integration approach is that differences in integration across countries will not distort relative measures of inputs and productivity. A simple example can illustrate this point.

Suppose that we want to compare output, input and productivity in motor car manufacturing in two countries, A and B. Assume for simplicity that in both countries 10 cars are produced, using 10 units of labour. The countries only differ in the number of firms: two in country A and only one in country B. The first firm in country A produces car components (engines, bodies, wheels etc.) using 5 units of labour. The second firm does the final assembly and produces 10 final cars, using 5 labour units to put together the car components produced by the other firm. In country B the two activities (car part production

---

[11] To be more precise, sectoral output at the aggregate level equals GDP at basic prices plus imports at purchasers' prices; see Aulin-Ahmavaara and Pakarinen (2007) for a discussion. The term 'sectoral' was suggested by Gollop (1979). This name is somewhat unfortunate, as the concept 'sector' is used by statisticians to indicate institutional sectors. Nevertheless, we keep to the use of sectoral output and input concepts to indicate the outputs and inputs of a fully integrated sector.

and assembly) are integrated in just one firm. So, by construction, the sectoral output (10 cars) and inputs (10 labour units) are the same in both countries, as the intra-industry trade of components between the two firms in country A is netted out. Similarly, productivity levels are identical by definition. However, when outputs and inputs are aggregated in country A without integration, differences will appear. Suppose that the output of car components of firm 1 is 5 units.[12] Then the total output in country A of firms 1 and 2 will be 15 (= 10 + 5), and the total intermediate inputs will be 5. This would suggest that car manufacturing in country A uses more intermediates than in country B. Similarly, standard multi-factor productivity (MFP) measures in A will be lower than in B, as the input–output ratio of the aggregated sector is higher than the input–output ratio of the integrated sector.[13] In the extreme case of infinite fragmentation, MFP would tend to zero, intermediate input–output ratios to unity and labour– and capital–output ratios to zero. Hence comparisons of input and productivity across countries will be sensitive to differences in the degree of integration. This is clearly an undesirable characteristic of standard non-integrated measures.

In addition, there is a statistical reason for using sectoral measures. National statistical offices are known to differ in their recording of intra-firm deliveries. This will partly depend on the unit of activity which is surveyed (establishments or enterprises) and the treatment of sub-contracting transactions. Therefore we prefer to use sectoral measures in international comparisons.[14] Inklaar and Timmer (2007b) provide a numerical example of the transport equipment manufacturing industry and show that the use of sectoral output measures is also empirically relevant, besides being conceptually preferable. Ratios of sectoral to gross output vary from a low 1.1 in the Netherlands, to over 1.3 in France and the USA. Also the shares of inputs in output change drastically. Typically, the share of material inputs declines

---

[12] For simplicity we abstract from incorporating prices in the example and assume unit prices for all goods.

[13] This follows from the identity that nominal output is equal to the value of intermediate inputs and value added. With integration, output and intermediate input are reduced by the same amount, while value added remains the same. Hence, the ratio of intermediates over output will be lower.

[14] When not all establishments of a firm belong to the same industry, this problem cannot be completely solved by using integrated measures.

when many of these inputs (parts and components) are produced in the same industry. In contrast the share of intermediate services and factor inputs increases.

Measures of sectoral output and input require industry-by-industry input-output tables (IOTs) with separate information on domestic and imported supplies of commodities. IOTs are not available for all countries in a common benchmark year and we used supply and use tables (see data description below) to construct comparable IOTs in the following way. Let S^D be the domestic supply matrix of a particular country (product×industry) of dimension $n \times m$ with n products and m industries, q^D the vector of total domestic supply by product ($n \times 1$), q^I a separate vector for imports ($n \times 1$) and q total supply ($q = q^D + q^I$). Further, let U indicate the intermediate part of the use table (product×industry) of dimension $n \times m$, to be split into domestic (U^D) and imported (U^I) such that $U = U^D + U^I$. Similarly Π^D and Π^I indicate the domestic and imported intermediate part of the input-output table (industry×industry) of dimensions $m \times m$ with $\Pi = \Pi^D + \Pi^I$.

The first step is to split the use table into domestic and imported. For this, we assume that the import-share of a product used by an industry is constant over all using industries. This import-share is derived from the supply table by dividing imports by total supply for each product as follows:

$$U^I = \hat{q}^I \hat{q}^{-1} U \qquad\qquad (6.15)$$

where $\hat{q}$ is the diagonal matrix with the elements of vector q on its main diagonal and zeroes elsewhere. The domestic use table is then easily derived as the difference between U and U^I:

$$U^D = U - U^I \qquad\qquad (6.16)$$

Next, one needs to transform supply and use tables into input-output tables. There are various ways to do this, depending on the assumptions made (see, for example, Eurostat 2002 chap. 11). We use the so-called 'fixed product-sales structure' assumption where each product has its own specific sales structure, irrespective of the industry where it is produced. This assumption is more plausible than its alternative (fixed industry-sales structure).[15] Under the assumption, the

---

[15] Plausibility will depend on the nature of secondary production. Often, the structure of demand for the secondary products is rather different from the

intermediate part of the domestic input-output table is derived as follows:

$$\mathbf{II}^D = (\mathbf{S}^D)'(\hat{\mathbf{q}}^D)^{-1}\mathbf{U}^D \qquad (6.17)$$

where a prime is used for transposition. Similarly, imported intermediates are derived as follows, implicitly assuming a similar industry-origin of the imported intermediates as for domestically produced:

$$\mathbf{II}^I = (\mathbf{S}^D)'(\hat{\mathbf{q}}^D)^{-1}\mathbf{U}^I \qquad (6.18)$$

Using these matrices, sectoral intermediate input can be defined as follows. Let II_{ij}^D be elements of $\mathbf{II}^D$, that is, domestic intermediate inputs from industry i used by industry j, and similarly for imports, then total sectoral intermediate input used by j (II_j) is given by:

$$II_j = \sum_i \left(II_{ij}^D + II_{ij}^I \right) - II_{jj}^D \qquad (6.19)$$

Similarly, sectoral output of industry j is defined as gross output minus the intra-industry deliveries (II_{jj}^D). The data sources for these variables are discussed next.

Input-output tables are not available for all countries in a common benchmark year and we used supply and use tables to construct these. The starting point of our analysis is the national supply and use table for each country, valued in national currency for 1997. Eurostat makes these tables available for the European countries on a common industry classification and at a sufficient level of industry detail for the purpose of this study. For non-European countries these tables are obtained from the national statistical offices. They had to be adjusted to the European industry classification. The value-added block of the tables distinguishes only two primary factors, namely capital and labour, so further disaggregation of these factor inputs is required. We use the labour and capital compensation as given in the EU KLEMS database in which a correction is made for the labour income of self-employed workers. Total hours worked and wages for each of the eighteen

primary products. But if, for example, secondary products are mainly trade and transport services which are delivered together with the primary products, the fixed-industry sales structure assumption might also be a plausible assumption. We follow the recommendation by Eurostat (2002).

labour types are taken from the EU KLEMS database and extended to thirty types by incorporating more detailed educational attainment data. Capital compensation is split into three ICT assets (computers, communication equipment and software) and five non-ICT assets (residential structures, non-residential structures, transport equipment, other non-ICT equipment and other assets). The share of each asset in total compensation is based on capital rental prices using the ex-ante approach. We multiply the asset- and industry-specific rental prices by the capital stock taken from the capital input files from the EU KLEMS database to derive the ex-ante capital compensation by asset (see below).[16]

Purchasing power parities (PPPs)

The theoretically most appropriate approach for international comparisons of output and productivity levels is to apply PPPs that are based on the industry-of-origin approach. The industry-of-origin approach was pioneered by Paige and Bombach (1959) in a comparison of the United Kingdom and the United States. The earlier work was conveniently summarised by Kravis (1976). In the past two decades, this method was further developed and used in the ICOP project (International Comparisons of Output and Productivity) at the University of Groningen (van Ark and Pilat 1993; Maddison and van Ark 2002; van Ark and Timmer 2009) and at the National Institute of Economic and Social Research (O'Mahony 1999). There are various alternative ways to obtain PPPs for gross output, partly depending on the data availability for individual industries. One way is to make use of producer prices for specified products, but these are scarce. The most widely used approach to obtain these PPPs is the unit-value-ratio method. This method makes use of production statistics such as censuses or business statistics surveys that record the output values and quantities for product items. By dividing the output value by the corresponding quantities, one obtains unit values, which can then be used for calculating unit value ratios for matched items between countries. Because of a lack of data, this approach can only be used for a limited set

---

[16] The summation of capital compensation over all assets will typically differ from the capital compensation as given in the National Accounts. The latter is used in the calculation of MFP; see below.

of industries. In addition, unit value ratios can suffer from quality-adjustment problems in international comparisons. Detailed product characteristics are difficult to observe directly from production statistics as they report quantity and values for product groups rather than for specified products, and descriptions are often brief.

An alternative to the industry-of-origin approach is to use data from internationally co-ordinated surveys on expenditure prices such as in the International Comparisons Program (ICP) under the auspices of the United Nations and the World Bank (Kravis *et al.* 1982). Since the early 1980s the OECD has regularly published estimates of expenditure PPPs, derived from its joint programme with Eurostat. Expenditure-based PPP comparisons are based on purchasers' prices of final goods and services with a detailed product specification. Hence, to apply them to output and productivity comparisons by industry, the PPPs need to be reallocated from expenditure categories to industry groups. The expenditure approach to sectoral PPPs was pioneered by Jorgenson, Kuroda and Nishimizu (1987) and most recently applied by van Biesebroeck (2009) and Sørensen and Schjerning (2008). In general, PPPs based on expenditure price surveys suffer less from quality problems as product comparisons are based on detailed specifications. However, the approach does also have a number of drawbacks for comparisons of output and productivity at industry level as it requires detailed adjustments for margins, taxes and international trade. Furthermore, by definition these PPPs only cover prices for final expenditure and do not reflect relative prices of intermediate goods. Following Pilat (1996), Timmer, Ypma and van Ark (2007) argue that a mixture of PPPs derived from the expenditure and industry-of-origin approach should be used for productivity comparisons at industry level, and this approach is followed in the construction of the GGDC Productivity Level database. Van Ark and Timmer (2009) provide further discussion of the alternative approaches to PPPs for productivity comparisons.

In the GGDC Productivity Level database, output PPPs are defined from the producer's point of view and are at basic prices. These PPPs have partly been constructed using unit value ratios for agricultural, mining and manufacturing products and transport and communication services. For the other market industries, PPPs are based on specified expenditure prices from Eurostat and the OECD, which were adjusted to industry level by using relative transport and distribution margins and adjusting for differences in relative tax rates. PPPs have been made transitive by applying the multilateral EKS-procedure for a set of thirty countries (Timmer, Ypma and van Ark 2007).

Intermediate input PPPs reflect the costs of acquiring intermediate deliveries and match the price concept used in the input-output tables, hence at basic prices plus net taxes. The data problems in obtaining input PPPs for individual industries are larger than for output. There is often no input price parallel to the output PPPs. Business statistics surveys and productivity censuses provide little or no information on quantities and values of inputs in manufacturing, and for non-manufacturing industries the information is largely absent. Moreover, PPPs from the expenditure side, by definition, do not reflect prices of intermediate inputs as they cover only final expenditure categories. Therefore, we rely on a transformation of output prices into intermediate input prices using the supply and use tables. We assume that the basic price of a good is independent of its use. That is, we use the same gross output PPP of an industry to deflate all intermediate deliveries from this industry to other industries. Unfortunately, (net) tax matrices are not available for most countries, so gross output PPPs cannot be adjusted for differences in tax rates across countries. As net taxes on products are minor for most market industries, this will probably not greatly affect our level estimates, but further investigation is needed to substantiate this claim, especially for comparisons at a detailed level. The aggregate intermediate input PPP for a particular industry can be derived by weighting intermediate inputs at the output PPP from the delivering industries. Imported goods are separately identified and exchange rates are used as conversion factors for imports.

PPPs for labour inputs are derived by dividing a country's wage rate by the corresponding US wage rate. This must be done at a detailed level of aggregation as characteristics of workers vary greatly across countries; see, for example, de la Fuente and Doménech (2006). For example, the share of college-educated workers in the USA is typically (much) higher than in the European countries. By having a detailed breakdown into various labour types, we try to minimise problems of composition in the determination of relative wages. Labour input is cross-classified by type of education (five types), age (three types) and gender, into thirty groups.[17] For each group in each industry, wages per hour worked are taken from the sources underlying the EU KLEMS labour composition estimates. They include all costs incurred by the producers in employment of labour including taxes levied, health cost payments, other types of insurance and contributions to retirement pensions paid by the employer and any other financial benefits.

Ex-ante approach to capital PPPs

Capital PPPs give the relative price of the use of a unit of capital in two countries from the purchasers' perspective. To obtain relative prices for capital input, we follow Jorgenson and Nishimizu (1978). Under the assumption that the relative efficiency of new capital goods is the same in both countries, the relative rental price of an asset k between country c and the base country, the USA ($PPP_{k,c}^K$) is calculated as

$$PPP_{k,c}^K = PPP_{k,c}^I \frac{\left(p_{k,c}^K/p_{k,c}^I\right)}{\left(p_{k,US}^K/p_{k,US}^I\right)} \tag{6.20}$$

with $PPP_{k,c}^I$ the relative investment price of asset k between country c and the USA, and $p_{k,c}^K/p_{k,c}^I$ the ratio of the user cost and the investment price of asset k in country c (in national prices). This expression is convenient as data on relative investment prices can be derived on the basis of price comparisons of investment goods across countries. In the absence of taxation the familiar cost-of-capital equation for asset type k is given by (introducing a time subscript):

$$p_{k,c,t}^K = p_{k,c,t-1}^I r_{t,c} + \delta_k p_{k,c,t}^I - \left[p_{k,c,t}^I - p_{k,c,t-1}^I\right] \tag{6.21}$$

This formula shows that the user cost is determined by the nominal rate of return (r), the rate of economic depreciation (δ) and the asset-specific capital gains. Note that the rate of return is the same for all asset types, and that the depreciation rate for an asset type is the same for all countries. Ignoring second-order effects, the ratio of the user

---

[17] Additional detail on types of education was added to the EU KLEMS database based on unpublished work by the National Institute of Economic and Social Research (NIESR).

cost and investment price needed for the calculation of the PPP can be
approximated by:

$$\frac{p_{k,c}^K}{p_{k,c}^I} \approx r_{t,c} + \delta_k - \left[\frac{\left(p_{k,c,t}^I - p_{k,c,t-1}^I \right)}{p_{k,c,t-1}^I} \right] \tag{6.22}$$

The last term on the right-hand side indicates the asset price change.
Note that this is done for each asset type k in each industry j, using
asset-industry-specific depreciation rates and investment prices.

The rate of return can be calculated in various ways. In the EU
KLEMS growth accounts we make use of the ex-post approach, backing out the industry rate of return as a residual on the basis of the
overall ex-post compensation of capital. In an alternative approach, the
rate of return is determined ex-ante. The ex-post approach is favoured
by most analysts of economic growth, although it has recently been
challenged (see discussion in Chapter 3). The practical and methodological reasons to opt for the ex-ante approach are especially strong in
the context of level comparisons. While in an analysis of growth over
time of one country it might be argued that possible deviations from
the assumptions of perfect markets and constant returns to scale only
change slowly, this is much harder to argue in the case of comparisons
across countries. Moreover, an important practical disadvantage of the
ex-post approach is the high volatility of the user cost of capital due to
its nature as a residual measure. Growth accounts are usually made for
analyses of growth during a period of, say, five or ten years in which
these errors are smoothed. However, level comparisons are made for
a benchmark year only and hence are highly sensitive to short-run
fluctuations in the rental prices. This causes problems especially at a
low industry and asset level, as capital compensation frequently turns
out to be low or even negative for some assets in some years. In addition, the ex-post approach is more sensitive to measurement errors,
for example concerning the classification of investment by asset type.
Given this, we base the rate of return on an ex-ante required rate of
return as indicated by ten-year government bond yields.

6.4 Productivity levels: crude versus data-intensive measures

The preceding discussion has demonstrated that a great deal of data
is required to get close to the theoretical concept of productivity as

based on neo-classical production theory. Detailed information about the composition and relative prices of labour and capital are needed for an accurate comparison of input across countries and industry-specific output prices are needed for an accurate comparison of output. But an important question is whether all these refinements matter in practice or whether a cruder measure that is easier to implement would give qualitatively similar results. To examine this, we look at various alternative comparative measures of inputs and outputs commonly used in the literature, and then compare a number of alternative productivity level estimates based on varying data intensity.

In Table 6.3 we present value-added PPPs for the market economy and four main sectors in the economy (ICT production, manufacturing, other goods and market services) for 1997. In addition we provide PPPs for aggregate GDP and exchange rates, as available from the OECD, that have both been used as alternatives. To deflate industry-level outputs and inputs, many studies rely on GDP PPPs, assuming that the following holds:

$$P\tilde{P}P_{c,j}^{Z} = PPP_{c}^{GDP} \quad \forall j \tag{6.23}$$

with PPP_{c}^{GDP} the overall PPP for aggregate GDP as regularly published by Eurostat and the OECD. As noted in the literature, this approach ignores the difference in prices across various industries as well as the differences in prices of intermediate inputs and outputs, and this has generally been seen as a major weakness (Sørensen 2001; Rogerson 2008). Instead, the value-added PPPs have been derived by separate deflation of output and intermediate inputs as in (6.12). As shown in Table 6.3, the ratio of sectoral value added to GDP PPP can vary between 75 per cent and more than 200 per cent. The PPPs for the market economy are generally higher than GDP PPPs. This is mainly due to the fact that the latter includes non-market services which, according to the OECD results, are expensive in the USA compared to other countries. Importantly, the table shows large differences in relative prices across sectors, confirming the findings by van Biesebroeck (2009) and Sørensen and Schjerning (2008). For example, the PPP for other goods in Japan is much higher than the PPP for manufacturing goods. This is mainly due to the high output prices in the agricultural sector, which is famous for its weak competitiveness and strong import protection (van Ark and Pilat 1993). The use of an overall GDP

Table 6.3. Various alternative PPP measures, 1997

	GDP PPP (OECD)	Market economy	Value added PPPs				Exchange rate
			ICT production	Manufacturing	Other goods	Market services	
Austria	0.92	1.26	1.20	1.36	1.19	1.22	0.89
Belgium	0.91	1.06	1.03	0.94	1.26	1.06	0.89
Czech Republic	12.7	16.0	30.0	15.2	15.4	18.1	31.7
Denmark	8.43	9.07	10.80	11.16	11.22	7.81	6.60
Finland	1.00	1.02	1.30	1.01	0.85	1.08	0.87
France	0.97	1.18	0.95	1.07	1.48	1.13	0.89
Germany	0.99	1.08	1.05	1.05	1.52	1.01	0.89
Hungary	85.0	96.5	115.5	89.9	132.1	90.9	186.8
Ireland	0.85	0.99	1.60	1.13	1.17	0.94	0.84
Italy	0.82	0.96	0.80	0.70	1.02	1.07	0.88
Netherlands	0.91	0.99	1.36	1.09	1.44	0.88	0.89
Portugal	0.67	0.75	1.33	0.91	0.82	0.68	0.87
Slovenia	0.46	0.59	0.62	0.53	0.69	0.62	0.67
Spain	0.72	0.86	0.92	0.87	0.93	0.84	0.88
Sweden	9.30	10.3	4.56	10.4	10.0	10.2	7.63
United Kingdom	0.63	0.75	0.48	0.74	0.85	0.71	0.61
European Union	0.91	1.04	0.91	0.91	1.22	1.03	0.89
Japan	168	229	158	166	366	230	121
United States	1.00	1.00	1.00	1.00	1.00	1.00	1.00

Notes: All entries in national currency per US$. For countries that joined the euro in 1999, the 1999 conversion rate was used on the old pre-euro currencies. European Union expressed in euro and refers to ten countries (EU-15ex): Austria, Belgium, Denmark, Finland, France, Germany, Italy, the Netherlands, Spain and the United Kingdom.

Sources: Value-added PPPs based on the GGDC Productivity Level database (Inklaar and Timmer 2008b). GDP PPP and exchange rate from OECD (2002).

Table 6.4. *Measures of labour input, 1997, market economy*

	Share of high-skilled workers (percentage)	Labour services per hour worked (USA = 1)	Average hours worked per worker	Labour services per worker (USA = 1)
Austria	5.9	0.86	1,659	0.77
Belgium	11.1	0.94	1,474	0.75
Czech Republic	8.5	0.86	2,049	0.96
Denmark	4.8	0.82	1,537	0.68
Finland	26.9	0.87	1,842	0.86
France	9.3	0.95	1,745	0.90
Germany	6.4	0.93	1,526	0.77
Hungary	10.1	0.98	2,111	1.12
Ireland	9.3	0.89	2,023	0.97
Italy	4.9	0.85	1,968	0.91
Netherlands	7.2	0.93	1,486	0.75
Portugal	4.8	0.60	1,912	0.62
Slovenia	9.7	0.83	1,897	0.85
Spain	10.1	0.86	1,768	0.83
Sweden	8.6	0.96	1,740	0.90
United Kingdom	11.0	0.88	1,797	0.86
European Union	8.3	0.89	1,710	0.82
Japan	19.0	0.97	1,837	0.97
United States	23.8	1.00	1,848	1.00

Notes: EU refers to ten countries; see Table 6.3.
Source: GGDC Productivity Level database (Inklaar and Timmer 2008b).

PPP would greatly overestimate productivity levels in this sector. On balance, the value-added PPPs for manufacturing differ by about 16 per cent from the GDP PPP across our set of countries (absolute log differences). This directly translates into a 16 per cent difference in measures of productivity levels. For market services the difference is comparable (15 per cent), while for other goods it is even bigger (32 per cent).

Next we look at data-intensive measures of labour and capital input. To ease exposition, we only present results for the aggregate market economy, though a similar comparison could be made for each of the detailed industries in our dataset. Table 6.4 presents our measures of labour services input per worker compared to those in the USA. When it comes to measuring labour input volumes, some studies only measure the relative number of persons engaged while others also account for differences in average hours worked across countries. Implicitly, these studies use the following PPP for labour:

$$PP\tilde{P}^L_{c,j} = \left(\frac{V^L_{c,j}}{H^L_{c,j}} \right) \Big/ \left(\frac{V^L_{US,j}}{H^L_{US,j}} \right) \tag{6.24}$$

with $H^L_{c,j}$ being the hours worked in industry j in country c, or, more crudely, the total number of workers, without adjustment for differences in hours worked. In contrast to our data-intensive measure given in (6.10), this measure does not account for differences in the composition of the work-force in different countries. The difference in skill levels across OECD countries is illustrated in the first column of Table 6.4, which provides the share of high-skilled workers in employment. This broadly corresponds to workers with a tertiary education, such as a bachelor's degree or higher. Apart from Finland, the USA appears to have the largest share of high-skilled workers, as also found by de la Fuente and Doménech (2006) and Cohen and Soto (2007). However, focusing only on workers with university education is potentially misleading as this approach ignores differences in lower levels of education. For example, Germany has a comparatively large share of workers in vocational education categories whose skills are highly valued in the labour market as reflected in relatively high skill premia. Vocational education is much less common in the USA. Furthermore, labour force characteristics such as age and gender are also relevant as indicators of work experience. Our detailed measures correct for all these differences. The second column of Table 6.4 shows the amount of labour services per hour worked based on (6.10). This indicator varies widely across countries, but all have lower inputs of labour services per hour worked than the USA. In addition, as shown in the third column of Table 6.4, average annual hours worked vary considerably across countries, between 1,474 hours in Belgium and 2,111 hours in Hungary, and this should be taken into account as well.[18] The final column of Table 6.4 shows the amount of labour services per worker,

---

[18] What is measured is actual hours worked, not hours paid, so in principle it takes differences in the number of vacation days, sick days, etc. into account.

which combines the effects of both differences in hours worked and compositional differences across countries. Except for Hungary, all countries have lower inputs of labour services per worker than the USA. For countries like Belgium, Denmark and the Netherlands, this is mainly due to lower working hours, while for countries like the Czech Republic, Portugal and Slovenia differences in labour composition are most important. These results show that a crude measure such as total workers leads to an overestimation of labour services in EU countries relative to the USA.

Finally, as a measure of capital input volumes, most studies use a measure of the relative capital stock. Typically, as data on capital stocks is given in national prices, a GDP PPP is used to make them comparable across countries, as follows:

$$P\tilde{P}P^K_{c,j} = PPP^{GDP}_c \left(\frac{V^K_{c,j}}{S^K_{c,j}} \right) \Big/ \left(\frac{V^K_{US,j}}{S^K_{US,j}} \right) \tag{6.25}$$

with $S^K_{c,j}$ the quantity of aggregate capital in industry j in country c, directly measured as the capital stock summed over all asset types. Consequently, this crude measure of capital does not take into account differences in investment prices or differences in the composition of capital. Our detailed measure given in (6.11) above is based on a comparison of capital service levels, accounting for asset heterogeneity and investment PPPs. Table 6.5 provides a comparison between the crude measure and our data-intensive measure of capital input for the market economy in our set of countries. All figures are on a per-hour worked basis to allow meaningful comparisons. The first column is based on comparisons of aggregate capital stock as in (6.25). The drawback of this measure is that it does not take into account differences in investment prices or the composition of the capital stock. Both issues are empirically important as indicated by Caselli and Wilson (2004) and Hsieh and Klenow (2007). Whereas in the past, capital stocks provided a good proxy for capital input levels, this is no longer the case in the ICT era. Jorgenson and Vu (2005) and Timmer and van Ark (2005) highlighted the diverging trends in the use of ICT capital and its impact on comparative productivity growth rates. This is illustrated in the second column which presents the share of ICT assets in total capital compensation. This share is more than 20 per cent in Denmark, Sweden, the UK and the USA, but less than 11 per cent in the Czech

Table **6.5.** *Measures of capital input per hour worked, 1997, market economy*

	Capital stock per hour worked (USA = 1)	ICT share in total capital compensation (percentage)	Capital services per hour worked (USA = 1)		
			Total	ICT	Non-ICT
Austria	1.44	13.4	1.12	0.43	1.37
Belgium	1.95	18.0	1.59	0.98	1.81
Czech Republic	0.93	8.3	0.45	0.16	0.55
Denmark	1.40	21.8	1.24	0.80	1.39
Finland	1.23	17.5	1.17	0.54	1.39
France	1.15	16.6	0.90	0.67	0.99
Germany	1.18	18.4	1.06	0.70	1.18
Hungary	0.95	12.9	0.47	0.23	0.55
Ireland	0.83	10.0	0.58	0.17	0.71
Italy	1.25	10.7	1.06	0.42	1.29
Netherlands	1.24	17.2	1.03	0.73	1.13
Portugal	0.49	10.9	0.40	0.13	0.49
Slovenia	0.78	26.9	0.49	0.35	0.54
Spain	1.01	17.0	0.69	0.44	0.77
Sweden	1.18	23.8	1.09	1.29	1.07
United Kingdom	0.84	22.0	0.75	0.68	0.78
European Union	1.14	14.8	0.93	0.60	1.05
Japan	1.18	19.4	1.19	0.91	1.29
United States	1.00	26.8	1.00	1.00	1.00

Notes and sources: Capital stock based on aggregate stocks in national currencies from EU KLEMS database, March 2008 (see Chapter 3), converted with GDP PPPs from OECD (2002). Share of ICT in total capital compensation and capital services based on GGDC Productivity Level database (Inklaar and Timmer 2008b). EU refers to ten countries; see Table 6.3.

Republic, Ireland, Italy and Portugal. Comparisons based on detailed measures of capital according to (6.11) are given in the final columns, for total assets and ICT and non-ICT assets separately. In 1997, capital intensity was higher in various European countries than in the USA. This was mainly because of the higher use of non-ICT capital. As almost all countries use less ICT than the USA, relative capital input services are lower than relative levels of stocks. In general, the lower the share of ICT, the bigger the difference is between the crude and data-intensive measures.

In addition, relative prices between equipment and other capital assets such as buildings and structures are known to differ, as the former are mostly imported, while the latter are domestically constructed. The price of structures depends largely on local wages and its PPP is usually close to the GDP PPP. In contrast, PPPs for equipment are closely related to exchange rates. For countries in which exchange rates are much higher than the overall GDP PPP, the crude capital input measures will be overestimated. This is the case, for example, for the Czech Republic, Hungary and Slovenia. All in all, for these countries, data-intensive measures of capital input can be as low as only half the crude measures. But also for other countries, differences can be sizeable. For example, for France we find a 25 percentage-point difference.

So far we have shown that crude and data-intensive measures of labour and capital inputs can differ widely. Each adjustment to output and input volumes discussed above has a direct impact on the measurement of MFP. Table 6.6 brings the previous tables together by comparing five alternative productivity level estimates using increasingly data-intensive methods in moving from left to right. Therefore the first column shows a crude measure, where GDP PPPs are used to convert output to a common currency, the number of persons engaged is used as the labour measure and capital stocks are the capital measure. This measure (MFP1) is comparable to the one used by Bernard and Jones (1996) and in many subsequent papers. MFP2 then adjusts MFP1 for differences in the average number of hours worked from Table 6.4. As this table showed, average hours worked are lower than in the USA in many countries, so MFP2 will be higher for those countries than MFP1. Indeed, while Belgium has a productivity level of 87 per cent of the USA according to MFP1, the level is 101 per cent according to MFP2. Conversely, since in Hungary the average number of hours worked is higher than in the USA, MFP2 is 40 per cent compared to the 44 per cent of MFP1. MFP3 then adjusts MFP2 for differences in the composition of the labour force. Compared to MFP2, MFP3 shows higher levels compared to the USA for all countries because, according to Table 6.4, the labour composition effect is smaller than unity in all countries compared to the USA. Differences in labour input measures do not translate one to one to MFP, since

Table 6.6. *Alternative measures of market economy MFP levels, 1997*
(USA = 1)

	MFP1	MFP2	MFP3	MFP4	MFP5
Austria	0.72	0.78	0.86	0.63	0.68
Belgium	0.87	1.01	1.05	0.90	0.96
Czech Republic	0.45	0.42	0.46	0.37	0.48
Denmark	0.75	0.85	0.97	0.90	0.94
Finland	0.76	0.76	0.84	0.82	0.84
France	0.88	0.91	0.94	0.78	0.84
Germany	0.82	0.94	0.98	0.90	0.93
Hungary	0.44	0.40	0.41	0.36	0.47
Ireland	0.99	0.94	1.01	0.87	0.99
Italy	0.82	0.79	0.88	0.74	0.78
Netherlands	0.79	0.92	0.97	0.89	0.94
Portugal	0.56	0.55	0.77	0.68	0.74
Slovenia	0.50	0.49	0.56	0.43	0.49
Spain	0.79	0.81	0.89	0.75	0.85
Sweden	0.84	0.88	0.90	0.82	0.84
United Kingdom	0.83	0.85	0.92	0.78	0.81
European Union	0.82	0.87	0.93	0.81	0.86
Japan	0.69	0.70	0.71	0.52	0.52
United States	1.00	1.00	1.00	1.00	1.00
Measurement alternatives					
Output PPP	GDP	GDP	GDP	Industry	Industry
Labour input	Persons	Hours	by type	by type	by type
Capital input	Stock	Stock	Stock	Stock	Services

Notes: EU refers to ten countries; see Table 6.3. Alternatives explained in main text.
Source: Authors' calculations based on GGDC Productivity Level database (Inklaar
and Timmer 2008b) and EU KLEMS database, March 2008 (see Chapter 3).

they are weighted with the labour costs in value added, which is about
two-thirds.

Instead of a GDP PPP, MFP4 is based on a value-added PPP. MFP4
levels are lower than MFP3 levels in all countries because value-added
PPPs are higher than GDP PPPs. Although this is true for the market
economy as a whole, this will not be the case for all detailed industries, as shown in Table 6.3. The final step towards our preferred
MFP alternative is an adjustment for capital PPPs and composition,

as shown in Table 6.5. Differences between capital stock and services input, weighted by the share of capital in value added (about one-third) account for the differences between MFP4 and MFP5. Because of lower levels of capital services per hour worked than capital stocks per hour worked relative to the USA, MFP5 levels are higher than MFP4 levels in all countries. For some countries, all these adjustments almost cancel out: for example, for Ireland both MFP1 and MFP5 are at 99 per cent of the US level and for Slovenia, MFP1 is 50 and MFP5 is 49 per cent of the US level. However, for most countries the effect is substantial, between 5 and almost 20 percentage points. For example, Germany would appear to be 18 percentage points less productive than the USA according to the crudest productivity measure but only 7 percentage points according to the data-intensive measure. Furthermore, differences at the detailed industry level tend to be even larger; see Inklaar and Timmer (2008b).

6.5 Reliability of level estimates

In the previous section we have shown that apart from being conceptually superior, data-intensive measures are also different from crude measures in practice. However, this does not imply that all data issues have been resolved. It should be stressed that the estimation of PPPs and MFP levels is still experimental. They are based on a wide variety of official data sources from national statistical institutes. The reliability of these sources differs and their consistency is far from perfect. In this section we first discuss two ways to check the reliability of the estimates: by using alternative methods on the same dataset and by comparing our industry-level results with estimates at the aggregate level based on alternative sources. Then we deal with more general problems in the construction of level estimates.

Single versus double deflation

A particular issue in level accounts is the issue of double deflation of value added. In theory, the price of value added should be based on the price of output and the price of intermediate inputs. As such, the data requirements for a value-added based MFP measure are exactly the same as for a gross-output based MFP measure. However, in practice, for reasons discussed below, the prices of intermediate inputs are often ignored, and the PPP for gross output is used instead. This approach is called single deflation, as opposed to double deflation in which the prices of intermediate inputs are taken into account as in (6.12).

Single deflation has some significant problems. It suffers from a so-called terms-of-trade bias[19] and a substitution bias. First, the terms-of-trade bias arises when relative prices of output and intermediate inputs differ for a particular industry. Second, differences in relative prices of primary factor inputs and intermediate inputs can lead to differences in the use of intermediate inputs, leading to substitution effects. Relatively lower intermediate input prices will lead to a higher use of intermediate inputs compared to the use of capital and labour inputs in the production process. When using single deflation, this substitution effect between intermediate inputs and value added is not reflected in the relative volume measure of value added. In practice, the terms-of-trade and the substitution biases are difficult to disentangle. The main point here is that as long as relative intermediate input prices do not move in tandem with relative output prices across countries, measures of single-deflated value added will be biased. The double-deflation procedure does not suffer from this bias and therefore most European countries and the USA have recently adopted double-deflation techniques in the compilation of value added time series in their National Accounts. We also apply double-deflation techniques in our level database.

However, in practice double deflation also has a number of well-known problems. First, double deflation puts larger requirements on data, as intermediate input PPPs are needed in addition to PPPs for gross output. These are not usually readily available and must be constructed on the basis of input prices for the various countries in combination with input shares derived from input-output tables (see section 6.3). Second, double deflation introduces a new possible source of error which is not present in single-deflation measures, i.e. errors associated with the measurement of input prices. In many sectors, material input prices are either unavailable or crudely measured. Hill (1971) suggests that the use of single deflation may be less misleading than using double deflation when material input prices are measured

---

[19] Note that the concept 'terms of trade' refers to relative prices of outputs and inputs in the domestic economy, and does not refer to 'terms of trade' as used in international trade literature, in which they refer to the differences in import and export prices.

with error. This problem is aggravated by the fact that double-deflated value added is defined as the output volume minus the intermediate input volume. A small percentage measurement error in the volume of gross output appears as a much larger percentage error in the volume of double-deflated value added than is the case for the volume of single-deflated value added.[20]

Inklaar and Timmer (2008b) show that the sensitivity of productivity level comparisons to the choice of single- or double-deflation techniques increases with the level of industry detail. At the market economy level, differences are only large for countries with exchange rates which are much higher than the GDP PPP in 1997 (for example, Eastern European countries, but also Denmark). For other countries, the differences are less than 5 per cent. The EU–US productivity gap would be 3 percentage points smaller if single deflation were used. Also at major sector levels, differences are generally small and can go either way. Differences are smallest for market services, as is to be expected given the low share of intermediates in output. As such, measurement errors in intermediate input prices have only a minor impact. Differences can be larger for goods-producing sectors as the intermediate input share is much larger; typically shares are 60 per cent, while only 30 per cent in the case of services.

Timmer and Inklaar (2008b) also discuss differences arising from the use of alternative sets of PPPs: PPPs from the OECD solely based on expenditure or a mixed set of production and expenditure PPPs. For example, based on the mixed-set market economy, MFP in the EU is 86 per cent of that in the USA, while 83 per cent when using only expenditure prices. More generally, differences can go either way and will be larger for more detailed industries. Differences are less for goods production than for market services and often within 5 per cent bounds. Differences for market services can be especially large for the trade and transportation sector; for example, the relative EU MFP level in trade based on expenditure PPPs only is 18 per cent lower than when based on our preferred mixed PPP set.

Comparison with total economy productivity estimates

The main aim of the GGDC Productivity Level database is to provide comparative labour and multi-factor productivity estimates at the

---

[20] See Hill (1971), p. 19.

industry level across a wide set of countries. However, there might be interest in the consistency of industry-level results with the well-known estimates of relative labour productivity levels regularly produced by the OECD and Eurostat. The main reason for making a comparison of results based on aggregated industry-level data and those based on aggregate data directly would be as a cross-check on our methodology and industry-level data sources. To this end, comparisons can be made of the labour productivity results for the total economy with estimates by the OECD and Eurostat. The estimates will differ for various reasons, both methodological and practical.

First of all, the measures will differ as they refer to two different concepts of GDP. In our study we measure GDP from the production side, while OECD/Eurostat measures GDP from the expenditure side. The former explicitly accounts for differences in domestic, import and export prices, while the latter does not adjust for differences in terms of trade across countries (see Feenstra *et al.* 2009). As such, the former measures the production capacity of a country, while the latter measures the consumption possibilities. For example, when a country has to pay relatively high prices for its imports, while receiving low prices for its exports, GDP measured from the production side will be higher than when it is measured from the expenditure side. For productivity comparisons we are interested in the former. Related to this, our estimates are built up in an input-output framework, deflating outputs and intermediate inputs with separate PPPs. The OECD/Eurostat estimates are made from the expenditure side, deflating expenditure with expenditure PPPs only. As is well known, there can be substantial discrepancies between output, intermediate input and expenditure prices in the National Accounts.

Second, there are differences in the underlying data. The differences for nominal GDP and persons engaged will be relatively small, but the differences in estimates of hours worked per person can be sizeable for some countries. One of the biggest obstacles is the conversion from simple job (or person) counts to estimates of total hours actually worked as the comparability of hours-worked measures is weak. The available evidence suggests that cross-country differences in the average hours worked per person are quite large. Even within the OECD, economy-wide measures of annual working hours range from just over 1,300 for countries like the Netherlands and Norway to over 2,400 for Korea. Eurostat provides estimates of hours actually worked which are (partly) harmonised across countries. Cross-country comparability can thus be improved in comparison with the use of original national sources for some countries, but there remains a margin of uncertainty (Ypma and van Ark 2006). Also, as yet it is unclear how these estimates match the output measures in the National Accounts, particularly at the industry level. This uncertainty can only be addressed by further methodological and statistical work to enhance international comparability, preferably within the System of National Accounts.

Finally, we adjust the treatment of non-market services, by setting its relative productivity to unity. If all countries measure output by inputs, this should be the case by definition. In contrast, using the expenditure PPPs for non-market services from OECD/Eurostat as output PPPs does not imply a relative productivity level of unity and suggests much higher productivity in Europe that in the USA in non-market services. We believe that as many countries still measure nominal output in these services (largely) by inputs, assuming equal productivity imparts less error than using the existing expenditure PPPs. As non-market services typically make up 20 to 30 per cent of total GDP this has a major impact on comparative GDP per hour levels. For this reason we prefer to make comparisons only of the market economy, excluding these sectors.

The conceptual differences between our estimates and those of the OECD for the aggregate economy can have major effects on comparative performance measures. By way of example, our estimates for GDP per hour worked in France relative to the USA are 22 per cent lower than the OECD estimates. Actually, our estimates for hours worked in the USA are 5 per cent higher, leaving 27 percentage points differences for the real GDP measure. Nine percentage points are due to our treatment of non-market services. Another 5 percentage points are due to the difference between GDP at basic prices and at purchasers' prices. The former is the right price concept for productivity comparisons, while the latter is used in OECD estimates. The differences due to treatment of non-market services and price concepts also have an approximately similar effect in comparisons of other European countries with the USA. The remaining 13 percentage points in the France–USA case are due to terms of trade and inconsistencies between production and expenditure PPPs. Unfortunately, the latter two cannot be disentangled and we can only guess about its relative importance. In the case of France, the exchange rate, which is used as PPP for imports, is much lower than the GDP PPP, while the output PPP is much higher. This indicates that the volume of imports is underestimated in the OECD estimates, while the volume of exports is overestimated. The impact of this mismeasurement depends on the size of the trade balance compared to GDP, and will be larger for small open economies.

Problems in level estimates

Difficulties in measuring productivity growth rates within a country based on the present system of National Accounts are also prevalent in comparisons of MFP levels between countries (see Chapter 3 and also Diewert 2001, 2008; Schreyer 2008). Of particular importance are data on capital assets such as land and inventories, which are not included in our set of assets because of missing data. Apart from software, we do not include other intangible capital, the importance of which has recently been highlighted.[21] Some of the industry output prices, in particular for services industries like finance and business services, are hard to measure, both over time and across countries, as discussed in Chapter 3. Sometimes, problems for level accounting are even more severe, such as in comparisons of levels of educational attainment (Mason *et al.* 2009) and hours worked (see discussion above). A major challenge in reducing measurement error lies in accounting for differences in the quality of goods and services produced. Piecemeal progress on this is being made both within statistical agencies and in the academic world, for example through using hedonic techniques. The country–product–dummy (CPD) method is a very simple hedonic model which can serve as a basis for relative price estimates that better take into account quality differences. Recent work also suggests that detailed barcode scanner data can be used to compare product prices across countries at a very detailed level, drastically reducing the problem of quality differences.[22] So far, studies have focused mainly on improving relative price measures for manufacturing products and attention increasingly needs to be given

[21] See discussion in Chapter 7.
[22] See, for example, Heravi *et al.* (2003) and Goldberg and Verboven (2005) for an application of hedonics. The former study is based on scanner data.

to comparisons of prices of services, given their rising importance in production.

More generally, it is true that more detailed measures of labour and capital are less reliable than more aggregate measures because of limited survey evidence, suggesting a trade-off between precision and measurement error. For example, while an estimate of total workers in an industry can be made relatively precisely, estimates of hours worked by university-educated workers are much more uncertain. Typically, these measures are based on additional survey data with a limited sample size, such as labour force surveys, and so looking at more detailed categories of workers tends to increase sampling error. Similarly, aggregate investment by asset type is normally available from the National Accounts. However, the allocation of assets to using industries is much less reliable than the aggregate series and depends on a wide variety of assumptions and scattered evidence. More generally, estimates based on sectoral data are less reliable due to sampling, reporting or other errors, while estimates based on aggregate data are more robust as errors tend to be averaged out (Griliches 1986; Diewert 2001).[23]

Clearly, the sophistication of the methodology followed in the construction of the level comparisons adds to the vulnerability of the estimates as it makes use of detailed measures of capital and labour services, separate industry-level PPPs for output and various types of inputs. Our point estimates will be more accurate than crude estimates derived solely on the basis of capital stocks, hours worked and GDP PPPs. But the variance of our estimates will be higher as well. The choice between an estimate which is precisely wrong or approximately correct ultimately depends on its use. Inklaar and Timmer (2009b) provide a new systematic approach to estimating measurement error in comparative measures of productivity. They find that although measurement error is higher for detailed measures, this seems to be outweighed by the improvements in precision of the estimates in cross-country regression studies. If there is an interest in specific estimates for a country at a detailed industry level, it would be advisable to consider alternative estimates as well. Some of these are provided in the GGDC Productivity Level database, such as single-deflated measures and alternative PPP measures. In general, detailed industry estimates

---

[23] For example, see the discussion of the findings in Inklaar *et al.* (2008) by Wendy Carlin, Jonathan Temple and a panel (Inklaar *et al.* 2008, pp. 171–8).

should never be interpreted without additional, more qualitative, evidence from careful industry case studies, for example such as described in Baily and Solow (2001). On the other hand, if a set of level estimates for econometric cross-country analyses is needed, then this database provides a unique opportunity to improve estimation models.

6.6 Productivity gaps and accounts

In this section we provide an overview of levels of output, input and productivity for European countries and the European Union as a whole, relative to the United States. In all tables, the European Union refers to ten countries of the old EU-15 as before: Austria, Belgium, Denmark, Finland, France, Germany, Italy, the Netherlands, Spain and the United Kingdom. We first present figures for the EU as a whole and in later tables take a more detailed look into levels in individual member states.

EU–US productivity accounts

The figures presented are all for the year 2005, which is the latest year available in the EU KLEMS March 2008 database. They are based on the benchmark level comparisons for the year 1997 discussed in the previous sections. Volume growth rates of output and inputs are taken from the EU KLEMS database and used to extrapolate the 1997 benchmark. Table 6.7 provides relative levels in the EU market economy and four major sectors for the year 2005, in comparison with the USA. In terms of labour productivity, a large gap looms between the two regions. In the market economy, value added per hour worked in the EU is less than 70 per cent of the US level. In Table 6.8 a breakdown of the labour productivity gap is made based on (6.14). Relative input levels from Table 6.7 are weighted by their average share in value added to calculate the contribution of inputs to the labour productivity gap. Table 6.8 reads as in the following example. The first row indicates that the (log) labour productivity gap between the EU market economy and the USA was 37 percentage points. Of this gap, 8 percentage points were due to labour composition differences. Differences in capital intensity mattered less, accounting for 5 percentage points. Although ICT intensity was much lower in the EU (see Table 6.7), non-ICT levels were higher and hence contributed positively. The

Table 6.7. Relative levels of inputs and productivity in the EU, major sectors, 2005 (USA = 1)

	Gross value added per hour worked	Labour input per hour worked	Capital input per hour worked	ICT capital input per hour worked	Non-ICT capital input per hour worked	Multi-factor productivity (value added)
Market economy	0.69	0.89	0.86	0.51	1.07	0.79
ICT production	0.60	0.88	0.59	0.45	0.80	0.77
Manufacturing	0.83	0.93	1.02	0.55	1.17	0.90
Other goods	0.63	0.92	0.65	0.34	0.70	0.79
Market services	0.70	0.87	0.87	0.51	1.18	0.79

Note: EU refers to ten countries; see Table 6.3.
Source: Inklaar and Timmer (2008b), appendix tables.

Table 6.8. *Accounting for the EU–US gap in labour productivity, 2005*

	Gross value added per hour worked	Contributions from					
		Labour composition	Capital input per hour worked	ICT capital per hour	Non-ICT capital per hour	Multi-factor productivity	Time–space inconsistency
Market economy	−0.37	−0.08	−0.05	−0.06	0.02	−0.24	−0.01
ICT production	−0.51	−0.08	−0.20	−0.18	−0.04	−0.26	0.03
Manufacturing	−0.19	−0.05	0.01	−0.04	0.04	−0.11	−0.04
Other goods	−0.46	−0.05	−0.17	−0.03	−0.13	−0.23	−0.01
Market services	−0.36	−0.10	−0.04	−0.06	0.03	−0.24	0.01

Notes: The gap is defined as the natural log of the ratio of the EU level to that of the USA. The contributions of the different inputs are calculated by multiplying the gap in input level from Table 6.7 by the share of each input in value added. Contribution in last column due to time–space consistency problem when extrapolating benchmark comparisons; see section 6.2. Contributions may not sum exactly due to rounding. EU refers to ten countries; see Table 6.3.

remaining gap of 24 per cent is explained by the differences in the efficiency with which labour and capital are used, as measured by multi-factor productivity.

Tables 6.7 and 6.8 also provide a decomposition for four major sectors in the economy. Gaps in labour productivity are rather different across the sectors and also the intensity with which labour and capital inputs are used varies. In all sectors, European labour productivity suffers because of the less qualified labour force compared to that of the USA. The gap in the use of capital plays an important role in explaining the lagging performance in ICT production and non-manufacturing goods production, but not in manufacturing and market services. In manufacturing, use of capital per hour is even higher than in the USA on account of the extensive use of non-ICT capital. The most important is the gap in multi-factor productivity which explains at least half of the gap in labour productivity for each sector, and as much as two-thirds in the case of market services.

Relative input and productivity levels for twenty-six detailed industries are given in Table 6.9. In 2005, the EU was leading the USA in labour productivity in seven industries, including mining, chemicals, rubber and plastics, and post and telecommunications. But in most industries the productivity gap between the EU and the USA is large: EU levels are less than half in agriculture, textiles, electrical equipment and utilities. In almost all industries, labour services per hour worked in the EU are lower than in the USA indicating a pervasive skill gap not only in most services but also in manufacturing industries. The use of capital, on the other hand, is frequently higher in the EU than in the USA, in particular in manufacturing. Out of thirteen manufacturing industries, eight have higher levels of capital services per hour worked. In services industries, however, capital use is generally lower, particularly in trade industries, finance and post and telecommunications. As before, in most industries it is not so much differences in the use of factor inputs that drive labour productivity gaps with the USA. Instead it is the lower efficiency with which factor inputs are used as measured by (value-added based) multi-factor productivity, given in the fourth column.

Based on the industry data a decomposition of the aggregate EU–US labour productivity gap can be made. The contribution of each industry is calculated by multiplying the log gap in labour productivity (log level of the EU over the USA) by the share of each industry in market

Table 6.9. *Relative levels of inputs and productivity in the EU, twenty-six industries, 2005 (USA = 1)*

	Value added per hour worked	Labour services per hour worked	Capital services per hour worked	Multi-factor productivity (value-added based)	Multi-factor productivity (gross-output based)
Agriculture	0.37	0.98	0.58	0.49	0.70
Mining	1.23	0.97	0.80	1.37	1.21
Food and beverages	0.93	1.07	1.17	0.89	0.96
Textiles and footwear	0.43	0.98	1.06	0.44	0.71
Wood products	1.05	0.90	1.39	1.06	1.00
Paper, print and publ.	0.84	0.96	1.29	0.82	0.90
Petroleum ref.	0.59	0.91	0.84	0.69	0.91
Chemicals	1.26	0.89	0.99	1.37	1.12
Rubber and plastics	2.21	0.92	1.09	2.30	1.38
Non-metallic mineral	1.79	0.95	1.41	1.70	1.26
Metal	0.87	0.94	1.13	0.89	0.95
Other machinery	0.85	0.97	0.60	1.06	1.02
Electrical equipment	0.25	0.82	0.67	0.31	0.60
Transport equipment	0.52	0.94	1.34	0.51	0.76
Other manufacturing	0.88	0.99	0.88	0.94	0.91

Utilities	0.47	0.96	0.70	0.63	0.73
Construction	0.95	1.00	0.96	0.94	0.97
Automotive trade	0.91	0.87	0.91	1.00	0.99
Wholesale trade	0.60	0.71	0.61	0.86	0.89
Retail trade	0.85	1.11	0.46	0.99	0.99
Hotels and rest.	0.59	1.02	1.04	0.62	0.79
Transport	0.59	0.93	0.90	0.63	0.76
Post and telecomms	1.39	0.91	0.61	1.78	1.42
Finance	0.99	0.97	0.76	1.18	1.13
Business services	0.57	0.86	0.85	0.58	0.69
Other services	1.03	0.92	2.76	0.80	0.88
Market economy	0.69	0.89	0.86	0.79	n.a.

Note: EU refers to ten countries; see Table 6.3.
Source: Inklaar and Timmer (2008b), appendix tables.

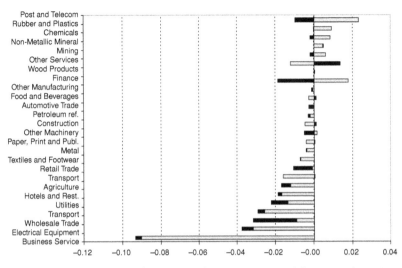

Figure 6.1. Industry contributions to the EU–US gap in labour productivity, market economy, 2005. The contribution of each sector is calculated by multiplying the log gap in labour productivity (log of the ratio of the EU level to that of the USA) by the share of each sector in market economy value added. The grey bar indicates the contribution of the log gap in multi-factor productivity and the black bar the contribution from log gaps in capital and labour services per hour worked. (*Sources*: Values for 1997 from GGDC Productivity Level database (Inklaar and Timmer 2008b) extrapolated with KLEMS database, March 2008 (see Chapter 3).)

economy value added. This is analogous to the method used for the industry contributions to aggregate growth described in Chapter 5. In Figure 6.1 we provide the contributions of twenty-six detailed industries. The bars indicate the contribution of each sector to the overall gap. Each bar is decomposed into the contribution of differences in input use and MFP. The grey part indicates the contribution of the log gap in multi-factor productivity and the black part the contribution from log gaps in capital and labour services per hour worked. By far the biggest contribution to the EU–US labour productivity gap is from business services, accounting for almost a third of the aggregate gap. The MFP gap in business services looms especially large and because of the large size of this sector in the economy, it makes a major contribution. Other sectors also contribute, but to a lesser degree, either because the productivity gaps in these sectors are relatively small (for example, for trade services) or because the sector is relatively unimportant in size (for example, ICT production, utilities and transport).

Productivity gaps in European countries

Next, we turn to an analysis of productivity gaps between individual European countries and the USA. Table 6.10 provides relative levels in the market economy for the year 2005, in comparison with the USA. As before, a breakdown of the labour productivity gap is made based on (6.14) and shown in Table 6.11. In terms of labour productivity, a wide range of levels is found within the European Union. In Belgium, the Netherlands and Sweden labour productivity levels are 85 per cent or more of the US level. Gaps in the use of human and physical capital are small, and efficient use is made of factor inputs as indicated by high MFP levels. In the new member states levels are 40 per cent or less of the US level in 2005, despite rapid growth in the preceding decade. This is partly based on gaps in the use of capital, but mainly due to weak MFP performance which is only half of the US level. Future growth must come not so much from increasing investment in physical and human capital, but much more from improvements in the way inputs are used. The long distances to the technological frontier suggest large potential gains from adopting new technologies developed elsewhere. A particular feature of the small Scandinavian countries, Denmark and Finland, is the gap in human capital that contributes 10 percentage points or more to the labour productivity gap. After a long decade of stagnation, the Mediterranean countries, Italy and Spain, have fallen to labour productivity levels just above half the US level. This is mainly due to low levels of MFP, but in Spain this is also due to the still existing gap in capital intensity. In the other major continental countries, France and Germany, gaps in input use are only minor and the labour productivity gap is mainly due to MFP gaps. In the UK, gaps in human and physical capital contribute about one-third to the gap with the USA and indicate some room for catch-up based on investment. In general, though, it can be concluded that gaps in MFP are by far the most important drivers of labour productivity gaps between European countries and the USA.

Table 6.10. *Relative levels of inputs and productivity, EU countries, market economy, 2005 (USA = 1)*

	Gross value added per hour worked	Labour input per hour worked	Capital input per hour worked	ICT-capital input per hour worked	Non-ICT capital input per hour worked	Multi-factor productivity (value added)
Austria	0.60	0.87	0.93	0.46	1.24	0.67
Belgium	0.96	0.94	1.56	1.16	1.79	0.86
Czech Republic	0.35	0.88	0.52	0.17	0.71	0.44
Denmark	0.78	0.82	1.23	1.02	1.35	0.84
Finland	0.81	0.87	0.96	0.45	1.21	0.90
France	0.73	0.98	0.81	0.44	1.02	0.80
Germany	0.79	0.91	1.02	0.62	1.26	0.85
Hungary	0.39	1.08	0.42	0.20	0.55	0.47
Ireland	0.80	0.95	0.63	0.13	0.93	0.93
Italy	0.57	0.86	0.91	0.26	1.31	0.65
Netherlands	0.86	0.96	0.89	0.62	1.07	0.92
Portugal	0.33	0.60	0.43	0.20	0.57	0.61
Slovenia	0.40	0.88	0.64	0.27	0.84	0.46
Spain	0.56	0.90	0.59	0.26	0.79	0.71
Sweden	0.88	0.97	1.09	0.77	1.26	0.84
United Kingdom	0.66	0.90	0.80	0.78	0.82	0.77
European Union	0.69	0.89	0.86	0.51	1.07	0.79
United States	1.00	1.00	1.00	1.00	1.00	1.00

Note: EU refers to ten countries; see Table 6.3.
Source: Inklaar and Timmer (2008b), appendix tables.

Table 6.11. *Accounting for the labour productivity gap with the USA, EU countries, market economy, 2005*

	Gap in gross value added per hour worked	Contributions to gap from			
		Labour composition	Capital per hour	Multi-factor productivity	Time–space inconsistency
Austria	−0.51	−0.10	−0.02	−0.39	0.00
Belgium	−0.04	−0.04	0.15	−0.15	0.00
Czech Republic	−1.05	−0.08	−0.24	−0.82	0.09
Denmark	−0.25	−0.13	0.07	−0.18	0.00
Finland	−0.21	−0.10	−0.01	−0.10	0.00
France	−0.31	−0.02	−0.07	−0.22	−0.01
Germany	−0.23	−0.06	0.01	−0.17	−0.01
Hungary	−0.95	0.05	−0.31	−0.74	0.06
Ireland	−0.22	−0.03	−0.18	−0.07	0.06
Italy	−0.56	−0.10	−0.03	−0.43	0.00
Netherlands	−0.15	−0.03	−0.04	−0.09	0.00
Portugal	−1.10	−0.33	−0.28	−0.49	0.00
Slovenia	−0.92	−0.10	−0.11	−0.77	0.06
Spain	−0.58	−0.07	−0.18	−0.34	0.00
Sweden	−0.13	−0.02	0.03	−0.17	0.04
United Kingdom	−0.41	−0.07	−0.07	−0.26	−0.02
European Union	−0.37	−0.08	−0.05	−0.24	−0.01

Notes: The gap is defined as the natural log of the ratio of the level of the European country to that of the USA. The contributions of the different inputs are calculated by multiplying the gap in input level by the share of each input in value added. EU refers to ten countries; see Table 6.3.

Source: Inklaar and Timmer (2008b), appendix tables.

Technology gaps

Relative MFP levels can also be used as indicators for the technological distance between countries. They are often used in analyses based on technology-gap models (see section 6.8). As argued by Jorgenson, Gollop and Fraumeni (1987) and Jorgenson *et al.* (2005), the best measure of technological change is multi-factor productivity growth based on gross output. This measure treats all inputs symmetrically and does not rely on separability of value added and intermediate inputs. As such it reflects technical change in the use of all inputs, not only labour and capital. Similarly, the best measure for the technological distance between countries is the relative level of gross-output based MFP as defined in (6.1). The last column of Table 6.9 provides these levels for our twenty-six detailed industries. It is shown that in 2005 the EU leads the USA in eight industries: mining, post and telecommunications, finance and five manufacturing industries. In other major industries, like construction, retail and automotive trade, MFP levels are on a par. Big gaps are found for industries like agriculture, business services and, in particular, electrical machinery. This wide range of gaps testifies to the importance of a detailed industry analysis. Aggregate productivity statistics might suggest that the EU is trailing the USA in terms of innovation and technological prowess, but the technological distance between the regions is highly industry-specific and the USA is not leading in all industries.

This becomes even more clear when we look at the levels of individual European countries. In Table 6.12 we provide for each industry the countries ranked first, second and third in terms of MFP levels in 2005. In addition, the average level of the set of thirteen countries to the frontier country is given in the last column. Clearly, countries seem to specialise in different manufacturing industries, ranging from the Netherlands in food to Finland in wood products, Ireland in chemicals and the USA in electrical equipment. Also in industries that are less open to international trade, technological leadership varies, with the USA leading in hotels and restaurants and business services, while the Netherlands leads in transport, Denmark in trade and other services and Sweden in telecommunications. At the same time, these estimates have to be evaluated with care, as discussed in the previous section.

Table 6.12. *Technology leaders, major sectors, 2005*

	Rank in MFP levels			Average level relative to frontier
	First	Second	Third	
Agriculture	USA	Denmark	Sweden	0.59
Mining	Netherlands	Belgium	Italy	0.27
Food and beverages	Netherlands	Italy	Ireland	0.63
Textiles and footwear	Belgium	USA	Netherlands	0.53
Wood products	Finland	France	Sweden	0.58
Paper, print and publ.	Ireland	Belgium	Finland	0.50
Petroleum ref.	France	UK	Ireland	0.34
Chemicals	Ireland	Finland	Netherlands	0.29
Rubber and plastics	Belgium	Portugal	France	0.43
Non-metallic mineral	Italy	Belgium	Germany	0.57
Metal	Italy	Netherlands	Sweden	0.80
Other machinery	UK	France	Germany	0.65
Electrical equipment	USA	Finland	Sweden	0.51
Transport equipment	Italy	USA	Spain	0.37
Other manufacturing	UK	Denmark	Finland	0.37
Utilities	Sweden	USA	Finland	0.46
Construction	Finland	Austria	Belgium	0.55
Trade	Denmark	Finland	Germany	0.67
Hotels and rest.	USA	Austria	Spain	0.65
Transport	Netherlands	Portugal	USA	0.32
Post and telecomms	Sweden	UK	France	0.30
Finance	Ireland	Denmark	Portugal	0.47
Business services	USA	Ireland	Portugal	0.67
Other services	Denmark	Germany	France	0.84

Notes: MFP is based on gross output. Average is over all EU-15 countries plus USA.
Source: Authors' calculations based on Inklaar and Timmer (2008b).

6.7 Convergence analysis

A key issue in modelling economic growth is whether there is a tendency for productivity levels to converge to a common level or whether differences in levels can continue indefinitely or even increase over time. Initially, this research was mainly focused on explaining patterns of convergence and divergence at the aggregate level.[24] More recently, studies of differences in performance at the sectoral level have appeared, motivated by the influential study of Bernard and Jones (1996). They found that across a set of selected OECD countries, convergence in the aggregate does not necessarily imply convergence at the industry level. In particular they found that during the period 1970–87 manufacturing showed little evidence of productivity convergence, in contrast to the services sector in which convergence was strong. These findings have not gone undisputed. Sørensen (2001) showed that the finding of non-convergence in manufacturing heavily depended on the choice of a set of purchasing power parities (PPPs) to convert national currencies into comparable units. Bernard and Jones (1996) used one set of aggregate GDP PPPs to convert all sectoral variables. However, as sectoral prices do not move in tandem over time, their findings became highly sensitive to the choice of the base year for the PPPs. Typically, manufacturing prices grow much slower than prices of services and a common PPP would not capture this difference. It was concluded that research relying on international comparisons of sectoral productivity and income should proceed with caution until sector-specific PPPs are available.[25] In this section we revisit the analysis of Bernard and Jones (1996) using the more data-intensive productivity measures presented in this chapter and extend their findings. For this we take our 1997 benchmark productivity levels and extrapolate them to 1970 and 2005 using relative MFP growth rates from the EU KLEMS database.[26]

As Islam (2003) argues in his survey, a test for productivity convergence should examine the dispersion of productivity levels over time (σ-convergence). A regression where productivity growth is explained by initial productivity levels can be used (β-convergence), but a significant coefficient on initial productivity levels is only a necessary, but not a sufficient condition for a smaller dispersion in productivity levels over time. Although β-convergence is useful in many economic models (see next section) we rely on σ-convergence here. Figure 6.2 shows

---

[24] See Islam (2003) and Barro and Sala-i-Martin (2004) for an overview.
[25] Bernard and Jones (2001), p. 1169; see also Harrigan (1999), Caselli (2005) and Rogerson (2008), p. 251.
[26] For the 1970–9 period, we partly rely on educational attainment data from de la Fuente and Doménech (2006) to estimate labour composition change.

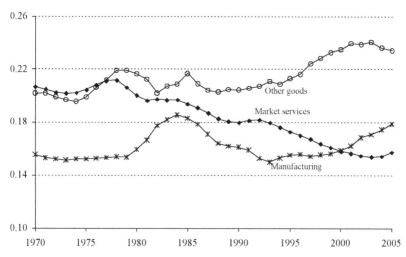

Figure 6.2. Standard deviation of multi-factor productivity levels, 1970–2005. Standard deviation based on MFP levels (value-added based) for thirteen countries (three-year moving average). (*Source*: Based on Inklaar and Timmer (2009a), fig. 1.)

the result of our industry group analysis for the 1970–2005 period. The figure plots the standard deviation of productivity levels relative to the USA for three industry groups, namely manufacturing, market services and other goods-producing industries. This latter group includes agriculture, mining, utilities and construction. Given the long time-span, we were forced to reduce our sample to the thirteen countries with sufficient data.[27] Looking at the 1970–87 period covered by Bernard and Jones (1996), their qualitative findings are confirmed: convergence in market services and no convergence in manufacturing and other goods-producing industries. This pattern does not change in subsequent years: market services continue to show convergence, while the other two sectors even show some evidence of divergence since the mid 1990s. This contrasting convergence pattern across sectors confirms the key message from Bernard and Jones (1996) that an industry perspective is very important in the convergence debate.

---

[27] These are Australia, Austria, Belgium, Denmark, Finland, France, Germany, Italy, Japan, the Netherlands, Spain, the United Kingdom and the United States.

Table 6.13. *Testing for convergence across countries*

	1980	2005	Difference	T3-test
Agriculture	0.22	0.22	0.00	−0.06
Mining	1.00	0.58	−0.41	4.04*
Food and beverages	0.08	0.10	0.02	−0.73
Textiles and footwear	0.15	0.13	−0.02	0.81
Wood products	0.23	0.24	0.02	−0.35
Paper, print and publ.	0.10	0.13	0.03	−2.19*
Petroleum ref.	0.20	0.21	0.02	−0.33
Chemicals	0.16	0.19	0.03	n.a.
Rubber and plastics	0.36	0.36	0.00	−0.04
Non-metallic mineral	0.21	0.18	−0.03	0.87
Metal	0.20	0.15	−0.05	1.90*
Other machinery	0.15	0.12	−0.02	0.80
Electrical equipment	0.17	0.17	0.00	−0.05
Transport equipment	0.17	0.15	−0.01	0.78
Other manufacturing	0.42	0.27	−0.15	3.13*
Utilities	0.12	0.12	0.00	0.02
Construction	0.14	0.18	0.04	n.a.
Trade	0.36	0.23	−0.13	3.09*
Hotels and rest.	0.18	0.15	−0.03	1.16
Transport	0.27	0.27	−0.01	0.31
Post and telecomms	0.19	0.34	0.14	−2.02*
Finance	0.19	0.23	0.05	−0.85
Business services	0.14	0.12	−0.02	0.79
Other services	0.20	0.11	−0.09	4.14*

Notes: * Denotes a standard deviation in 2005 that is significantly different from that in 1980 at the 5% level. T3-test is a test for a significant difference between standard deviations. This statistic asymptotically has a standard normal distribution. 'n.a.' denotes that the test statistic could not be calculated on account of specific parameter values; see Carree and Klomp (1997). Columns 1 and 2 show standard deviation based on data for twenty countries.
Source: Inklaar and Timmer (2009a), table 5.

This is further confirmed in Table 6.13 where we look at patterns of convergence in each of our twenty-four detailed industries. Data limitations require us to restrict the analysis to the 1980–2005 period. Across industries, the evidence for convergence and divergence is also diverse: thirteen industries have lower standard deviations in 2005 than in 1980 while eleven have higher standard deviations. The final column of Table 6.13 shows a test statistic for the equality of standard deviations from Carree and Klomp (1997). Taking into account that the standard deviations over time are not independent, they formulate a test statistic that is asymptotically normally distributed. Five of the industries have a significantly positive test statistic, implying significant convergence, while two show significant divergence. Interestingly, two of the significantly converging industries are in manufacturing, which does not converge in aggregate. Similarly, post and telecommunications, an industry in market services, is one of the industries that show significant divergence, while aggregate market services show convergence. In summary, the detailed industry perspective reinforces Bernard and Jones' (1996) main message that convergence patterns differ substantially across industries.[28]

Given the fact that learning and knowledge spillovers typically take place at the level of firms, rather than industries, it will be interesting to link the industry-level convergence analysis to the burgeoning literature on firm-level productivity. Typically, it is found that within countries there is a large dispersion in productivity across firms, such that it is quite possible that the top firms in a lagging country are above some firms in a leading country. This naturally raises the question of the frontier to which firms are converging. Further linking of industry- and firm-level databases might throw new light on these issues (Bartelsman *et al.* 2008; Griffith *et al.* 2009).

6.8 Determinants of productivity growth

In the previous chapters we showed how investment in physical capital and human capital account for a substantial portion of labour productivity growth in many countries. At the same time we found that cross-country differences in labour productivity growth are mainly due to differences in the efficiency with which the inputs are used, as measured by MFP growth. To gain further insight into the causes of MFP growth differences, it is necessary to move beyond the growth accounting framework and explain differences in MFP growth. Such analysis crucially requires estimates of relative levels as well as growth

[28] Using PPPs based on expenditure prices only, van Biesebroeck (2009) arrives at the same conclusion; see also Sørensen and Schjerning (2008).

rates. In this section we use regression analysis to gauge statistically the importance of a number of potential determinants of MFP growth, based on a dynamic catching-up, or technology-gap, model as is commonly used in the literature.[29] Of the many possible determinants, we focus on whether ICT use and the use of skilled labour generates externalities and whether regulatory barriers to entry hamper productivity growth.

A technology-gap model of productivity growth

Following the technology-gap model, MFP growth in an industry is determined by the strength of the domestic innovation process and the speed of imitation of best-practice technologies developed elsewhere.[30] The potential for technology transfer is captured by the technology gap relative to the global productivity leader. But the social and technological capabilities of an economy determine to what extent an industry innovates and exploits imitation opportunities.[31] Aghion and Howitt (2006) argue that traditional European institutions are mostly suited to catching up to the technology frontier and not so much to fostering innovation. For example, educational systems are more geared towards vocational schooling rather than higher education; capital markets are biased towards large incumbent firms rather than start-ups; labour market regulation promotes on-the-job training but hinders reallocations across firms; and innovation systems, including, for example, patent protection laws and public R&D institutes, stimulate incremental innovation rather than major breakthroughs. To capture this idea, additional variables reflecting these institutional differences across countries are added to a standard catch-up model. Such variables might influence MFP growth by affecting the pace of innovation and the speed of technology imitation. For example, Griffith *et al.* (2004) find that spending on research and development (R&D) in manufacturing industries increases the pace of innovation but also speeds up technology imitation.

---

[29] See, for example, Nicoletti and Scarpetta (2003), Griffith *et al.* (2004), Cameron *et al.* (2005), and Vandenbussche *et al.* (2006).

[30] Innovation is defined as the development of technologies which are not only new to a country, but also new to the world.

[31] Fagerberg (1994) surveys the earlier literature; see also note 1 above.

The basic model to be estimated is then:

$$\Delta \ln \text{MFP} = \beta \,(\text{Technology gap}) + \gamma X + \delta (X * \text{Technology gap})$$

$$(6.26)$$

where X denotes one of several possible determinants of MFP of policy interest. The key parameters are β, which quantifies the importance of technology imitation that depends on the size of the technology gap, γ which shows the direct effect of X on productivity growth and δ which gauges whether X has a larger effect on productivity growth for industries that are farther away from the frontier (positive sign) or closer to the frontier (negative sign). The regressions will also include dummies to control for fixed country-specific, industry-specific and time-specific factors. In this section, we look at three possible determinants of MFP growth, namely the use of ICT capital, the use of university-educated workers and regulatory barriers to entry, as all three have been suggested as important drivers of productivity growth. Moreover, the latter two also play a prominent role in the recommendations of the Sapir Report (Sapir *et al.* 2004). Based on our technology-gap measures presented in the previous sections, we can begin testing the importance of our potential explanatory variables for cross-country differences in MFP growth.[32]

Spillovers from ICT capital

The first variable to be tested is ICT use. ICT, like other types of fixed capital, contributes to labour productivity growth by increasing the amount of capital input per hour worked. In previous chapters we showed that ICT use accounted for a major part of labour productivity growth, under the assumption that the benefits of ICT capital are reflected by the price paid for its use. A more contentious hypothesis is that ICT generates positive externalities, i.e. benefits that are higher than the costs being paid by the investor. Such externalities could be caused by, for example, network effects or complementary investments, such as organisational change, that go unmeasured. The evidence on externalities from ICT use is mixed. There is some firm-level

---

[32] The analysis in this section is based on an earlier vintage of data than used in the rest of this book, namely the March 2007 version of the EU KLEMS database and a preliminary version of the GGDC Productivity Level database.

Table 6.14 *Relationship between technology gaps, ICT use and productivity growth*

Dependent variable: MFP growth

	1	2	3
Technology gap	0.016***	0.016***	0.012***
	(0.004)	(0.004)	(0.004)
ICT use		−0.090**	−0.212***
		(0.041)	(0.068)
Technology gap * ICT use			0.221**
			(0.108)
Number of observations	6,864	6,864	6,864

Notes: The table shows OLS regression estimates, explaining annual MFP growth by the gap relative to the frontier, ICT use and the interaction between the technology gap and ICT use. *, ** and *** denote coefficients significantly different from zero at, respectively, the 10%, 5% and 1% levels. Standard errors, consistent for heteroscedasticity and autocorrelation, are in parentheses. The industry-level data are a balanced panel for twenty-six market industries in each of the eleven countries for the period 1980–2004 and all regressions include country, industry and year dummies.

and industry-level research for the USA that suggests super-normal returns to ICT, but a recent survey and meta-analysis concludes that the hypothesis of normal returns seems to hold (Stiroh 2004). The evidence for countries other than the USA is more scattered and these national studies are generally not directly comparable.[33] Using the EU KLEMS database, we can focus on MFP and test for externalities of ICT use across a larger group of countries and industries. The externalities should show up as a positive correlation between ICT use and MFP growth, as indicated in the model above.

Table 6.14 shows the results of this exercise. We first show a regression in which only the technology gap is used to explain MFP growth. The technology gap is defined as minus the log of the relative MFP

---

[33] See, for example, Brynjolfsson and Hitt (2003) for a firm-level study and Stiroh (2002) and Basu *et al.* (2004) for industry-level studies. OECD (2004) provides a collection of national studies. Basu *et al.* (2004) and O'Mahony and Vecchi (2005) are among the very few cross-country studies of the productive impact of ICT and find super-normal returns to ICT use in the USA, but not in the UK. Draca *et al.* (2007) provide an overview.

level, so that a larger gap equals a lower relative level. Column 1 indicates that industries that are further away from the technological frontier show faster MFP growth. In the light of the theoretical models discussed above, this might be interpreted as the result of international technology transfers, which benefit laggard countries more than countries close to the frontier. This finding of β-convergence of MFP levels within service industries confirms earlier analysis by, for example, Bernard and Jones (1996) and Nicoletti and Scarpetta (2003).

The results in Table 6.14 show that the evidence of positive externalities of ICT on MFP growth is weak. We measure ICT adoption as the share of ICT-capital compensation in gross output. Column 2 actually shows a significant negative relationship between ICT use and MFP growth. This would imply that the returns to ICT investments are lower than their costs. The size of this effect depends on the distance to the technology frontier as indicated by the interaction effect in column 3. Countries that are further away from the frontier benefit more from ICT investment than countries that are close to the frontier. Nevertheless, the marginal effects of ICT use are significantly negative for the majority of industries (about 90 per cent of the observations). This is also economically significant. For example, the median MFP gap of all industries is 0.33, so at the median ICT use (0.9 per cent), MFP growth is overestimated by 0.14 percentage points. As a result, our cross-country analyses do not suggest any positive externalities to the use of ICT. If anything, the contribution of ICT to labour productivity growth is somewhat overestimated by the growth accounting method. However, this possible overestimation cannot explain the large cross-country differences in MFP growth.

Spillovers from skilled labour

Skilled labour has also been suggested as another driver of technological change and an important source of productivity growth. Vandenbussche *et al.* (2006) present a model where economies with a larger share of university-educated workers exhibit a faster rate of innovation, because skilled labour has a comparative advantage for innovation compared to imitation. Hence the growth-enhancing effect of skilled labour will be stronger for economies closer to the frontier as the opportunities for growth through imitation decrease. Vandenbussche *et al.* (2006) present cross-country evidence supporting this model and their study has been used in the Sapir Report (Sapir *et al.*

2004) to support the policy argument that higher education stimulates innovation. Their finding of skill externalities is all the more important because in an earlier study, Krueger and Lindahl (2001) conclude that while there is a high private return to education, the evidence for externalities at the level of industries or aggregate economies is far from conclusive.

However, the study of Vandenbussche *et al.* (2006) has two important drawbacks. First, growth differences between countries are only analysed at the aggregate level, instead of across industries within countries, which leaves open the possibility that the positive correlation between human capital and MFP growth is due to a country-specific factor that is correlated with both human capital and growth.[34] The second drawback is that they rely on crude MFP measures that do not take into account differences in hours worked or in the educational attainment of the labour force. This means that their analysis cannot make a distinction between private and social returns to education. Only findings of social returns (or externalities) would provide a solid basis for policy initiatives.

In Table 6.15, we show that while the use of crude MFP measures provides a weak confirmation of the Vandenbussche *et al.* (2006) results, when using data-intensive MFP measures, the positive correlation between human capital and MFP growth is absent. In the left panel, we replicate the set-up by Vandenbussche *et al.* (2006), using aggregate economy data, no country fixed effects and crude MFP measures. Columns 1 and 2 show a significant positive effect of high-skilled workers on MFP growth. The interaction term also has a negative sign as predicted by the model of Vandenbussche *et al.* (2006), but is not significant. However, the positive effect of the share of high-skilled workers disappears once data-intensive MFP measures are used, as shown in columns 3 and 4. In the last columns, we rework the analysis for our set of twenty-six market industries. The industry-level estimates are consistent throughout and do not provide evidence that a larger share of high-skilled workers has an impact on MFP growth. Our results for the use of skilled labour are therefore similar to those

---

[34] See Temple (2000) for a more extensive discussion of the problem with cross-country growth regressions. This possibility is not entirely dispelled by the fact that the positive correlation between human capital and MFP growth disappears once taking into account country-fixed effects.

Table 6.15. *Relationship between high-skilled workers and productivity growth at the aggregate and services industry levels*

Dependent variable: MFP growth

	Total economy				Industry level	
	Crude MFP		Data-intensive MFP		Data-intensive MFP	
	1	2	3	4	5	6
Technology gap	0.027**	0.044**	0.015*	0.007	0.016***	0.017***
	(0.011)	(0.020)	(0.008)	(0.014)	(0.014)	(0.016)
High-skilled share	0.043**	0.065**	0.004	−0.009	0.003	0.004
	(0.020)	(0.027)	(0.016)	(0.034)	(0.014)	(0.016)
Technology gap × high-skilled share		−0.106		0.056		−0.004
		(0.126)		(0.121)		(0.028)
Number of observations	264	264	264	264	6,864	6,864

Notes: The table shows OLS regression estimates, explaining MFP growth by the gap relative to the frontier, the share of high-skilled (university-educated) workers in total hours worked and the interaction between the technology gap and the high-skilled share. *, **, and *** denote coefficients significantly different from zero at, respectively, the 10%, 5% and 1% levels. Standard errors, consistent for heteroscedasticity and autocorrelation, are in parentheses. For definitions of crude and data-intensive MFP, see Table 6.6. The total economy data are a balanced panel for eleven countries, while the industry-level data are a balanced panel for twenty-six market industries in each of the eleven countries, all of these for the period 1980–2004. The total economy results include year dummies and the industry-level results include country, industry and year dummies.

for ICT use: there is no evidence of productivity externalities from employing university-educated workers. As for ICT, this means that the contribution of a higher-educated work-force to labour productivity growth is well captured in the growth accounting exercises in this book.

The impact of regulatory barriers to entry on MFP growth

Analysing the effect of competition on productivity growth has taken great flight in recent years (see, for example, Aghion and Griffith 2005 and Crafts 2006 for overviews). The outcome of recent theoretical work is that more competition in product markets stimulates productivity growth because it stimulates innovation. Moreover, this effect might be stronger when an industry is closer to the technology frontier as those industries need to rely more on innovation compared to imitation.[35] Testing this prediction is not straightforward, as competition in product markets cannot be observed directly. In some cases, changes in the regulatory regime can be used as a proxy for changes in competition. For example, Griffith *et al.* (2006) use information on the implementation of the European Single Market Programme in different years and different countries and assume a stronger effect in some manufacturing industries than others in order to establish that deregulation improved productivity growth in manufacturing by stimulating spending on R&D. Eventually, the liberalisation of market services that is mandated in the EU Services Directive may provide a similar testing ground for the effects of regulation on productivity growth in market services.

In the meantime, the product market regulation measures compiled by the OECD are the most useful for the purpose of measuring the impact of regulation on productivity. Nicoletti and Scarpetta (2003) describe the OECD Product Market Regulation Database measures in detail and provide the first systematic empirical analysis of the impact of regulation on productivity in a cross-country setting. Their study has been highly influential and has been another source of inspiration for the Sapir Report (Sapir *et al.* 2004). Nicoletti and Scarpetta (2003) find some evidence that entry liberalisation in services increases

---

[35] See, for example, Acemoglu, Aghion and Zilibotti (2006) for such a model.

productivity growth, which supports the theoretical notion that entry barriers decrease the intensity of competition. Paradoxically, they find an impact of deregulation in services on productivity growth in manufacturing industries, but not in services industries.[36] The mixed nature of the results may be due to the fact that there is insufficient change over time in the barriers to entry in some industries. For example, in most countries, barriers to entry in retail trade hardly changed in the period for which data are available. To identify the effects of barriers to entry, an even more detailed focus on an industry with more variation in the regulatory measures might be needed.

Inklaar *et al.* (2008) provide such a detailed analysis and some of their main results are reproduced here.[37] In particular, they looked at barriers to entry in two individual industries: transport and storage services and post and telecommunication services. For both industries, the OECD constructed a time-series of barriers to entry covering the entire sample period from 1980 onwards and both industries experienced substantial entry liberalisation in most countries. This is most strongly so in post and telecommunications, which changed during the 1990s from a very restrictive to an almost fully liberalised industry environment in nearly all countries.[38] Table 6.16 shows that there is little effect of changes in barriers to entry in the transport industry, but that in post and telecommunications, lower barriers are strongly related to higher MFP growth (columns 3 and 4). This finding provides support for the notion that lower barriers to entry promote productivity growth by increasing competition in the latter sector. In general though, for other services sectors, no evidence could be found. It might be that the OECD summary measures of regulation do not capture all the complexities of product market regulation and their interaction with labour market regulation. Also, most regulations are fine-grained and industry-specific such as land zoning in retailing, accounting standards in business services or sanitation requirements in

---

[36] In their Table 8, Nicoletti and Scarpetta (2003) report a significant impact of entry liberalisation in services on productivity growth across all industries. However, in Table 7 they show that this entry liberalisation trend in services did not significantly affect productivity growth in services.

[37] The full details of the approach, including extensive robustness analyses, can be found in Inklaar *et al.* (2008).

[38] See Conway and Nicoletti (2006) on the trends and also Boylaud and Nicoletti (2000) on regulation and performance in telecommunications.

Table 6.16. *The effect of barriers to entry on productivity growth in services*

Dependent variable: MFP growth

	Transport and storage		Post and telecommunications	
	1	2	3	4
Technology gap	0.115***	0.128***	0.077***	0.068***
	(0.035)	(0.041)	(0.023)	(0.023)
Barriers	−0.012	−0.007	−0.041***	−0.060***
	(0.008)	(0.008)	(0.012)	(0.021)
Barriers * technology gap		−0.011		0.037
		(0.014)		(0.029)
Number of observations	264	264	264	264

Notes: Dependent variable is MFP growth in the transport industry or the telecommunications industry. All regressions include country and year dummies. For further notes, see Table 6.15.
Source: Inklaar *et al.* (2008), table 11.

the hotel business. In addition, overall entry barriers will also include other costs such as fixed start-up costs.[39] This points to the importance of detailed regulatory and productivity measures to analyse the impact of regulation on productivity. Chapter 7 provides a further discussion.

6.9 Concluding remarks

Economic growth analysis has been hampered by a lack of data of sufficient quality on industry productivity levels. Neo-classical production theory implies that accurate productivity level estimates require industry-specific relative output and input prices and a thorough accounting for the heterogeneity of inputs. Although each of these problems is widely acknowledged and has been partially addressed in various studies, the GGDC Productivity Level database presented in this chapter is the first that provides a comprehensive treatment.

---

[39] See Baily and Kirkegaard (2004) and Crafts (2006) on some of these considerations. Also see Kox and Lejour (2005) on the impact of differences in regulation across countries.

It does so at an industry level and using detailed data on inputs and outputs. As shown in this chapter, the differences between crude and data-intensive measures are very important in practice: there are considerable differences across countries in average hours worked; the composition of the work-force in terms of educational attainment and experience; the use of ICT and non-ICT capital; and prices of both industry output, intermediate inputs and investment. Accounting for these differences has a substantial impact on productivity level estimates. In particular, this chapter has emphasised the importance of having detailed industry measures for analyses of catch-up and convergence based on technology-gap models. Results are sensitive to the type of data used, and industry trends differ from the aggregate.

Our preferred productivity measures take into account many of the criticisms that have been raised against cruder estimates. However, this does not imply that all data issues have been resolved. As discussed in section 6.5 and Chapter 3, there are a number of areas for further improvement in the basic statistics underlying the measurement of productivity growth and levels. Of particular importance is extending data on capital assets, such as land and intangible capital. Some of the industry output prices, in particular for services industries like finance and business services are hard to measure, both over time and across countries. And international comparisons of educational attainment levels and hours worked need to be improved. More generally, it is true that more detailed measures of labour and capital are less reliable than more aggregate measures on account of limited survey evidence. Notwithstanding these remaining issues, we would argue that our productivity level estimates provide a fruitful starting point for further research. They should increase the degree of trust in cross-country growth analyses, especially research employing econometric specifications that include technology-gap variables.

7 | Drivers of productivity growth in Europe

7.1 Paths for productivity growth in Europe

In this book we have documented and analysed Europe's productivity performance since the mid 1990s and compared it to growth since the 1970s, as well as to the productivity record of the United States. On both counts, Europe's performance has been disappointing as labour productivity growth has seriously slowed since 1995, while it has accelerated in the United States. In this book we have analysed the determinants of Europe's poor productivity performance using a new database on productivity at the industry level, the EU KLEMS database.

While our findings confirm the established view that the growing role of ICT and continued improvements in human capital are important drivers of labour productivity growth, this appears not to be the main reason that Europe has failed to show faster productivity growth. While there are differences across European countries and between Europe and the USA, ICT investment has become a more important source of growth everywhere, as illustrated in Chapter 3. Slower productivity growth in Europe since the mid 1990s has been mainly related to a slowdown in the efficiency with which labour and capital are used, as measured by multi-factor productivity (MFP) growth. Indeed one key finding of Chapter 2 is that European growth could benefit from exploiting the increased potential for productivity growth in market services. In contrast to earlier suggestions in the literature, services industries such as trade and business services may see rapid labour productivity growth, as evidenced by the US experience. Given that market services are likely to continue to grow as a share of the economy in both regions, they are potentially a major source of economic growth. But until the mid 2000s Europe had not exploited this opportunity, leading to a growing gap in the productivity level between Europe and the USA. By 2005, the market services sector in Europe was 20 per cent less productive than in the USA.

In addition to slow productivity growth in market services, labour productivity growth in goods production, a traditional European strength, also slowed considerably after 1995. In part, this is related to the end of the catching-up in traditional sectors of the economy, such as agriculture in France, Italy and Spain. But labour productivity growth has also slowed down across most manufacturing industries. To some extent, this can be traced to slower capital deepening. Indeed if investment rates do not adjust, faster employment growth and falling unemployment numbers will lead to slower increases in capital per hour worked. Most importantly though, MFP growth has slowed down in virtually all goods-producing industries, as discussed in Chapter 5.

European economies therefore face a major challenge if they are to increase economic performance and living standards through productivity growth. To grasp the significance of this challenge we illustrate a few productivity growth scenarios, making use of the historical MFP performance in the periods 1980–95 and 1995–2005. Figure 7.1 illustrates a number of possible scenarios. The baseline scenario for both the USA and Europe assumes that the industry growth rates of MFP for 1995–2005 will be maintained, using the 2005 value-added shares to compute market economy growth. This implies a widening productivity gap between Europe and the USA since US MFP growth was quite rapid over this period, while European MFP was close to stagnation. We also look at two alternatives for European growth. In the first, labelled 'manufacturing renaissance', we assume that MFP growth in manufacturing industries would return to its 1980–95 rates. This scenario considerably raises the contribution of the manufacturing sector to aggregate MFP growth, but since manufacturing makes up a shrinking part of Europe's economies (see also Chapter 4), market economy MFP growth in the USA would still outpace that of Europe. The other, more optimistic, alternative assumes that Europe will be able to close the current MFP level gap of 20 per cent by 2020 by way of faster market services MFP growth. As the figure shows, this would require aggregate MFP growth in Europe to increase to almost double the US growth rate, sustained for fifteen years and with three-quarters of aggregate growth coming from market services industries. This suggests a major challenge for Europe in closing the productivity gap with

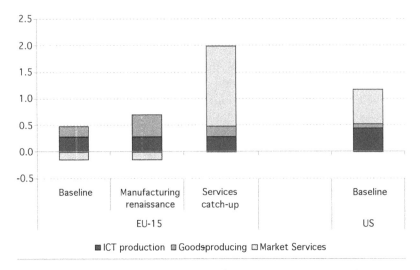

Figure 7.1. Sector contributions to market economy MFP growth scenarios, Europe and USA (*Sources*: Authors' estimates using MFP growth rates and value-added shares from the EU KLEMS database March 2008 (see Chapter 3) and market economy productivity levels from the GGDC Productivity Levels database (Inklaar and Timmer 2009a).)

the United States.[1] Whatever scenario is ultimately realised, there are a number of areas for research on growth that will be important for researchers, statisticians and policy analysts for years to come. In this chapter we briefly discuss a number of important areas for empirical research, without the intention of providing an exhaustive overview of the studies in the field of economic growth.[2]

To begin, efforts should be made to improve measures of output in services to better monitor the performance of this sector. Specifically, this requires more research into how we should conceptualise output

---

[1] We also considered a slower growth scenario for the USA, assuming a slowdown of the MFP growth rate to the average growth rate between 1980 and 1995. This puts US MFP growth at a similar rate as the baseline scenario in Europe. So if US MFP growth stagnates while Europe continues its growth rate as before, the productivity gap between the two regions will at best stay the same. Only if one of the two more optimistic scenarios in Europe were to be realised, could it overtake the US level if the latter grows at the slower rate.

[2] The *Handbook of Economic Growth*, edited by Aghion and Durlauf (2005), provides a good starting point for those interested in a wider overview.

in financial services but also a renewed focus on non-market services such as health and education (section 7.2). To better understand the process of innovation, and its relation to productivity, the crucial role of intangible capital needs to be recognised. Expenses on intangibles such as R&D, licences and organisational innovations can be important sources of productivity growth. By considering these expenses as investments in knowledge, their contribution to growth can be measured within the standard growth accounting framework (section 7.3). This research will require a further integration of the research fields of innovation and economic growth.

There are other areas within the innovation research field that are also of immediate relevance for productivity. The growth accounting approach, which has been applied in the EU KLEMS project reported in this book, is essentially a supply-side approach to the sources of economic growth. The role of demand in inducing innovation paths and boosting productivity growth is still not well understood and deserves further attention (section 7.4).

There is also a significant literature on how competition impacts on innovation, but more empirical research is needed to determine the optimal level of competition to support innovation. Competition will also have a direct effect on productivity as more intense competition increases the rate of resource reallocation. It can lead to a faster exit of less productive firms and a greater chance for more productive entrants to gain a foothold and grow quickly after start-up. Government policy can have a large influence on resource reallocation through its regulation of entry barriers and the resulting degree of competition in an industry. This is discussed in section 7.5. Section 7.6 concludes.

7.2 Measuring services productivity

A key obstacle to a better understanding of services productivity and its determinants is the challenge of measuring output in services. As we discussed in Chapter 3, measurement practices in the framework of today's National Accounts are less than perfect in providing an accurate measure of the productivity performance of these industries. In market services, there are major challenges in the measurement of output and productivity in financial and business services. In addition, there is an increased need for improvement in measurement practices in the non-market services of government, health and education, if only because of their large shares in the economy. Both financial services and non-market services deserve attention in view of the difficulties in conceptualising their output and productivity performance, which go beyond standard statistical measurement issues such as adequately capturing quality improvements in deflators.

Financial services

While there have been many (anecdotal) suggestions that the financial sector has been one of the sectors that has perversely driven US growth during the past decade or so,[3] measured productivity growth in financial services has in fact been quite low in both the USA and Europe (see Table 2.4). However, it is questionable whether the estimates of productivity growth in the financial sector adequately reflect the performance of the financial sector. As the discussion on bank output in Chapter 3 showed, current statistical practices are not up to the task of measuring output and productivity adequately. There is some circumstantial evidence that measured growth in European banking has been overstated in recent years. By the same token, the benefits of financial innovation are often called upon in discussions of regulation in the financial sector, but their quantitative importance is generally unknown.[4] Before we are able to measure these factors, we still need more clarity on what it is that banks and other financial institutions actually provide: is it mostly transaction services or does it also include intermediation services such as providing information on risk profiles, and to what extent is bearing risk a 'productive service'? There is a large literature on what banks do (see, for example, Stiroh 2000), but more effort is needed to translate new conceptual insights into the coherent measurement framework of the National Accounts and to find ways of implementing these output and productivity concepts in day-to-day statistical practice.[5]

As is well known, the importance of the financial sector for economic growth goes beyond its direct contribution to aggregate output. One

---

[3] See, for example, Paul Krugman's query on 'how much of the apparent US productivity miracle, a miracle not shared by Europe, was a statistical illusion created by our bloated finance industry?' (http://krugman.blogs.nytimes. com/2009/04/16/reconsidering-a-miracle/)

[4] See, for example, Frame and White (2004).

[5] See Basu *et al.* (2009) for an initial attempt.

of its key roles is to allocate financial resources to stimulate economic activity in other industries. There is considerable empirical evidence that a better-developed financial system enhances economic growth and financial institutions can help to select and finance the most profitable investment projects (Levine 2005). However, important questions remain. For instance, the role of finance in resource allocation has only recently started to receive empirical attention in new studies based on firm-level data. Furthermore, recent evidence suggests that the growth benefits from a more efficient financial system level off beyond a certain level of financial development.[6] And following the global financial crisis in 2008–9, the issue of the optimal business model and structure in the banking industry to safeguard the stability of the financial system and deliver growth-enhancing competition has become pressing.

Non-market services

The growing share of economic activity in non-market services, such as health and education, has made a better understanding of productivity growth increasingly important. Measurement of output in non-market services is still the Achilles' heel of empirical productivity studies. By definition, output measurement in this sector defies the current practice of deflating revenue or sales by an appropriate price index. Instead, input measures are often used, implicitly assuming no productivity growth. In recent years, much effort has been devoted to this issue by national and international bodies responsible for developing performance statistics for these sectors, mainly by experimenting with genuine output measures based on quantity indicators. But many conceptual and practical issues remain in attempts to apply the concepts in international comparisons.[7] It is common practice to divide non-market services into those individually consumed (health, social services, education) and collective services (criminal justice and policing, defence, general government administration). The conceptual issues

---

[6] On resource allocation, see, for example, Wurgler (2000) and Aghion *et al.* (2007). On efficiency, see, for example, Manning (2003) and Inklaar and Koetter (2008).

[7] See, for example, Eurostat (2001), the Atkinson Review (Atkinson 2005) and recent work at the Centre for the Measurement of Government Activity at the UK Office for National Statistics and at the OECD.

that need to be addressed for individual services include the use of 'activities' rather than costs as output measures, and the choice of weights to employ to aggregate across activities. Activities or other volume indicators need to be enhanced to yield quality-adjusted output measures and need to take account of product and process innovations in service provision. Conceptual problems are more severe for collective services.

A few examples illustrate some of the issues that face researchers attempting to tackle these problems. Recent studies on output measurement in the health sector have resorted to readily available measures of survival rates and reductions in waiting times in adjusting for quality.[8] However, in order to estimate properly the effect of treatment on the health of individuals, studies should go beyond these traditional measures and somehow include quality-of-life or disability-free metrics based on characteristics such as mobility, absence of pain, etc.

In the case of education services, arguably the best available evidence on quality in schools comes from standardised academic achievement tests, which are designed to be as comparable as possible across different schools and regions and, more recently, across countries in the OECD PISA study. Indeed there are arguments that improvements in quality, as measured by performance in tests, might have a considerably larger impact on economic growth than a proportionate increase in average years of schooling (Hanushek and Kimko 2000). However, there is some concern about whether tests provide sufficiently comparable indicators of academic performance, especially when used to assess students from different educational systems.

Even greater conceptual and practical problems arise when dealing with collective services, with difficulties even in defining activities. The Atkinson Review (Atkinson 2005) implied that, other things being equal, the volume of protective services should increase in line with the quantity protected. A number of problems are faced when applying this principle to protective services (police, fire service, defence services). For example, as both people and property are protected, the volume of the former is probably best measured by a head-count, while the latter is measured by an index of the capital stock. But the relative degree of protection offered by these services to different groups of

---

[8] For example, Dawson *et al.* (2005).

people and property may differ. For defence, a balanced view needs to be formed of what the armed services actually provide defence against (O'Mahony and Stevens 2006).

7.3 The role of intangible capital

As advanced economies become more knowledge-intensive, they make increasing use of a whole range of intangible assets, related to information technology, knowledge and firm-specific competencies. These are assets that are not physically present, but rather are embedded in the firm's organisational structure or in its human resources. They crucially contribute to the firm's and the economy's innovation and productivity performance. To the extent that such unmeasured investments in intangibles generate additional output growth in the future, their growth benefits end up in the measured multi-factor productivity (MFP) residual. There is scope, however, to measure such investments and their productivity impact more explicitly.

Until the mid 1990s, conventional measures of investment, as included in the National Accounts of countries, consisted primarily of tangible assets such as equipment and structures. In the 1993 version of the System of National Accounts (ISWGNA 1993) the treatment of intangibles began to change with the decision to capitalise software expenditures and include them as an investment that contributes to GDP. This treatment has recently been extended to include scientific R&D in National Accounts measures, mostly as a satellite account (for example, in Canada, the Netherlands and the USA), and by the decision of the United Nations in the 2008 revision of the System of National Accounts. Still, the full range of value-building intangible assets are not yet likely to be accorded the same treatment as software and scientific R&D in the National Accounts, even though surveys show that assets like management capability, marketing and employee-training expenditures are important complementary investments to R&D. According to Corrado *et al.* (2005), there is no clear-cut distinction between tangibles and intangibles that would justify a distinction between the former being capitalised and the latter being expensed. In fact, any outlay that is intended to increase future, rather than current, consumption should be treated as a capital investment.

Various definitions of intangible capital are possible, with different coverage of activities, but most definitions are offspring from

Schumpeter's classification, including the development of new products and production processes, organisational change, management, marketing and finance (Schumpeter 1934). Corrado *et al.* (2005) were the first to develop an estimate of a broad range of intangibles for the USA in the 1990s, distinguishing three categories:

(1) Computer software, which is already capitalised in the National Accounts.
(2) Innovative property, which includes both scientific property and 'non-scientific' R&D. The latter includes the development of innovative new financial products and architectural modelling. Spending on this exceeded the amount spent on the conventional science-lab type.
(3) Firm-specific competencies, which is the largest category, covering brand capital, worker training and management capability. For example, investment in brand names was measured as a fraction of advertising spending. As discussed below, the choice of what to include in this broad category is still an important issue of discussion and requires further research.

The key finding of the research by Corrado *et al.* (2005) is that intangible investment by US businesses averaged $1.2 trillion per year during the 1998–2000 period, an amount that is roughly the same as investment in tangible capital at that time.[9] Replication of this study for a number of European countries suggests that levels in Europe were lower than in the USA: the percentage of intangible investment relative to GDP ranged from around 5% in Italy and Spain, to 7–8% in France and Germany, 10% in the United Kingdom and 13% in the United States (Hao *et al.* 2008; Marrano *et al.* 2009).

By capitalising intangibles, their impact on growth can also be analysed with the standard growth accounting approach. This has been done first for the USA by Corrado *et al.* (2009) and more recently for several European countries following the same methodology.

---

[9] This is also the amount by which nominal GDP is increased by the capitalisation of this broad list of intangibles. In percentage terms, the resulting estimate of GDP is 10 per cent larger. The software portion of this is already included in current GDP estimates, but this amounts to only 13 per cent of the $1.2 trillion increase. Even if scientific R&D were added, as suggested in the new System of National Accounts, this percentage would rise to 28 per cent, leaving more than 70 per cent of intangibles unaccounted for.

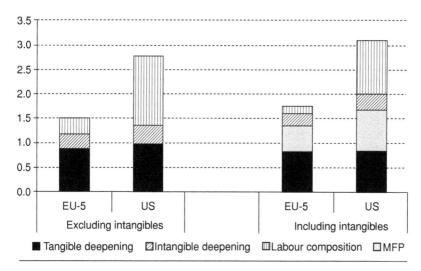

Figure 7.2. Intangibles and labour productivity growth in Europe and the USA, 1995–2003, market economy. EU-5 is a weighted average of growth accounts for France, Germany, Italy, Spain and the UK. Data is from Hao *et al.* (2008). The original source for the USA is Corrado *et al.* (2009) and for the UK, Marrano *et al.* (2009). For Germany, France, Italy and Spain, intangible investment is estimated from a combination of National Accounts, surveys of statistical offices and trade associations and corporate financial reports. EU KLEMS provides the output of industries that produce intangibles, deflators and depreciation rates of tangible assets and software and databases. Corrado *et al.* (2009) provides the deflators of all intangible assets and the depreciation rates of intangible assets excluding software and databases.

Figure 7.2 shows a summary of the growth accounting results for the market economy in the five largest European economies (France, Germany, Italy, Spain and the United Kingdom) and the United States. Labour productivity growth is decomposed both by excluding and including intangibles as investment. The figure shows that the contribution from intangibles to labour productivity growth is rather high. In the USA the intangibles' contribution is even as high as the contribution of tangible investment. In Europe, the contribution of intangibles is somewhat lower, both compared to the USA and compared to tangibles, but still sizeable. The MFP residual is somewhat smaller, but there are no large differences in this respect between Europe and the USA, and a large MFP gap remains.

Despite the significant progress in measuring intangible capital, there are important remaining challenges in adequately determining its contribution to growth and growth differentials (Hulten and van Ark 2008; Nakamura 2010). Intangibles are often created within firms and not mediated by the market, which makes it particularly challenging to include them in an accounting system that typically relies on market prices to measure marginal revenues. In addition, the rate and profiles of depreciation of intangible assets are difficult to determine, and may be different from what standard geometric depreciation patterns for tangible capital imply. An important conceptual concern is the non-rival nature or, more generally, the externalities created by several intangible investments (Nakamura 2010). These drive a wedge between productivity effects at firm level and at higher levels of aggregation. Positive externalities may be large for some intangibles, such as R&D, while negative externalities may also exist, for example from market stealing through the benefits of advertising.[10] But for other types of intangible capital, such as brand equity and organisational competencies, many effects are firm-specific, meaning that firms can exclude competitors from gaining access to its benefits.[11]

Despite these conceptual and measurement challenges, the inclusion of intangibles in a growth accounts framework is an important research track to pursue, despite the marginalistic principles of the underlying model, as it provides an important benchmark for further research. For example, it is very useful to provide a breakdown of intangible investment by industry in view of the different nature of intangibles in services from those in manufacturing, as the latter relies more on scientific R&D.[12] The linkages between technology, investment, organisation and productivity can also be further analysed in a firm-level regression framework. For example, Bloom and van Reenen (2007) link the intangible of corporate management practices to productivity and show significant cross-country differences, with US firms on average better managed and more productive than European firms. In particular, it is suggested that US multi-nationals are organised in a way that allows them to use new technologies such as ICT more efficiently than non-US firms (Bloom *et al.* 2009).

---

[10] See, for example, Bloom *et al.* (2007) who find that (positive) technology spillovers quantitatively dominate negative market spillovers.
[11] See Corrado *et al.* (2009).   [12] See, for example, Baldwin *et al.* (2008).

7.4 Demand, productivity and innovation

Research on productivity and innovation has typically been characterised by a strong emphasis on the supply side: what investments are needed to drive growth and raise productivity, and what resources are required to support innovation. In comparison there has been little attention paid to the demand side of innovation and productivity. Schmookler (1966) was an early contributor who argued that the pace of patenting followed demand for the industry's products, and Ruttan (2001) more broadly argues that innovation is often induced by market demand. Recent research has found some support for this in the pharmaceutical industry, but other studies suggest these effects are not ubiquitous.[13] Moreover, Bartelsman *et al.* (1994) find that industry productivity is affected by the activity level of its customers in the short run, but this effect disappears over longer time horizons.

In general most demand-induced innovation studies have focused on manufacturing. While one might equate 'technology upgrading' with the introduction of new vintages of machinery, formal R&D and other hard science, in particular in manufacturing, the concept of technology as used in economic theory is actually much broader and therefore also applicable to services. 'Technology' describes the available knowledge about the various ways in which inputs, such as capital and labour, can be combined in the production of goods and services (Hulten 2001). For service industries in particular, this may be more strongly related to changes in organisational structure, management and work practices than 'hard' technological changes. Service activities also tend to be less standardised and more customised than manufacturing production, and depend strongly on the interaction with the consumer, and are therefore more embedded in company and management cultures and other intangibles. These types of technology might less easily spill over from one firm to another than manufacturing technologies.

---

[13] For instance, Finkelstein (2004) finds that vaccine research is stimulated by policies that increase the market size for these vaccines. Acemoglu and Linn (2004) find support for demand-induced innovation in the pharmaceutical industry when using demographic trends as an exogenous determinant of market size. On the other hand, Acemoglu, Cutler, Finkelstein *et al.* (2006) do not find such an effect using the introduction of Medicare as a determinant of market size.

In Chapter 2 we argued that the slow but steady shift of demand towards services seems to have had a negative impact on aggregate productivity growth in Europe, as productivity growth in services in general is lower than in goods production. Baumol already put this hypothesis forward in his cost-disease model for services (Baumol 1967, 2007).[14] According to this model the rapid rise in the share of services in total economic output reflects the perverse increase in demand for services that are characterised by rapid cost increases and low productivity. Recently however, the cost-disease model has been challenged in the light of rapid productivity growth in US services (Triplett and Bosworth 2006). In Chapter 2 we also showed that trade and business services were responsible for the lion's share of the productivity growth gap between the USA and the EU. While supply factors such as innovation and market reforms certainly played a role, these sectors were also the ones that experienced a very rapid increase in demand during the 2000s. In the US retail sector, for example, the rapid rise in consumption strengthened scale effects, through the spread of 'big boxes', and efficiency effects, through high adoption rates of new innovations. Gordon (2007) argues that the big-box effect represents an 'exceptional' advantage to the USA due to preferences, long distances, infrastructure, etc. and might not be easily repeated in Europe. Scale and efficiency effects may also have resulted from a rapid rise in outsourcing of ancillary processes such as accounting, marketing, legal, etc. by US firms, leading to high demand for more productive business services.

Demand factors may also play a role in personal services, such as food preparation, childcare and cleaning services, and impact on the measured productivity differential between Europe and the United States. For example, Freeman and Schettkat (2005) show how different shares of household and market-based provision of those personal services impact on employment growth, but there could also be implications for productivity. The argument would be that in many European countries the current market for these services is not large enough to justify investment in innovation through intangible assets. More research is required to establish those links between demand, innovation and productivity in services.

---

[14] See Oulton (2002) for a moderated view, taking into account the role of services as intermediate inputs.

7.5 Resource reallocation, competition and regulation

Productivity growth in Europe may also benefit from a more flexible approach towards labour, product and capital markets in which resources can flow to their most productive uses. In general, the efficiency of resource allocation is an area of growing interest given the wider availability of firm-level datasets and theoretical work that recognises the importance of differences across firms in productivity and other factors. There is a wide range of studies that have identified the impact of exit and entry on productivity and stress the importance of more productive firms increasing their market share relative to less productive competitors.[15] For instance, Klapper *et al.* (2006) have shown that legal entry barriers across Europe hold back entry of new firms and retard the subsequent growth of new entrants. There is also evidence emerging that the dynamics of entry and exit and subsequent growth play a role in explaining part of the productivity differential between Europe and the USA, as suggested for example by Bartelsman *et al.* (2004) and Bartelsman *et al.* (2005).

Based on newly developed measures of regulation in the OECD Product Market Regulation Database, Nicoletti and Scarpetta (2003) provide the first systematic empirical analysis of the impact of regulation on productivity in a cross-country setting, in particular for manufacturing.[16] Alesina *et al.* (2005) provide evidence that various measures of regulation in product markets, in particular entry barriers, are negatively related to investments. However, industry-level evidence on the impact of regulations on productivity in market services is still weak, except for telecommunications, as we have also shown in Chapter 6. A related strand of literature focuses on the indirect effects of regulation on growth through its impact on innovation.[17] Griffith *et al.* (2006) argue that the European Single Market Programme has increased the degree of competition within manufacturing industries

---

[15] Foster *et al.* (2001) and Foster *et al.* (2008) provide recent overviews of the empirical literature. Restuccia and Rogerson (2008) and Hsieh and Klenow (2009) provide theoretical models that permit the quantification of the role of market distortions in the allocation of resources.

[16] Conway and Nicoletti (2006) present updates of their indicators for non-manufacturing industries.

[17] See Aghion and Griffith (2005) for an overview.

and as a result, innovation. This relationship is not necessarily linear. Aghion *et al.* (2005) show that competition should not be too tough since firms need to earn enough rents to pay for innovative investments, but competition should also be tough enough to provide a motive for innovation. Also, the impact of product market deregulation on employment and productivity might be mediated by labour market institutions (Gust and Marquez 2004; Griffith *et al.* 2007). In an overview, Crafts (2006) argues that there is substantial evidence that restrictive product market regulations hinder technology transfer and have a negative impact on productivity, in particular in the wake of a new technology era based on ICT.

More empirical research is needed to identify the optimal level of competition and study the relationship to productivity. Most likely, the productivity effects will be highly industry-specific, depending, for example, on the size and maturity of the industry and the industry concentration, but also on the nature of the education system, the availability of capital for start-ups, the sophistication of the consumer and the characteristics of the legislative framework. These studies should provide the tools not only to quantify the importance of resource reallocation but also to explain why it is greater in some countries and industries than in others. Indeed, our analysis in this book has demonstrated that industry heterogeneity should not be ignored and could be exploited. This is demonstrated by, for example, Bassanini *et al.* (2009), who show that the effect of strict dismissal regulations differs systematically across industries, and, likewise, Klapper *et al.* (2006) show that the effect of entry barriers is industry-specific. These systematic differences are useful in part because they allow for methodologically more convincing evidence, but also because they provide new insights into why some industries are showing faster growth than others.

The findings will prove particularly relevant for policy analysts as well, since this research could provide further motivation for changing market entry regulations. The drive in Europe during the first decade of the twenty-first century towards a greater openness of service product markets, for example through the adoption of a Services Directive specifically aimed at creating a common market for services across the European Union, may hold the potential to increase productivity across Europe in the coming decades.

7.6 Concluding remarks

The aim of this final chapter has been to outline the main findings of this book and suggest a number of implications and new directions for research and policy analysis based on those findings. In particular, we emphasise that the key to faster productivity growth in Europe is in market services. Here lie the opportunities in terms suggested by a large productivity gap with the USA; a weight in the economy sizeable enough to have a substantial impact on aggregate growth; and challenges in understanding and influencing the drivers of productivity growth in this sector. We have highlighted a number of areas where we believe a greater emphasis on research and analysis is required to support economic policy. In particular, we discussed important challenges in the measurement of output, but also of crucial inputs in the form of intangible capital. A greater understanding of how developments in the financial sector influence productivity in the rest of the economy also seems highly relevant. We also emphasised how the role of demand factors in services innovation and productivity growth is poorly understood and how more effort is needed to understand the patterns of resource reallocation between firms.

We started this book with two main perspectives on Europe's falling behind, with some observers focusing on the restrictive regulations of product and labour markets and others stressing the failings of the European innovation system. As the discussion in this chapter has made clear, we believe that these are still the most relevant perspectives for understanding Europe's growth performance. Throughout this book we have aimed to demonstrate the limitations of looking only at aggregate trends and growth performance at the macro level. We have shown that the industry sources of the European slowdown are different from the sources of the US growth advantage; that the use of ICT and human capital differs considerably across sectors; that productivity dynamics vary widely by industry and that European productivity levels are ahead of the USA in some industries and behind in others. Indeed, the industry perspective adopted here helps to understand better the effects of regulation and innovation on European growth and productivity. We believe that these findings are the tip of the iceberg and that there is great promise in further exploiting differences across industries to gain a deeper understanding of European growth.

References

Abel, J. R., E. R. Berndt and A. G. White (2007), 'Price Indexes for Microsoft's Personal Computer Software Products', in E. R. Berndt and C. R. Hulten (eds.), *Hard-to-Measure Goods and Services: Essays in Honor of Zvi Griliches*, University of Chicago Press, Chicago, pp. 269–89.

Abernathy, F. H., J. T. Dunlop, J. H. Hammond and D. Weil (1999), *A Stitch in Time: Lean Retailing and the Transformation of Manufacturing – Lessons from the Apparel and Textile Industries*, Oxford University Press, Oxford.

Abraham, K. G. (2005), 'What We Don't Know Could Hurt Us: Some Reflections on the Measurement of Economic Activity', *Journal of Economic Perspectives*, 19(3), pp. 3–18.

Abramovitz M. (1989), *'Thinking about Growth' and Other Essays on Economic Growth and Welfare*, Cambridge University Press, Cambridge.

Acemoglu, D. and J. Linn (2004), 'Market Size in Innovation: Theory and Evidence from the Pharmaceutical Industry', *Quarterly Journal of Economics*, 119(3), pp. 1049–90.

Acemoglu, D., P. Aghion and F. Zilibotti (2006), 'Distance to Frontier, Selection, and Economic Growth', *Journal of the European Economic Association*, 4(1), pp. 37–74.

Acemoglu, D., S. Johnson and J. A. Robinson (2002), 'Reversal of Fortune: Geography and Institution in the Making of the Modern World Income Distribution', *Quarterly Journal of Economics*, 117(4), pp. 1231–94.

Acemoglu, D., D. Cutler, A. Finkelstein and J. Linn (2006), 'Did Medicare Induce Pharmaceutical Innovation', *American Economic Review*, 96(2), pp. 103–7.

Aghion, P. and S. N. Durlauf (2005), eds., *Handbook of Economic Growth*, North-Holland, Amsterdam.

Aghion, P. and R. Griffith (2005), *Competition and Growth: Reconciling Theory and Evidence*, MIT Press, Cambridge, MA.

Aghion, P. and P. Howitt (2006), 'Joseph Schumpeter Lecture. Appropriate Growth Policy: A Unifying Framework', *Journal of the European Economic Association*, 4(2–3), pp. 269–314.

(2007), 'Capital, Innovation, and Growth Accounting', *Oxford Review of Economic Policy*, 23(1), pp. 79–93.

(2009), *The Economics of Growth*, MIT Press, Cambridge, MA.

Aghion, P., T. Fally and S. Scarpetta (2007), 'Credit Constraints as a Barrier to the Entry and Post-Entry Growth of Firms', *Economic Policy*, 22(52), pp. 731–79.

Aghion, P., N. Bloom, R. Blundell, R. Griffith and P. Howitt (2005), 'Competition and Innovation: An Inverted-U Relationship', *Quarterly Journal of Economics*, 120(2), pp. 701–28.

Ahmad, N. (2003), 'Measuring Investment in Software', OECD/STI Working Papers, no. 2003/6, Paris.

Aizcorbe, A. and S. Kortum (2005), 'Moore's Law and the Semiconductor Industry: A Vintage Model', *Scandinavian Journal of Economics*, 107(4), pp. 603–30.

Akkermans, D. H. M., C. Castaldi and B. Los (2009), 'Do "Liberal Market Economies" Really Innovate More Radically than "Coordinated Market Economies"? Hall & Soskice Reconsidered', *Research Policy*, 38, pp. 181–91

Alesina, A., S. Ardagna, G. Nicoletti and F. Schiantarelli (2005), 'Regulation and Investment', *Journal of the European Economic Association*, 3(4), pp. 791–825.

Allen, R. C. and W. E. Diewert (1981), 'Direct versus Implicit Superlative Index Number Formulae', *Review of Economics and Statistics*, 63(3), pp. 430–5.

Atkinson, T. (2005), *Measurement of Government Output and Productivity for the National Accounts* (Final Report of the Atkinson Review), HMSO.

Aulin-Ahmavaara, P. and P. Pakarinen (2007), 'Integrated Industry and Economy-wide TFP-Measures with Different Prices in Different Uses', *Economic Systems Research*, 19(3), pp. 253–76.

Autor, D. H., L. F. Katz and A. B. Krueger (1998), 'Computing Inequality: Have Computers Changed the Labour Market?' *Quarterly Journal of Economics*, 113(4), pp. 1169–210.

Baily, M. N. and J. F. Kirkegaard (2004), *Transforming the European Economy*, Institute for International Economics, Washington, DC.

Baily, M. N. and R. M. Solow (2001), 'International Productivity Comparisons Built from the Firm Level', *Journal of Economic Perspectives*, 15(3), pp. 151–72.

Baldwin, J. R. and W. Gu (2007), 'Multifactor Productivity in Canada: An Evaluation of Alternative Methods of Estimating Capital Services', *Canadian Productivity Review*, 9, pp. 1–53.

Baldwin, J., W. Gu, A. Lafrance and R. MacDonald (2008), 'Intangible Capital in Canada: R&D, Innovation, Brand, and Mining, Oil and Gas Exploration Expenditures', paper for the 30th General Conference of the International Association for Research in Income and Wealth, Portoroz, Slovenia, 24–30 August, 2008.

Balk, B. M. (2003), 'The Residual: On Monitoring and Benchmarking Firms, Industries and Economies with Respect to Productivity', *Journal of Productivity Analysis*, 20(1), pp. 5–47.

(2009), 'Measuring Productivity Change without Neoclassical Assumptions: A Conceptual Analysis', Statistics Netherlands Discussion Papers, 09-023, The Hague.

Barro, R. J. and X. Sala-i-Martin (2004), *Economic Growth*, 2nd edn, MIT Press, Cambridge, MA.

Bartelsman, E. J. and M. Doms (2000), 'Understanding Productivity: Lessons from Longitudinal Microdata', *Journal of Economic Literature*, 38(3), pp. 569–95.

Bartelsman, E. J., R. J. Caballero and R. K. Lyons (1994), 'Customer- and Supplier-Driven Externalities', *American Economic Review*, 84(4), pp. 1075–84.

Bartelsman, E. J., J. Haltiwanger and S. Scarpetta (2004), 'Microeconomic Evidence of Creative Destruction in Industrial and Developing Countries', Tinbergen Institute Discussion Papers, no. 04-114, Amsterdam.

Bartelsman, E. J., J. Haskel and R. Martin (2008), 'Distance to Which Frontier? Evidence on Productivity Convergence from International Firm-level Data', CEPR Discussion Papers, no. 7032, London.

Bartelsman, E. J., S. Scarpetta and F. Schivardi (2005), 'Comparative Analysis of Firm Demographics and Survival: Evidence from Micro-level Sources in OECD Countries', *Industrial and Corporate Change*, 14(3), pp. 365–91.

Basker, E. (2007), 'The Causes and Consequences of Wal-Mart's Growth', *Journal of Economic Perspectives*, 21(3), pp. 177–98.

Bassanini, A., L. Nunziata and D. Venn (2009), 'Job Protection, Legislation and Productivity Growth in OECD Countries', *Economic Policy*, 24(58), pp. 349–402.

Basu, S., J. Fernald, N. Oulton and S. Srinivasan (2004), 'The Case of the Missing Productivity Growth: Or, Does Information Technology Explain Why Productivity Accelerated in the United States but not in the United Kingdom?', in M. Gertler and K. Rogoff (eds.), *NBER Macroeconomics Annual*, MIT Press, Cambridge, MA, pp. 9–63.

Basu, S., R. Inklaar and J. C. Wang (2009), 'The Value of Risk: Measuring the Service Output of U.S. Commercial Banks', *Economic Inquiry*, forthcoming.

Baumol, W. J. (1967), 'Macroeconomics of Unbalanced Growth: The Anatomy of Urban Crisis', *American Economic Review*, 57(3), pp. 415–26.

—— (2007), 'On Mechanisms Underlying the Growing Share of Service Employment in the Industrialized Economies', in M. B. Gregory, W. Salverda and R. Schettkat (eds.), *Services and Employment: Explaining the U.S.–European Gap*, Princeton University Press, Princeton, pp. 63–80.

Baumol, W. J., S. A. B. Blackman and E. N. Wolff (1985), 'Unbalanced Growth Revisited: Asymptotic Stagnancy and New Evidence', *American Economic Review*, 75(4), pp. 806–17.

Bélorgey, N., R. Lecat, and T. Maury (2004), 'Déterminants de la productivité apparente du travail', *Bulletin de la Banque de France*, January.

Berman, E., J. Bound and S. Machin (1998), 'Implications of Skill-Biased Technological Change: International Evidence', *Quarterly Journal of Economics*, 113(4), pp. 1245–79.

Bernard, A. and C. I. Jones (1996), 'Comparing Apples to Oranges: Productivity Convergence and Measurement Across Industries and Countries', *American Economic Review*, 86(5), pp. 1216–38.

—— (2001), 'Comparing Apples to Oranges: Reply', *American Economic Review*, 91(4), pp. 1168–9.

Berndt, E. R. and M. A. Fuss (1986), 'Productivity Measurement with Adjustments for Variations in Capacity Utilizations and Other Forms of Temporary Equilibrium', *Journal of Econometrics*, 33(1), pp. 7–29.

Biatour, B., G. Bryon and C. Kegels (2007), 'Capital Services and Total Factor Productivity Measurements: Impact of Various Methodologies for Belgium', EU KLEMS Working Paper Series, no. 13, Groninger.

Biatour, B. and C. Kegels (2008), 'Growth and Productivity in Belgium', Federal Planning Bureau Working Paper, no. 17-08, Brussels.

Blanchard, O. J. (1997), 'The Medium Run', *Brookings Papers on Economic Activity*, 2, pp. 89–141.

—— (2004), 'The Economic Future of Europe', *Journal of Economic Perspectives*, 18(4), pp. 3–26.

Bloom, N. and J. van Reenen (2007), 'Measuring and Explaining Management Practices across Firms and Nations', *Quarterly Journal of Economics* 122(4), pp. 1351–408.

Bloom, N., R. Sadun and J. van Reenen (2009), 'Americans do IT better: US Multinationals and the Productivity Miracle', unpublished paper, Stanford University.

Bloom, N., M. Schankerman and J. van Reenen (2007), 'Identifying Technology Spillovers and Product Market Rivalry', NBER Working Papers, no. 13060, Cambridge, MA.

Bourlès, R., and G. Cette (2007), 'Trends in "Structural" Productivity Levels in the Major Industrialized Countries', *Economics Letters*, 95(1), pp. 151–6.

Boylaud, O. and G. Nicoletti (2000), 'Regulation, Market Structure and Performance in Telecommunications', OECD Economics Department Working Papers, no. 237, Paris.

Bresnahan, T. F. and M. Trajtenberg (1995), 'General Purpose Technologies: "Engines of Growth"?', *Journal of Econometrics*, 65(1), pp. 83–108.

Broadberry, S. N. (1998), 'How Did the United States and Germany Overtake Britain? A Sectoral Analysis of Comparative Productivity Levels, 1870–1990', *Journal of Economic History*, 58(2), pp. 375–407.

(2006), *Market Services and the Productivity Race, 1850–2000: British Performance in International Perspective*, Cambridge University Press, Cambridge.

Bruno, M. (1984), 'Raw Materials, Profits, and the Productivity Slowdown', *Quarterly Journal of Economics*, 99(1), pp. 1–30.

(2003), 'Computing Productivity: Firm-Level Evidence', *Review of Economics and Statistics*, 85(4), pp. 793–808.

Cameron, G., J. Proudman and S. Redding (2005), 'Technological Convergence, R&D, Trade and Productivity Growth', *European Economic Review*, 49(3), pp. 775–807.

Carré, J.-J., P. Dubois and E. Malinvaud (1975), *French Economic Growth*, Stanford University Press, Stanford.

Carree, M. A. and L. Klomp (1997), 'Testing the Convergence Hypothesis: A Comment', *Review of Economics and Statistics*, 79(4), pp. 683–6.

Caselli, F. (2005), 'Accounting for Cross-Country Income Differences', in P. Aghion and S. N. Durlauf (eds.), *Handbook of Economic Growth*, North-Holland: Amsterdam, pp. 679–741.

Caselli, F. and D. J. Wilson (2004), 'Importing Technology', *Journal of Monetary Economics*, 51(1), pp. 1–32.

Castaldi, C. and B. Los (2009), 'The Identification of Superstar Innovations Using Tail Estimators', unpublished paper, University of Groningen.

Castelli, A., D. Dawson, H. Gravelle, R. Jacobs, P. Kind, P. Loveridge, S. Martin, M. O'Mahony, P. Stevens, L. Stokes, A. Street and M. Weale (2007), 'A New Approach to Measuring Health System Output and Productivity', *National Institute Economic Review*, 200 (April), pp. 105–17.

Caves, D. W., L. R. Christensen and W. E. Diewert (1982a), 'The Economic Theory of Index Numbers and the Measurement of Input, Output, and Productivity', *Econometrica*, 50(6), pp. 1392–414.

(1982b), 'Multilateral Comparisons of Output, Input and Productivity Using Superlative Index Numbers', *Economic Journal*, 92(365), pp. 73–86.

Chenery, H., S. Robinson and M. Syrquin (1986), *Industrialization and Growth: A Comparative Study*, Oxford University Press for the World Bank, New York.

Christensen, L. R., D. Cummings and D. W. Jorgenson (1981), 'Relative Productivity Levels, 1947–1973: An International Comparison', *European Economic Review*, 16(1), pp. 61–94.

Chun, H. (2003), 'Information Technology and the Demand for Educated Workers: Disentangling the Impacts of Adoption versus Use', *Review of Economics and Statistics*, 85(1), pp. 1–8.

Coelli, T. J., D. S. Prasada Rao, C. J. O'Donnell and G. E. Battese (2005), *An Introduction to Efficiency and Productivity Analysis*, Springer, New York.

Cohen, D. and M. Soto (2007), 'Growth and Human Capital: Good Data, Good Results', *Journal of Economic Growth*, 12(1), pp. 51–76.

Colangelo, A. and R. Inklaar (2010), 'Banking Sector Output Measurement in the Euro Area – a Modified Approach', GGDC Research Memoranda, no. GD-117, Groningen.

Colecchia, A. and P. Schreyer (2002), 'ICT Investment and Economic Growth in the 1990s: Is the United States a Unique Case? A Comparative Study of Nine OECD Countries', *Review of Economic Dynamics*, 5(2), pp. 408–42.

Collins, S. M. and B. P. Bosworth (1996), 'Economic Growth in East Asia: Accumulation versus Assimilation', *Brookings Papers on Economic Activity*, 2, pp. 135–203.

Conway, P. and G. Nicoletti (2006), 'Product Market Regulation in the Non-Manufacturing Sectors of OECD Countries: Measurement and Highlights', OECD Economics Department Working Paper, no. 530, paris.

Corrado, C. A., C. R. Hulten and D. E. Sichel (2005) 'Measuring Capital and Technology: An Expanded Framework', in C. A. Corrado, J. C. Haltiwanger and D. E. Sichel (eds.), *Measuring Capital in the New Economy*, University of Chicago Press, Chicago, pp. 11–46.

(2009), 'Intangible Capital and U.S. Economic Growth', *Review of Income and Wealth*, 55(3), pp. 661–85.

Corrado, C. A., P. Lengermann, E. J. Bartelsman and J. J. Beaulieu (2006), 'Sectoral Productivity in the United States: Recent Developments and the Role of IT', *German Economic Review*, 8(2), pp. 188–210.

Crafts, N. F. R. (2006), 'Regulation and Productivity Performance', *Oxford Review of Economic Policy*, 22(2), pp. 186–202.

Crafts, N. F. R. and T. Mills (2005), 'TFP growth in British and German Manufacturing, 1950–1996', *Economic Journal*, 115(505), pp. 649–70.

Crafts, N. F. R. and G. Toniolo (1996), eds., *Economic Growth in Europe since 1945*, Cambridge University Press, Cambridge.

Crespi, G., C. Criscuolo, J. Haskel and D. Hawkes (2006), 'Measuring and Understanding Productivity in UK Market Services', *Oxford Review of Economic Policy*, 22(4), pp. 560–72.

Daveri, F. (2002), 'The New Economy in Europe, 1992–2001', *Oxford Review of Economic Policy*, 18(3), pp. 345–62.

(2004), 'Delayed IT Usage: Is It Really the Drag on Europe's Productivity?', *CESifo Economic Studies*, 50(3), pp. 397–421.

Daveri, F. and C. Jona-Lasinio (2005), 'Italy's Decline: Getting the Facts Right', IGIER Working Papers, no. 301, Milan.

Daveri, F. and M. Maliranta (2007), 'Age, Seniority and Labour Costs: Lessons from the Finnish IT Revolution', *Economic Policy*, 22(49), pp. 117–75.

Daveri, F. and O. Silva (2004), 'Not only Nokia: What Finland Tells Us about New Economy Growth', *Economic Policy*, 19(38), pp. 117–63.

Dawson, D., H. Gravelle, A. Street, A. Castelli, R. Jacobs, P. Kind, P. Loveridge, M. O'Mahony, P. Stevens and L. Stokes (2005), 'Developing New Approaches to Measuring NHS Outputs and Productivity', NIESR Discussion Papers, no. 264, London.

de la Fuente, A. and R. Doménech (2006), 'Human Capital in Growth Regressions: How Much Difference does Data Quality Make?', *Journal of the European Economic Association*, 4(1), pp. 1–36.

Denison, E. F. (1962), *The Sources of Economic Growth in the United States and the Alternatives Before Us*, Committee for Economic Development, New York.

(1967), *Why Growth Rates Differ*, Brookings Institution, Washington, DC.

Dew-Becker, I. and R. J. Gordon (2008), 'The Role of Labor Market Changes in the Slowdown of European Productivity Growth', NBER Working Papers, no. 13840, Cambridge, MA.

Diewert, W. E. (1976), 'Exact and Superlative Index Numbers', *Journal of Econometrics*, 4, pp. 114–45.

(2001), 'Which (Old) Ideas on Productivity Measurement Are Ready to Use?', in C. R. Hulten, E. R. Dean and M. J. Harper (eds.), *New Developments in Productivity Analysis*, NBER Studies in Income and Wealth, 63. University of Chicago Press, Chicago, pp. 85–102.

(2007), 'Measuring Productivity in the System of National Accounts', UBC Discussion Papers, no. 07-06.

(2008), 'What is to be Done for Better Productivity Measurement', *International Productivity Monitor*, 16, 40–52.

Diewert, W. E. and C. J. Morrison (1986), 'Adjusting Output and Productivity Indexes for Changes in the Terms of Trade', *Economic Journal*, 96(383), 659–79.

Domar, E. D. (1961), 'On the Measurement of Technical Change', *Economic Journal*, 71(284), pp. 709–29.

Doms, M. E. (2005), 'Communications Equipment: What Has Happened to Prices', in C. A. Corrado, J. C. Haltiwanger and D. E. Sichel (eds.), *Measuring Capital in the New Economy*, University of Chicago Press, Chicago, pp. 323–62.

Doms, M. E., W. E. Dunn, S. D. Oliner and D. E. Sichel (2004), 'How Fast Do Personal Computers Depreciate? Concepts and New Estimates', in J. M. Poterba (ed.), *Tax Policy and the Economy*, vol. XVIII, MIT Press, Cambridge, MA, pp. 37–81.

Draca, M., R. Sadun and J. van Reenen (2007), 'Productivity and ICTs: a Review of the Evidence', in R. Mansell, C. Avgerou, D. Quah and R. Silverstone (eds.), *The Oxford Handbook of Information and Communication Technologies*. Oxford University Press, Oxford, pp. 100–47.

Durand, R. (1996), 'Canadian Input-Output-Based Multi-factor Productivity Accounts', *Economic Systems Research*, 8(4), pp. 367–89.

Eichengreen, B. (2007), *The European Economy since 1945: Coordinated Capitalism and Beyond*, Princeton University Press, Princeton.

Eicher, T. S. and T. Strobel (2009), *Information Technology and Productivity Growth: German Trends and OECD Comparisons*, Edward Elgar, Cheltenham.

Erumban, A. A. (2008), 'Rental Prices, Rates of Return, Capital Aggregation and Productivity: Evidence from EU and US', *CESifo Economic Studies*, 54(3), pp. 499–533.

European Commission (1996), *European System of Accounts ESA 1995*, Office for Official Publications of the EC, Luxembourg.

(2004), *The EU Economy, 2004 Review*, Office for Official Publications of the EC, Luxembourg.

Eurostat (2001), *Handbook on Price and Volume Measures in National Accounts*, Office for Official Publications of the EC, Luxembourg.

(2002), *The ESA95 Input–Output Manual: Compilation and Analysis*, Office for Official Publications of the EC, Luxembourg.

Fagerberg, J. (1994), 'Technology and International Differences in Growth Rates', *Journal of Economic Literature*, 32(3), pp. 1147–75.

Färe, R., S. Grosskopf and D. Margaritis (2006), 'Productivity Growth and Convergence in the European Union', *Journal of Productivity Analysis*, 25(1), pp. 111–41.

Feenstra, R. C., H. Ma and D. S. P. Rao (2009), 'Consistent Comparisons of Real Incomes Across Time and Space', *Macroeconomic Dynamics* 13(S2), pp. 169–93

Feenstra, R. C., A. Heston, M. P. Timmer and H. Deng (2009), 'Estimating Real Production and Expenditures Across Nations: A Proposal for Improving the Penn World Tables', *Review of Economics and Statistics*, 91(1), pp. 201–12.

Finkelstein, A. (2004), 'Static and Dynamic Effects of Health Policy: Evidence from the Vaccine Industry', *Quarterly Journal of Economics*, 119(2), pp. 527–64.

Foster, L., J. Haltiwanger and C. J. Krizan (2001), 'Aggregate Productivity Growth: Lessons from Microeconomic Evidence', in C. R. Hulten, E. R. Dean and M. J. Harper (eds.), *New Developments in Productivity Analysis*, NBER Studies in Income and Wealth, 63. University of Chicago Press, Chicago, pp. 303–72.

Foster, L., J. Haltiwanger and C. J. Krizan (2006), 'Market Selection, Reallocation, and Restructuring in the U.S. Retail Trade Sector in the 1990s', *Review of Economics and Statistics*, 88(4), pp. 748–58.

Foster, L., J. Haltiwanger and C. Syverson (2008), 'Reallocation, Firm Turnover, and Efficiency: Selection on Productivity or Profitability?', *American Economic Review*, 98(1), pp. 394–425.

Frame, W. S. and L. J. White (2004), 'Empirical Studies of Financial Innovation: Lots of Talk, Little Action?', *Journal of Economic Literature*, 42(1), pp. 116–44

Fraumeni, B. M. (1997), 'The Measurement of Depreciation in the U.S. National Income and Product Accounts', *Survey of Current Business*, July, pp. 7–23.

Freeman, R. B. and R. Schettkat (2005), 'Marketization of Household Production and the EU–US gap in work', *Economic Policy*, 20(41), pp. 6–50.

Fuchs, V. R. (1968), *The Service Economy*, NBER, New York.

Fukao, K., S. Hamagata, T. Inui, K. Ito, H.U. Kwon, T. Makino, T. Miyagawa, Y. Nakanishi and J. Tokui (2007), 'Estimation Procedures and TFP Analysis of the JIP Database 2006', RIETI Discussion Papers, no. 07-E-003, Tokyo.

Garibaldi, P. and P. Mauro (2002), 'Employment Growth: Accounting for the Facts', *Economic Policy* 17(1), pp. 67–113.

Gerschenkron, A. (1962), *Economic Backwardness in Historical Perspective. A Book of Essays*, Harvard University Press: Cambridge, MA.

Gilchrist, S. and E. Zakrajsek (2007), 'Investment and the Cost of Capital: New Evidence from the Corporate Bond Market', NBER Working Papers, no. 13174, Cambridge, MA.

Goldberg, P. K. and F. Verboven (2005), 'Market Integration and Convergence to the Law of One Price: Evidence from the European Car Market', *Journal of International Economics*, 65(1), pp. 49–73.

Gollin, D. (2002), 'Getting Income Shares Right', *Journal of Political Economy*, 110(2), pp. 458–74.

Gollop, F. (1979), 'Accounting for Intermediate Input: the Link between Sectoral and Aggregate Measures of Productivity', in *Measurement and Interpretation of Productivity*, National Academy of Sciences, Washington, DC, pp. 318–33.

Gordon, R. J. (2000), 'Does the "New Economy" Measure up to the Great Inventions of the Past?', *Journal of Economic Perspectives*, 14(4), pp. 49–74.

(2007), 'Why was Europe Left at the Station when America's Productivity Locomotive Departed?', in M. Gregory, W. Salverda and R. Schettkat (eds.), *Services and Employment: Explaining the U.S.–European Gap*, Princeton University Press, Princeton, pp. 176–97.

Görzig, B. (2007), 'Depreciation in EU Member States: Empirical and Methodological Differences', EU KLEMS Working Paper Series, no. 17, Groningen.

Görzig, B., M. Gornig, L. Nayman and M. O'Mahony (2010), 'Productivity transitions in large mature economies: France, Germany, and the UK', EU KLEMS Working Paper Series, Groningen, forthcoming.

Greenwood, J., Z. Hercowitz, and P. Krusell (1997), 'Long-run Implications of Investment-specific Technological Change', *American Economic Review*, 87(3), pp. 342–62.

Griffith, R., R. Harrison and G. Macartney (2007), 'Product Market Reforms, Labour Market Institutions and Unemployment', *Economic Journal*, 117(519), pp. C142–C166.

Griffith, R., R. Harrison and H. Simpson (2006), 'Product Market Reform and Innovation in the EU', CEPR Discussion Papers, no. 5849.

Griffith, R., S. Redding and H. Simpson (2009), 'Technological Catch-up and Geographic Proximity', *Journal of Regional Science*, 49(4), pp. 689–720.

Griffith, R., S. Redding and J. van Reenen (2004), 'Mapping the Two Faces of R&D: Productivity Growth in a Panel of OECD Industries', *Review of Economics and Statistics*, 86(4), pp. 883–95.

Griliches, Z. (1986), 'Economic Data Issues', in Z. Griliches and M. D. Intriligator (eds.), *Handbook of Econometrics*, vol. III, Elsevier, Amsterdam, pp. 1465–514.

(1992), ed., *Output Measurement in the Service Sectors*, NBER Studies in Income and Wealth, 56, University of Chicago Press, Chicago.

(1994), 'Productivity, R&D, and the Data Constraint', *American Economic Review*, 84(1), pp. 1–23.

Gust, C. and J. Marquez (2004), 'International Comparisons of Productivity Growth: the Role of Information Technology and Regulatory Practices', *Labour Economics*, 11(1), pp. 33–58.

Hall, R. E. (1988), 'The Relation between Price and Marginal Cost in US Industry', *Journal of Political Economy*, 96(5), pp. 921–47.

Hanushek, E. A. and D. Kimko (2000), 'Schooling, Labour Force Quality and the Growth of Nations', *American Economic Review*, 90(5), pp. 1184–208.

Hao, J., V. Manole and B. van Ark (2008), 'Intangible Capital and Growth – An International Comparison', Economics Program Working Paper Series, #08 – 14, The Conference Board, New York.

Harberger, A. C. (1998), 'A Vision of the Growth Process', *American Economic Review*, 88(1), pp. 1–32.

Harrigan, J. (1999), 'Estimation of Cross-country Differences in Industry Production Functions', *Journal of International Economics*, 47(2), pp. 267–93.

Hartwig, J. (2008), 'Productivity Growth in Service Industries: Are the Transatlantic Differences Measurement-Driven?', *Review of Income and Wealth*, 54(3), pp. 494–505.

Havlik, P., S. Leitner and R. Stehrer (2008), 'Growth Resurgence, Productivity Catching-up and Labour Demand in CEESs', *WIIW Statistical Reports*, no. 3.

Heravi, S., A. W. Heston and M. Silver (2003), 'Using Scanner Data to Estimate Country Price Parities: A Hedonic Regression Approach', *Review of Income and Wealth*, 49(1), pp. 1–21.

Hill, T. P. (1971), *The Measurement of Real Product: A Theoretical and Empirical Analysis of Growth Rates, for Different Industries and Countries*, OECD, Paris.

Hornstein, A., P. Krusell and G. Violante (2005), 'The Effects of Technical Change on Labor Market Inequalities', in P. Aghion and S. N. Durlauf (eds.), *Handbook of Economic Growth*, vol. 1B, Elsevier, Amsterdam, pp. 1275–370.

Hsieh, C.-T. and P. J. Klenow (2007), 'Relative Prices and Relative Prosperity', *American Economic Review*, 97(3), pp. 562–85.

(2009), 'Misallocation and Manufacturing TFP in China and India', *Quarterly Journal of Economics*, 124, pp. 1403–48.

Hulten, C. R. (2001), 'Total Factor Productivity: A Short Biography', in C. R. Hulten, E. R. Dean and M. J. Harper (eds.), *New Developments in Productivity Analysis*, NBER Studies in Income and Wealth, 63, University of Chicago Press, Chicago, pp. 1–47.

(2010), 'Growth Accounting', in B. H. Hall and N. Rosenberg (eds.), *Handbook of the Economics of Innovation*, Elsevier North-Holland, Amsterdam, vol. II, ch. 7.

Hulten, C. R. and B. van Ark (2008), 'Innovation, Intangibles and Economic Growth: Towards a Comprehensive Accounting of the Knowledge Economy', *Yearbook on Productivity 2007, Papers Presented at the Saltsjobaden Conference, October 2007*, Statistics Sweden, Stockholm, pp. 127–46.

Inklaar, R. (2010), 'The Sensitivity of Capital Services Measurement: Measure All Assets and the Cost of Capital', *Review of Income and Wealth*, forthcoming.

Inklaar, R. and M. Koetter (2008), 'Financial Dependence and Industry Growth in Europe: Better Banks and Higher Productivity', GGDC Research Memoranda, no. GD-100, Groningen.

Inklaar, R. and M. P. Timmer (2007a), 'Of Yeast and Mushrooms: Patterns of Industry-level Productivity Growth', *German Economic Review*, 8(2), pp. 174–87.

(2007b), 'International Comparisons of Industry Output, Inputs and Productivity Levels: Methodology and New Results', *Economic Systems Research* 19(3), pp. 343–63.

(2008a), 'Accounting for Growth in Retail Trade: An International Productivity Comparison', *Journal of Productivity Analysis*, 29(1), pp. 23–31.

(2008b), 'GGDC Productivity Level Database: International Comparisons of Output, Inputs and Productivity at the Industry Level', GGDC Research Memoranda, no. GD-104, Groningen.

(2009a), 'Productivity Convergence Across Industries and Countries: The Importance of Theory-based Measurement', *Macroeconomic Dynamics*, 13(S2), pp. 218–40.

(2009b), 'Measurement Error in Productivity Levels: Is more Detailed Data Better?', GGDC Research Memoranda, no. GD-111, Groningen.

Inklaar, R. and J. C. Wang (2009), 'Not your Grandfather's Bank Anymore; Consistent Measurement of Traditional and Novel Bank Output', unpublished paper, University of Groningen and Federal Reserve Bank of Boston.

Inklaar, R., M. O'Mahony and M. P. Timmer (2005), 'ICT and Europe's Productivity Performance: Industry-level Growth Account Comparisons with the United States', *Review of Income and Wealth*, 51(4), pp. 505–36.

Inklaar, R., M. P. Timmer and B. van Ark (2007), 'Mind the Gap! International Comparisons of Productivity in Services and Goods Production', *German Economic Review*, 8(2), pp. 281–307.

(2008), 'Market Services Productivity Across Europe and the U.S.', *Economic Policy*, 23(53), pp. 139–94.

Inter-Secretariat Working Group on National Accounts (1993), *System of National Accounts 1993*, Brussels/Luxembourg, New York, Paris, Washington, DC.

Islam, N. (2003), 'What Have We Learnt from the Convergence Debate?', *Journal of Economic Surveys*, 17(3), pp. 309–62.

Jalava, J. and I. K. Kavonius (2009), 'Measuring the Stock of Consumer Durables and its Implications for Euro Area Savings Ratios', *Review of Income and Wealth*, 55(1), pp. 43–56.

Jalava, J. and M. Pohjola (2008), 'The Roles of Electricity and ICT in Economic Growth: The Case of Finland', *Explorations in Economic History*, 45(3), pp. 270–87.

Jorgenson, D. W. (1995a), *Productivity*, vol. I: *Postwar U.S. Economic Growth*, MIT Press, Cambridge, MA.

(1995b), *Productivity*, vol. II: *International Comparisons of Economic Growth*, MIT Press, Cambridge, MA.

(2001), 'Information Technology and the U.S. Economy', *American Economic Review*, 91(1), pp. 1–32

Jorgenson, D. W. and Z. Griliches (1967), 'The Explanation of Productivity Change', *Review of Economic Studies*, 34(3), pp. 249–83.

Jorgenson, D. W. and M. Nishimizu (1978), 'U.S. and Japanese Economic Growth, 1952–1974: An International Comparison', *Economic Journal*, 88(352), pp. 707–26.

Jorgenson, D. W. and K. Nomura (2007), 'The Industry Origins of the US–Japan Productivity Gap', *Economic Systems Research*, 19(3), pp. 315–42.

Jorgenson, D. W. and K. J. Stiroh (2000), 'Raising the Speed Limit: U.S. Economic Growth in the Information Age', *Brookings Papers on Economic Activity*, 1, pp. 125–211.

Jorgenson, D.W. and M. P. Timmer (2009), 'Structural Change in Advanced Nations: A New Set of Stylised Facts', GGDC Research Memoranda, no. GD-115, Groningen.

Jorgenson, D. W. and K. Vu (2005), 'Information Technology and the World Economy', *Scandinavian Journal of Economics*, 107(4), pp. 631–50.

Jorgenson, D. W. and E. Yip (2001), 'Whatever Happened to Productivity Growth? Investment and Growth in the G-7', in C. R. Hulten, E. R. Dean and M. J. Harper (eds.), *New Developments in Productivity Analysis*, NBER Studies in Income and Wealth, 63. University of Chicago Press, Chicago, pp. 205–46.

Jorgenson, D. W. and K.-Y. Yun (1991), *Tax Reform and the Cost of Capital*, Oxford University Press, New York.

Jorgenson, D. W., F. M. Gollop and B. M. Fraumeni (1987), *Productivity and U.S. Economic Growth*, Harvard Economic Studies, Cambridge, MA.

Jorgenson, D. W., M. S. Ho and K. J. Stiroh (2003), 'Lessons for Europe from the U.S. Growth Resurgence', *CESifo Economic Studies*, 49(1), pp. 27–47.

(2005), *Information Technology and the American Growth Resurgence*, MIT Press, Cambridge, MA.

Jorgenson, D. W., M. Kuroda and M. Nishimizu (1987), 'Japan–U.S. Industry-level Productivity Comparisons, 1960–1979', *Journal of the Japanese and International Economies*, 1(1), pp. 1–30.

Kaldor, N. (1963), 'Capital Accumulation and Economic Growth', in F. A. Lutz and D. C. Hague (eds.), *Proceedings of a Conference Held by the International Economics Association*, Macmillan, London.

Kegels, C., M. Peneder and H. van der Wiel (2008), 'Productivity Performance in Three Small European Countries: Austria, Belgium and the Netherlands', EU KLEMS Working Paper Series, no. 21, Groningen.

Keller, W. (2002), 'Trade and the Transmission of Technology', *Journal of Economic Growth*, 7(1), pp. 5–24.

Klapper, L., L. Laeven and R. Rajan (2006), 'Entry Regulation as a Barrier to Entrepreneurship', *Journal of Financial Economics*, 82(3), pp. 591–629.

Koeniger, W. and M. Leonardi (2007), 'Capital Deepening and Wage Differentials: Germany versus US', *Economic Policy*, 22(49), pp. 71–116.

Kohli, U. (1990), 'Growth Accounting in the Open Economy: Parametric and Nonparametric Estimates', *Journal of Economic and Social Measurement* 16(4), pp. 125–36.

Kox, H. and A. Lejour (2005), 'Regulatory Heterogeneity as Obstacle for International Services Trade', CPB Discussion Papers, no. 49, The Hague.

Kratena, K. (2007), 'Technical Change, Investment and Energy Intensity', *Economic Systems Research*, 19(3), pp. 295–314.

Kravis, I. B. (1976), 'A Survey of International Comparisons of Productivity', *Economic Journal*, 86(341), pp. 1–44.

Kravis, I. B., A. Heston and R. Summers (1982), *World Product and Income*, Johns Hopkins University Press, Baltimore.

Krijnse-Locker, H. and H. D. Faerber (1984), 'Space and Time Comparisons of Purchasing Power Parities and Real Values', *Review of Income and Wealth*, 30(1), pp. 53–84.

Krueger, A. B. (1999), 'Measuring Labor's Share', *American Economic Review, Papers and Proceedings*, 89 (2), pp. 45–51.

Krueger, A. B. and M. Lindahl (2001), 'Education for Growth: Why and for Whom?', *Journal of Economic Literature*, 39(4), pp. 1101–36.

Krüger, J. J. (2008), 'Productivity and Structural Change: A Review of the Literature', *Journal of Economic Surveys*, 22(2), pp. 330–63.

Krugman, P. (1994), 'The Myth of Asia's Miracle', *Foreign Affairs*, 73(6), pp. 62–78.

Krugman, P. R. and A. J. Venables (1995), 'Globalization and the Inequality of Nations', *Quarterly Journal of Economics*, 110(4), pp. 857–80.

Kuznets, S. (1971), *Economic Growth of Nations: Total Output and Production Structure*, Harvard University Press, Cambridge, MA.

Lee, F. and J. Tang (2000), 'Productivity Levels and International Competitiveness between Canadian and U.S. Industries', *American Economic Review*, 90(2), pp. 176–9.

Lengellé, M. (1980), 'Development of the Service Sector in OECD Countries: Economic Implications', in I. Leveson and J. Wheeler (eds.), *Western Economies in Transition: Structural Change and Adjustment Policies in Industrial Countries*, Westview Press: Boulder, CO, pp. 139–57.

Levine, R. (2005), 'Finance and Growth: Theory and Evidence', in P. Aghion and S. N. Durlauf (eds.), *Handbook of Economic Growth*, North-Holland, Amsterdam.

Losch, M. (2006), ed., *Deepening the Lisbon Agenda: Studies on Productivity, Services and Technologies*, Austrian Federal Ministry of Economics and Labour: Vienna.

Machin, S. and J. van Reenen (1998), 'Technology and Changes in Skill Structure: Evidence from Seven OECD Countries', *Quarterly Journal of Economics*, 113(4), pp. 1215–44.

Maddison, A. (1980), 'Economic Growth and Structural Change in Advanced Countries', in I. Leveson and J. Wheeler (eds.), *Western Economies in Transition: Structural Change and Adjustment Policies in Industrial Countries*, Westview Press: Boulder, CO, pp. 41–60.

(1987), 'Growth and Slowdown in Advanced Capitalist Economies: Techniques of Quantitative Assessment', *Journal of Economic Literature*, 25(2), pp. 649–98.

(1995), *Explaining the Economic Performance of Nations. Essays in Time and Space*, Edward Elgar, Aldershot.

Maddison, A. and B. van Ark (2002), 'The International Comparison of Real Product and Productivity', in A. Maddison, D. S. P. Rao and W. F. Shepherd (eds.), *The Asian Economies in the Twentieth Century*, Edward Elgar: Cheltenham, pp. 5–26.

Manning, A. (2003), *Monopsony in Motion: Imperfect Competition in Labour Markets*, Princeton University Press, Princeton.

Manser, M. (2005), 'Productivity Measures for Retail Trade: Data and Issues', *Monthly Labor Review*, July, pp. 30–8.

Marrano, M. G., J. Haskel and G. Wallis (2009), 'What Happened to the Knowledge Economy? ICT, Intangible Investment, and Britain's Productivity Record Revisited', *Review of Income and Wealth*, 55(3), 686–716.

Mas, M., C. Milana and L. Serrano (2008), 'Spain and Italy: Catching Up and Falling Behind. Two Different Tales of Productivity Slowdown', EU KLEMS Working Papers, no. 37, Groningen.

Mason, G., B. O'Leary and M. Vecchi (2009), 'Cross-country Analysis of Productivity and Skills at Sector Level', Report to Sector Skills Development Agency, National Institute of Economic and Social Research, London.

Matthews, R. C. O., C. H. Feinstein and J. C. Odling-Smee (1982), *British Economic Growth 1856–1973*, Stanford University Press, Stanford.

McGuckin, R. H. and B. van Ark (2005), 'Productivity and Participation: An International Comparison', GGDC Research Memoranda, no. GD-78, Groningen.

McGuckin, R. H., M. Spiegelman and B. van Ark (2005), 'The Retail Revolution: Can Europe Match the U.S. Productivity Performance?', in *Perspectives on a Global Economy*, The Conference Board, New York.

McKinsey Global Institute (2002), *Reaching Higher Productivity Growth in France and Germany – Retail Trade Sector*, McKinsey, New York.

Meade, D. S., J. Stanislaw, S. J. Rzeznik and D. C. Robinson-Smith (2003), 'Business Investment by Industry in the U.S. Economy for 1997', *Survey of Current Business*, November, pp. 18–70.

Nakamura, L. (2010), 'Intangible Assets and National Income Accounting: Measuring a Scientific Revolution', *Review of Income and Wealth*, forthcoming.

Nelson, R. R. and H. Pack (1999), 'The Asian Miracle and Modern Growth Theory', *Economic Journal*, 109(457), pp. 416–36.

Ngai, L. R. and C. A. Pissarides (2007), 'Structural Change in a Multisector Model of Growth', *American Economic Review*, 97(1), pp. 429–43.

Nickell, S. (1997), 'Unemployment and Labor Market Rigidities: Europe versus North America', *Journal of Economic Perspectives*, 11(3), pp. 55–74.

Nicoletti, G. and S. Scarpetta (2003), 'Regulation, Productivity and Growth: OECD Evidence', *Economic Policy*, 18(36), pp. 9–72.

Nordhaus, W. D. (2002), 'Productivity Growth and the New Economy', *Brookings Papers on Economic Activity*, 2, pp. 211–44.

(2008), 'Baumol's Diseases: A Macroeconomic Perspective', *B.E. Journal of Macroeconomics: Contributions to Macroeconomics*, 8(1), art. 9.

O'Mahony, M. (1999), *Britain's Relative Productivity Performance, 1950–1996: An International Perspective*, National Institute of Economic and Social Research, London.

O'Mahony, M. and F. Peng (2008), 'Skill Bias, Age and Organisational Change', EU KLEMS Working Papers, no. 36.

O'Mahony, M. and P. Stevens (2006), 'International Comparisons of Output and Productivity in Public Services Provision: A Review', in G. A. Boyne, K. A. Meier, L. J. O'Toole and R. M. Walker (eds.), *Public Service Performance: Perspectives on Measurement and Management*, Cambridge University Press, Cambridge, pp. 233–53.

O'Mahony, M. and M. P. Timmer (2009), 'Output, Input and Productivity Measures at the Industry Level: the EU KLEMS Database', *Economic Journal*, 119(538), pp. F374–F403.

O'Mahony, M. and B. van Ark (2003), eds., 'EU Productivity and Competitiveness: An Industry Perspective. Can Europe Resume the Catching-up Process?' Office for Official Publications of the EC, Luxembourg.

O'Mahony, M. and M. Vecchi (2005), 'Quantifying the Impact of ICT Capital on Output Growth: A Heterogeneous Dynamic Panel Approach', *Economica*, 72, pp. 615–33.

O'Mahony, M., C. Robinson and M. Vecchi (2008), 'The Impact of ICT on the Demand for Skilled Labour: A Cross-country Comparison', *Labour Economics*, 15(6), pp. 1435–50.

Obstfeld, M. and K. Rogoff (1996), *Foundations of International Macroeconomics*, MIT Press, Cambridge, MA.

OECD (2001), *Measuring Productivity – Measurement of Aggregate and Industry-level Productivity Growth*, OECD, Paris.

(2002) *Purchasing Power Parities and Real Expenditures, 1999 Benchmark Year*, OECD, Paris.

(2004), *The Economic Impact of ICT: Measurement, Evidence and Implications*, OECD, Paris.

(2008), *OECD Compendium of Productivity Indicators 2008*, OECD, Paris.

Oliner, S. D. and D. E. Sichel (2000), 'The Resurgence of Growth in the Late 1990s: Is Information Technology the Story', *Journal of Economic Perspectives*, 14(4), pp. 3–22.

Oulton, N. (2002), 'ICT and Productivity Growth in the United Kingdom', *Oxford Review of Economic Policy*, 18(3), pp. 363–79.

(2007), 'Ex Post versus Ex Ante Measures of the User Cost of Capital', *Review of Income and Wealth*, 53(2), pp. 295–317.

Paige, D. and G. Bombach (1959), *A Comparison of National Output and Productivity of the United Kingdom and the United States*, OECD, Paris.

Pilat, D. (1996), 'Labour Productivity Levels in OECD Countries: Estimates for Manufacturing and Selected Service sectors', OECD Economics Department Working Papers, no. 162, paris.

Pilat, D., F. Lee and B. van Ark (2002), 'Production and Use of ICT: a Sectoral Perspective on Productivity Growth in the OECD Area', *OECD Economic Studies*, 35(2), pp. 47–78.

Pissarides, C. A. (2007), 'Unemployment and Hours of Work: the North Atlantic Divide Revisited', *International Economic Review*, 48(1), pp. 1–36.

Prescott, E. C. (2004) 'Why Do Americans Work So Much More Than Europeans?' *Federal Reserve Bank of Minneapolis Quarterly Review*, 28, July, pp. 2–13.

Restuccia, D. and R. Rogerson (2008), 'Policy Distortions and Aggregate Productivity with Heterogeneous Plants', *Review of Economic Dynamics* 11(4), pp. 707–20.

Restuccia, D., D. T. Yang and X. Zhu (2008), 'Agriculture and Aggregate Productivity: A Quantitative Cross-country Analysis', *Journal of Monetary Economics*, 55(2), pp. 234–50.

Rogerson, R. (2008), 'Structural Transformation and the Deterioration of European Labor Market Outcomes', *Journal of Political Economy*, 116(2), pp. 235–59.

Ruttan, V. (2001), *Technology, Growth, and Development: An Induced Innovation Perspective*, Oxford University Press, Oxford.

Sapir, A., P. Aghion, G. Bertola, M. Hellwig, J. Pisani-Ferry, D. Rosati, J. Viñals and H. Wallace (2004), *An Agenda for a Growing Europe: The Sapir Report*, Oxford University Press, Oxford.

Schettkat, R. and L. Yokarini (2006), 'The Shift to Services: A Review of the Literature', *Structural Change and Economic Dynamics*, 17(2), pp. 127–47.

Schmookler, J. (1966), *Invention and Economic Growth*, Harvard University Press, Cambridge, MA.

Schreyer, P. (2000), 'The Contribution of Information and Communication Technology to Output Growth: a Study of the G7 Countries', OECD/STI Working Papers, no. 2000/2, Paris.

    (2001), *Measuring Productivity – OECD Manual. Measurement of Aggregate and Industry-level Productivity Growth*, OECD, Paris.

    (2002), 'Computer Price Indices and International Growth and Productivity Comparisons', *Review of Income and Wealth*, 48(1), pp. 15–31.

    (2008), 'International Comparisons of Levels of Capital Input and Multifactor Productivity', *German Economic Review*, 8(2), pp. 237–54.

    (2009), *Measuring Capital OECD Manual*, OECD, Paris.

Schumpeter, J. A. (1934), *The Theory of Economic Development: an Inquiry into Profits, Capital, Credit, Interest, and the Business Cycle*, Harvard University Press, Cambridge, MA.

Sichel, D. E. (1997), 'The Productivity Slowdown: Is a Growing Unmeasurable Sector the Culprit?', *Review of Economics and Statistics*, 79(3), pp. 367–70.

Solow, R. M. (1957), 'Technical Change and the Aggregate Production Function', *Review of Economics and Statistics*, 39(3), pp. 312–20.

(1987), 'We'd better watch out', *New York Times Book Review*, 12 July, p. 36.

Sørensen, A. (2001), 'Comparing Apples to Oranges: Productivity Convergence and Measurement Across Industries and Countries: Comment', *American Economic Review*, 91(4), pp. 1160–7.

Sørensen, A. and B. Schjerning (2008), 'Productivity Measurement in Manufacturing and the Expenditure Approach', *Review of International Economics*, 16(2), pp. 327–40.

Statistical Commission and Economic Commission for Europe (2004), 'Survey of National Practices in Estimating Service Lives of Capital Assets', paper presented at Joint UNECE/Eurostat/OECD meeting on National Accounts, Geneva, 28–30 April.

Stiroh, K. J. (2000), 'How Did Bank Holding Companies Prosper in the 1990s?', *Journal of Banking and Finance*, 24(11), pp. 1703–45.

(2002), 'Information Technology and the US Productivity Revival: What Do the Industry Data Say?', *American Economic Review*, 92(5), pp. 1559–76.

(2004), 'Reassessing the Impact of IT in the Production Function: A Meta-Analysis and Sensitivity Tests', unpublished paper, Federal Reserve Bank, New York.

Summers, R. and A. Heston (1991), 'The Penn World Table (Mark 5): an Expanded Set of International Comparisons, 1950–1988', *Quarterly Journal of Economics*, 106(2), pp. 327–68.

Temple, J. (2000), 'Growth Regressions and What the Textbooks Don't Tell You', *Bulletin of Economic Research*, 52(3), pp. 181–205.

(2005), 'Dual Economy Models: A Primer for Growth Economists', *Manchester School*, 73(4), pp. 435–78.

Timmer, M. P. and G. J. de Vries (2009), 'Structural Change and Growth Accelerations in Asia and Latin America: a New Sectoral Data Set', *Cliometrica*, 3(2), pp. 165–90.

Timmer, M. P. and B. van Ark (2005), 'Does Information and Communication Technology Drive EU–US Productivity Growth Differentials?', *Oxford Economic Papers*, 57(4), pp. 693–716.

Timmer, M. P., G. Ypma and B. van Ark (2007), 'Industry-of-Origin Prices and Output PPPs: a New Dataset for International Comparisons', GGDC Research Memoranda, no. GD-82, Groningen.

Timmer, M. P., T. van Moergastel, E. Stuivenwold, G. Ypma, M. O'Mahony and M. Kangasniemi (2007), 'EU KLEMS Growth and Productivity Accounts: *Part I (Methodology) and Part 2 (Sources)*', Groningen (March).

Tinbergen, J. (1942), 'Zur Theorie der Langfirstigen Wirtschaftsentwicklung', *Weltwirtschaftliches Archiv*, 55, pp. 511–49.

Triplett, J. E. (1996), 'High Tech Industry Productivity and Hedonic Price Indices', in *Industry Productivity. International Comparison and Measurement Issues*, OECD, Paris, pp. 119–42.

(2006), *Handbook on Hedonic Indexes and Quality Adjustments in Price Indexes. Special Application to Information Technology Products*, OECD, Paris.

Triplett, J. E. and B. P. Bosworth (2004), *Productivity in the U.S. Services Sector: New Sources of Economic Growth*, Brookings Institution, Washington, DC.

(2006), 'Baumol's Disease Has Been Cured: IT and Multi-factor Productivity in U.S. Service Industries', in D. W. Jansen (ed.), *The New Economy and Beyond: Past, Present, and Future*, Edward Elgar, Cheltenham, pp. 34–71.

(2008), 'The State of Data for Services Productivity Measurement in the United States', *International Productivity Monitor*, 16, pp. 53–70.

van Ark, B., and D. Pilat (1993), 'Productivity Levels in Germany, Japan and the United States', *Brookings Papers on Economic Activity, Microeconomics*, 2, pp. 1–48.

van Ark, B., and M. P. Timmer (2009), 'Purchasing Power Parity Adjustments for Productivity Level Comparisons', in D. S. P. Rao (ed.), *Purchasing Power Parities: Methods and Applications*, Edward Elgar, Cheltenham, pp. 334–66.

van Ark, B., R. Inklaar and R. H. McGuckin (2003), 'ICT and Productivity in Europe and the United States, Where Do the Differences Come From?', *CESifo Economic Studies*, 49(3), pp. 295–318.

van Ark, B., M. O'Mahony and M. P. Timmer (2008), 'The Productivity Gap between Europe and the U.S.: Trends and Causes', *Journal of Economic Perspectives*, 22(1), pp. 25–44.

van Ark, B., J. Melka, N. Mulder, M. P. Timmer and G. Ypma (2002), 'ICT Investments and Growth Accounts for the European Union 1980–2000', GGDC Research Memoranda, no. GD-53, Groningen.

van Biesebroeck, J. (2009) 'Cross-Country Conversion Factors for Sectoral Productivity Comparisons', *Journal of Productivity Analysis*, 32(2), pp. 63–79.

van den Bergen, D. M. van Rooijen-Horsten, M. de Haan and B. M. Balk (2008), 'Productivity Measurement at Statistics Netherlands', Statistics Netherlands Discussion Papers no. 08-041, The Hague.

Van Reenen, J. (2006), 'The Growth of Network Computing: Quality-adjusted Price Changes for Network Servers', *Economic Journal* 116(509), F29–F44.

Vandenbussche, J., P. Aghion and C. Meghir (2006), 'Growth, Distance to the Frontier and Composition of Human Capital', *Journal of Economic Growth*, 11(2), pp. 97–127.

Vijselaar, R. and F. Albers (2004), 'New Technologies and Productivity Growth in the Euro Area', *Empirical Economics*, 29(3), pp. 621–46.

Wölfl, A. (2003), 'Productivity Growth in Service Industries: An Assessment of Recent Patterns and the Role of Measurement', OECD/STI Working Paper Series, no. 2003/7, Paris.

Wurgler, J. (2000), 'Financial Markets and the Allocation of Capital', *Journal of Financial Economics*, 58(1–2), pp. 187–214.

Young, A. (1995), 'The Tyranny of Numbers: Confronting the Statistical Realities of the East Asian Growth Experience', *Quarterly Journal of Economics*, 110(3), pp. 641–80.

Ypma, G. and B. van Ark (2006), 'Employment and Hours Worked in National Accounts: A Producer's View on Methods and a User's View on Applicability', EU KLEMS Working Paper Series, no. 10, Groningen.

Index

9 780521 198875